Humanities in Review

HUMANITIES IN REVIEW

VOLUME 1

Board of Editors
RONALD DWORKIN
KARL MILLER
RICHARD SENNETT

General Editor
DAVID RIEFF

The New York Institute for the Humanities

Cambridge University Press
CAMBRIDGE
LONDON   NEW YORK   NEW ROCHELLE
MELBOURNE   SYDNEY

Published by the Press Syndicate of the University of Cambridge
The Pitt Building, Trumpington Street, Cambridge CB2 1RP
32 East 57th Street, New York, NY 10022, USA
296 Beaconsfield Parade, Middle Park, Melbourne 3206, Australia

Copyright © 1982 by The New York Institute for the Humanities

First published 1982

Printed in the United States of America

Library of Congress Cataloging in Publication Data
Main entry under title:
Humanities in review.
I. Rieff, David (David Sontag)
AC5.H82   1982   081   82-4589
ISBN 0 521 24971 6 hard covers   AACR2
ISBN 0 521 27105 3 paperback

This publication was prepared with support
(partial support) from the National Endowment
for the Humanities.

Contents

List of contributors	*page* vii
Foreword by Richard Sennett	ix

I. THE BODY AND SOCIETY

Sexuality and solitude *Michel Foucault and Richard Sennett*	3
A short history of body consciousness *Jean Starobinski*	22
The sacred and the body social in sixteenth-century Lyon *Natalie Zemon Davis*	40

II. THE NATURE OF ACTING

Acting in everyday life and everyday life in acting *Victor Turner*	83
The actor as a celebrity *Richard Gilman*	106

III. HOW FORM IN ART IS RELATED TO CULTURE

The breaking of form *Harold Bloom*	127
The "I" as an other in poetry *Stephen Spender*	157
Music does not flow: constant and variable elements in music's patterning *Virgil Thomson*	186

Contents

IV. STUDIES IN CULTURAL HISTORY
The occult philosophy in the Elizabethan age 201
Frances Yates
Triumph or downfall of civil society 218
Alain Touraine

Contributors

Harold Bloom is Professor of Humanities at Yale University. His books include *Poetry and Repression, Figures of Capable Imagination,* and *The Flight to Lucifer: A Gnostic Fantasy.*

Natalie Zemon Davis is Henry Charles Lea Professor of History at Princeton. Her published works include "Poor Relief, Humanism and Heresy" in *Studies in Medieval & Renaissance History* and "The Reasons of Misrule: Youth Groups and Charivaris in 16th Century France" in *Past and Present.*

Michel Foucault is Professor (Chair of the history of systems of thought) at the Collège de France. Recent books in translation include *The Archaeology of Knowledge; Discipline and Punish: The Birth of the Prison;* and *The History of Sexuality: Volume 1.*

Richard Gilman is an author and critic, and is currently President of the American PEN Center. His most recent books include *Common and Uncommon Masks, The Making of Modern Drama,* and *Decadence: The Strange History of an Epithet.*

Richard Sennett is Director of the New York Institute for the Humanities and University Professor of the Humanities at New York University. His most recent books include *The Frog Who Dared to Croak, Authority,* and *The Fall of Public Man.*

Stephen Spender is a poet and critic. His most recent books include *Love-Hate Relations: A Study of Anglo-American Sensibilities, T. S. Eliot,* and *The Thirties and After, Poetry, Politics, People.*

Jean Starobinski is Professor of Literature at the University of Geneva. His books include *Les Mots sous les mots, Les Emblèmes de la raison,* and *Les Trois fureurs.*

Virgil Thomson is a composer and author. His compositions include *Four*

Contributors

Saints in Three Acts and the opera *Lord Byron*. His books include *Music Reviewed 1940–1954*, and *American Music since 1910*.

Alan Touraine is Director of Studies at the Ecole des Hautes Etudes. His books include *The Voice and the Eye*, *La Prophétie anti-nucléaire*, and *L'Après-socialisme*.

Victor Turner is William R. Kenan Professor of Anthropology at the University of Virginia, Charlottesville. His books include *Dramas, Fields and Metaphors; Revelation and Divination in Ndembu Ritual;* and *Image and Pilgrimage in Christian Culture*.

Dame Frances Yates is an Honorary Fellow at the Warburg Institute in London. Her books include *Astraea: The Imperial Theme in the Sixteenth Century*, *Elizabethan Neoplatonism Reconsidered: Spenser and Francesco Giorgi*, and *The Occult Philosophy in the Elizabethan Age*.

Foreword

This book represents work commissioned from 1978 to 1980 by the New York Institute for the Humanities, founded in 1976 as a college without students. New York and its environs contain many universities; the city is a thriving literary and artistic center. But these two worlds within the city, rather surprisingly, seldom meet. The Institute was to be a place, therefore, where academics and nonacademics could have a chance to talk with each other. In its first years the Institute's activities were, for the most part, informal seminar groups, meeting once or twice a month, each seminar organized by a Fellow of the Institute. One seminar, for example, explored the place of metaphorical thought in science and in the arts; the seminar consisted of a mathematician, a physicist, a poet, a painter, an art historian, and an anthropologist. Another seminar on the culture of New York City mixed historians of the city with critics, artists, and administrators of the city's cultural institutions.

When the Institute began, it had no program. It consisted of several rooms in a basement on Washington Square, donated by New York University – a place where people could hold meetings or simply gather for lunch or drinks. The staff consisted of one harassed secretary. The occasions the Institute created proved attractive enough that it began to expand as an organization. As it expanded, some semblance of a program became necessary. My colleagues Aryeh Neier and Thomas Bender and I (all three of us have served as the Institute's director at one time or another) decided the Institute should focus on three immediate problems and one long-term issue in the humanities.

The first of the immediate problems had to do with the state of American culture in the wake of the Vietnam War. The disaster of the war had turned American culture isolationist; the internationalism of the Kennedy era had gone sour or seemed politically suspect. Given the

Foreword

hand-to-mouth finances of our Institute, there was obviously nothing we could do about this in any major way. But New York City is an international city, both because of its long history of foreign immigration and its present status as an international diplomatic and economic center. We thought, therefore, that we might create an audience in New York for the writing of distinguished foreign scholars and artists, an audience composed not of specialists but of a more general mix of academics and nonacademics, in the way the Institute's seminars had been mixed. With the help of John Sawhill, then president of New York University, we founded the James lectures, a series of five to seven lectures each year that bring writers from abroad to New York to talk about their work. We also decided to invite foreign writers – such as Alberto Moravia, Nadine Gordimer, Vladimir Voinovich, and Leszak Kolakowski – to come talk to smaller groups on more specialized topics.

The second immediate problem we decided to address was what has been called "the new diaspora," the exiling of writers and intellectuals from Eastern Europe and Latin America in the last decade by repressive political regimes. The Institute is not a political organization. But it did seem to us that we could at least provide a home for distinguished exiled writers in New York City and (not incidentally) enrich the culture of the city by their presence. The Russian poet Joseph Brodsky, the Cuban poet Herberto Padilla, and the Argentinian novelist Luisa Valenzuela are now Fellows of the Institute as part of this effort. The Institute has also sponsored an international conference on writing and censorship to explore, with a group of writers from around the world, the consequences of repression on the act of writing, and we shall continue such efforts in the future.

The third practical matter the Institute seeks to address unfortunately knows no national boundaries. It is the perennial lack of money for artists and intellectuals who do not have teaching jobs. The problem is always bad, but in the last decade it has become worse, as universities, after a period of expansion, are now cutting back. In these retrenchments the first to be fired are often "marginal people" – that is, writers or researchers doing exploratory work that does not fit neatly into academic categories and departments. Thanks to grants from the National Endowment for the Humanities and the Exxon Education Foundation, we have supported some of these "marginal" intellectuals.

The reader of this volume will find, however, that it is not a kind of sample case of the activities I have described. We have chosen to focus

Foreword

this volume on the larger and less practical question that hangs over many of the particular discussions in our seminars and conferences: What constitutes "humanistic understanding" of a subject? This volume is about the role history and historical thinking plays in answering that question.

Richard Sennett

I

The body and society

MICHEL FOUCAULT AND RICHARD SENNETT

Sexuality and solitude

RICHARD SENNETT

A few years ago, Michel Foucault and I discovered we were interested in the same problem, in very different periods of history. The problem is why sexuality has become so important to people as a definition of themselves. Sex is as basic as eating or sleeping, to be sure, but it is treated in modern society as something more. It is the medium through which people seek to define their personalities, their tastes. Above all, sexuality is the means by which people seek to be conscious of themselves. It is that relationship between self-consciousness, or subjectivity, and sexuality that we want to explore. Few people today would subscribe to Brillat-Savarin's dictum, "Tell me what you eat, and I will tell you who you are," but a translation of this dictum to the field of sex does command assent: Know how you love, and you will know who you are.

Michel Foucault and I are working, as I say, on two very different historical periods in which this theme of self-consciousness via sexuality appears. He focuses on how Christianity in its early phases, from the third to the sixth centuries, assigned a new value to sexuality and redefined sexuality itself. I focus on the late eighteenth and nineteenth centuries, and within that period on how medical doctors, educators, and judges took a new interest in sexuality. When it became apparent to us in our conversations together during the last few years that we were asking rather similar questions about our two historical periods, we decided to set up a seminar to see what connections we could make.

Comparing two eras separated by fifteen hundred years should give any good historian the shudders. But the seminar is more than an idle experiment. We hope to get some rough, tentative ideas about the continuing influence of Christianity on modern culture. How do Christian ideas of sexuality continue as unspoken assumptions in the secular literature on this subject? Our purpose has been to answer that question.

MICHEL FOUCAULT AND RICHARD SENNETT

The first part of what follows is a short statement by each of us on how we came to focus on this particular problem, at these particular moments of history: These are two short overviews of the subject in general. The second part is an analysis of a specific text: Concrete textual analysis is the work we are conducting in the seminar. M. Foucault discusses the problem of sexuality and solitude as it appears in the work of the early church father Augustine. I then discuss medical analyses of masturbation, which begin with the work of the French-Swiss doctor Samuel Tissot in the mid-eighteenth century.

Let me begin the first part with something of a short intellectual autobiography. I did not set out to study sexuality at all. I set out to study the history of solitude in modern society. I wanted to understand the evolution to experiences of solitude because it seemed to be a good way to study a vast but amorphous subject: the development of subjectivity in modern culture. How has the concept of "I" changed in the last two centuries? To tame this very general subject, I sought to understand the changing circumstances in which people felt alone with themselves – the conditions of family, work, and political life that prompted people to consider themselves to be alone. Originally I focused on such tangible matters as how people felt alone in the middle of city crowds (an incomprehensible notion to someone of the mid-seventeenth century) and how factory conditions changed so that people felt more or less isolated from each other. This history of the circumstances in which people felt alone appeared to me after a while, however, to be inadequate to the subject. In particular, it did not account for the mental tools people use to think about themselves when they are alone. In the nineteenth century, one tool of self-definition was the perception of one's own sexuality; this has grown ever more important. For instance, by the end of the century, there existed the notion that when one left the family and went out into the crowd, one was free to have all kinds of sexual experiences that one would have been ashamed to admit one could desire, thinking of oneself as a member of a family. Thus there appeared two kinds of desire, one for the anonymous man, one for the family man.

Let me now say something about what the word *solitude* means. We know three solitudes in society. We know a solitude imposed by power. This is the solitude of isolation, the solitude of anomie. We know a solitude that arouses fear in those who are powerful. This is the solitude of the dreamer, of the *homme révolté*, the solitude of rebellion. Finally, there is a solitude that transcends the terms of power. It is a solitude based on the idea of Epictetus that there is a difference between being

Sexuality and solitude

lonely and being alone. This is the sense of being one among many, of having an inner life that is more than a reflection of the lives of others. It is the solitude of difference.

Each of these solitudes has a history. In the ancient world, the solitude imposed by power was exile; in seventeenth-century France, the solitude imposed by power was banishment to the countryside. In a modern office, the solitude created by power is a sense of loneliness in the middle of the mass. In the ancient world, the detached dreamer whom the powerful feared was one like Socrates – one who set against the laws of the state a discourse of superior law, an ideal against an established order of power. The modern *homme révolté*, an Artaud or a Genet, sets against the order of power the truth of lawlessness. The solitude of difference, of an inner life that is more than a reflection of others' lives, is similarly historical.

In most of the writings on this subject, the emphasis is put on the first two solitudes: people in isolation perceived either as victims or as rebels. Emile Durkheim is probably the greatest spokesman for the solitary as a victim, Jean-Paul Sartre for the solitary as a rebel. The sense of apartness, of difference, is more often neglected, and for a good reason. This is an immensely confused experience in modern society, and one reason for the confusion is that our ideas of sexuality as an index of self-consciousness make it hard for us to understand how we stand apart from other individuals in society. It is this third solitude upon which M. Foucault and I have focused.

Confusion about standing apart because of one's sexuality is bred partly of fear. The first modern researchers on sexuality believed they were opening up a terrifying Pandora's box of unrestrained lust, perversion, and destructiveness in looking at the sexual desires of people alone without the civilizing restraints of society. When we come to analyze the texts about masturbation of Tissot and others, I hope some sense of this terror will become apparent. A person alone with his or her sexuality appeared to be a person alone with a very dangerous force. In our seminar we have sought to understand these late Enlightenment and Victorian fears of the Pandora's box within a person to be not simply blind prejudices, or aberrations of scientific inquiry. These fears expressed ideas about the relation between mind and body, speech and desire, of which the Victorian doctors were themselves unaware. Their attitudes are buried in fundamental Christian formulas about the relationship among desire, discourse, and political domination. What is inherited blindly is likely to be passed on blindly. Victorian morality provides not simply the moral foundation of the sort of right-wing clamor for social repression that appeared in the last American election; it is also the foundation of the belief, in more benign circles, that contemplation of one's sexuality is the contemplation of "a problem," of mysteries inside oneself that can do great damage in the course of giving one pleasure. This highly charged psychological value put on sexuality is a legacy of Victorian wisdom, even though we flatter ourselves that we no longer share the Victorians' repressive prejudices. This idea of having an identity composed of one's sexuality puts a tremendous burden on one's erotic feelings, a burden that someone in the eighteenth century would find very hard to understand.

The second way in which our seminar has focused on the disorientations of sexual self-awareness concerns the act of relating the mind to the body. We have used in the seminar the phrase *the technology of the self* to describe how sexuality is used to measure human character. Part of the modern technology of the self consists in using bodily desire to measure whether or not a person is being truthful. "Do you really mean it?" "Are you being honest with yourself?" These are questions people have come to answer through trying to chart what the body desires: If your body doesn't desire it, then you aren't being honest with yourself. Subjectivity has become yoked to sexuality: The truth of subjective self-consciousness is conceived in terms of measured bodily stimulation. The practice in American speech of asking whether "you really feel what I am saying," that idea of using the word *feeling* as a measure of truth between people, is a consequence of yoking sexuality to subjectivity and carries with it the connotation that if something isn't felt, it isn't true. The origins of telling the truth through bodily desire have been traced back in our seminar work, again, to Christian sources. The modern consequence is that the wayward course of sexual desire has acted like acid on the confidence in one's self-consciousness: As bodily desires change, people have to keep telling themselves new or different or contradictory truths about themselves. Faith in oneself, in the integrity of self-consciousness, is eroded as the truth of one's self is yoked to the standards of the body.

Sexuality, then, has introduced elements of both fear and self-doubt into the experience of this third solitude, the condition of knowing oneself as a distinct, separate human being. It is a psychological truism that what is feared or ambiguous becomes urgent to a person. The very uncertainties that sexuality creates for subjectivity magnify the importance of the experience: That is, as sexuality becomes more problematic, it becomes more important to us in defining ourselves. I think the rhetorical and political view M. Foucault and I share is that sexuality has become too important, that it has become charged with tasks of self-definition and self-knowledge it cannot and should not perform.

Let me add a final introductory note. One logical response to this problem of sexuality and solitude is to maintain: "Forget it. Enjoy the sex and stop thinking about yourself." I would like to close my initial presentation by saying why I do not think the issue of solitude can be disposed of in this way.

There is a direct relationship between solitude and sociability: Unless a human being can be comfortable alone, he or she cannot be comfortable with others. There is a rhythm between the solitude of difference and sociability that ought to obtain in society, and it is a rhythm we do not feel because, in part, the experience of being alone with ourselves is so troubled. This rhythm is possible for us to experience in a way that it was not in the past, because an immense opportunity has opened up in Western bourgeois society, which is to live in a fragmented society.

There exists today an opportunity to escape the organic bonds of religion, family, work, and community, which have held many societies together before – if not completely in fact, at least as a common ideal. The love of the organic is a love we can begin to do without. Large bureaucracies are not held together by principles of organic solidarity, as Durkheim was the first to point out; the family and the workplace are no longer joined, even physically in the same household, as they were in the eighteenth-century city or countryside. Religion no longer plays the integrating role it played in traditional Catholic or Jewish life. Rather than bewailing these changes as signs of decline in society, I think we have to accept them and try to see what good they serve. The good I see them serving is to create a new opportunity for both solitude and sociability.

The loosening of organic bonds means that sociable relations could become more and more matters of choice. The less often social relations appear embedded in a scheme of nature, of divine law, of organic necessity, the more often people should be able to imagine themselves as creatures with a life apart from their social roles. When we choose to enter into social relations, they matter more. But that sense of choosing or not choosing whom a person cares about in a fragmented society depends on knowing how to see oneself as a distinct human being in one's own right. The inflation of sexuality to a measure of psychological truth has come to disorient this kind of self-knowledge.

Michel Foucault and Richard Sennett

MICHEL FOUCAULT

In a work consecrated to the moral treatment of madness and published in 1840, a French psychiatrist, Louren, tells of the manner in which he treated one of his patients – treated and, of course, as you may imagine, cured. One morning he places Mr. A., his patient, in a shower room. He makes him recount in detail his delirium. "But all that," says the doctor, "is nothing but madness. Promise me not to believe in it any more." The patient hesitates, then promises. "That is not enough," replies the doctor. "You have already made me similar promises and you haven't kept them." And he turns on the cold shower above the patient's head. "Yes, yes! I am mad!" the patient cries. The shower is turned off, the interrogation is resumed. "Yes. I recognize that I am mad," the patient repeats. He adds, however: "I recognize it because you are forcing me to do so." Another shower. "Well, well," says Mr. A., "I admit it. I am mad, and all that was nothing but madness."

To make somebody suffering from mental illness recognize that he is mad is a very ancient procedure in traditional therapy. In the works of the seventeenth and eighteenth centuries, one finds many examples of what one might call truth therapies. But the technique used by Louren is altogether different. Louren is not trying to persuade his patient that his ideas are false or unreasonable. What happens in the head of Mr. A. is a matter of perfect indifference for Louren. The doctor wishes to obtain a precise act, the explicit affirmation: "I am mad." Since I first read this passage of Louren about twenty years ago, I have kept in mind the project of analyzing the form and the history of such a bizarre practice. Louren is satisfied when and only when his patient says, "I am mad" or, "That was madness." Louren's assumption is that madness as a reality disappears when the patient asserts the truth and says that he is mad.

We have, then, the reverse of the performative speech act. The affirmation destroys in the speaking subject the reality that made the same affirmation true. What conception of truth of discourse and of subjectivity is taken for granted in this strange and yet widespread practice? In order to justify the attention I am giving to what is seemingly so specialized a subject, let me take a step back for a moment. In the years that preceded World War II, and even more so after the war, philosophy in continental Europe and in France was dominated by the philosophy of subject. I mean that philosophy took as its task par excellence the foundation of all knowledge and the principle of all

Sexuality and solitude

signification as stemming from the meaningful subject. The transcendence of the "A" group reigned. The importance given to this question was, of course, the result of the impact of Husserl, but the centrality of the subject was also tied to an institutional context, because the French university, since philosophy began with Descartes, could only advance in a Cartesian manner. But we must also take into account the political conjunct. Given the absurdity of wars, slaughters, and despotism, it seemed to be up to the individual subject to give meaning to his existential choices. With the leisure and distance that came after the war, this emphasis on the philosophy of subject no longer seemed so self-evident. Hitherto-hidden theoretical paradoxes could no longer be avoided. This philosophy of consciousness had paradoxically failed to found a philosophy of knowledge, and especially of scientific knowledge. Also, this philosophy of meaning had failed to take into account the formative mechanisms of signification and the structure of systems of meaning.

With the all too easy clarity of hindsight – of what Americans call the Monday-morning quarterback – let me say that there were two possible paths that led beyond this philosophy of subject. The first of these was the theory of objective knowledge as an analysis of systems of meaning, of semiology. This was the path of logical positivism. The second was that of a certain school of linguistics, psychoanalysis, and anthropology – all grouped under the rubric of structuralism. These were not the directions I took. Let me announce once and for all that I am not a structuralist, and I confess, with the appropriate chagrin, that I am not an analytic philosopher. Nobody is perfect. But I have tried to explore another direction. I have tried to get away from the philosophy of the subject, through a genealogy of the modern subject as a historical and cultural reality. That means as something that can eventually change, which is of course politically important. One can proceed with this general project in two ways. In dealing with modern theoretical constructions, we are concerned with the subject in general. In this way, I have tried to analyze the theories of subject as a speaking, living, working being in the seventeenth and eighteenth centuries. One can also deal with the more practical understanding found in those institutions where certain subjects became objects of knowledge and at the same time objects of domination: asylums, prisons, and so on.

I wished to study those forms of understanding that the subject creates about himself. But since I started with this last type of problem, I have been obliged to change my mind on several points. Let me introduce a kind of auto-critique. It seems, according to some suggestions of Habermas, that one can distinguish three major types of techniques: techniques that permit one to produce, to transform, to manipulate things; techniques that permit one to use sign systems; and, finally, techniques that permit one to determine the conduct of individuals, to impose certain ends or objectives – that is, techniques of production, techniques of signification or communication, and techniques of domination. But I became more and more aware that in all societies there is another type of technique: techniques that permit individuals to affect, by their own means, a certain number of operations on their own bodies, their own souls, their own thoughts, their own conduct, and this in a manner so as to transform themselves, modify themselves, and attain a certain state of perfection, happiness, purity, supernatural power. Let us call this kind of technique technologies of the self.

If one wants to analyze the genealogy of subject in Western civilization, one has to take into account not ony techniques of domination but also techniques of the self. One has to show the interaction between these two types of self. When I was studying asylums, prisons, and so on, I perhaps insisted too much on techniques of domination. What we call discipline is something extremely important in this kind of institution. But it is only one aspect of the art of governing people in our societies. Having studied the field of power relations and taken that as a point of departure, I would like, in the years to come, to study power relations starting from techniques of the self. In every culture, I think, this self technology implies a set of truth obligations: learning what is truth, discovering the truth, being enlightened by truth, telling the truth. All of these are considered important either for the constitution or for the transformation of the self.

What about truth as a duty in our Christian societies? As everybody knows, Christianity is a confession. This means that Christianity belongs to a very special type of religion – one that imposes obligations of truth on its practitioners. Such obligations in Christianity are numerous. For instance, there is the obligation to hold as truth a set of propositions that constitute dogma, the obligation to hold certain books as a permanent source of truth, and obligations to accept the decisions of certain authorities in matters of truth. Christianity requires another form of truth obligation: Everyone in Christianity has the duty to explore who he is, what is happening within himself, the faults he may have committed, the temptations to which he is exposed. Moreover, everyone is obliged to tell these things to other people and, hence, to bear witness against himself.

These two ensembles of obligation – those regarding the faith, the book, and the dogma, and those regarding the self, the soul, and the heart – are linked together. A Christian needs the light of faith when he wants to explore himself, and, conversely, his access to the truth cannot be conceived of without the purification of the soul. One can object that the same two obligations are found in Buddhism. The Buddhist also has to go to the light and discover the truth about himself. But the relation between these two obligations is quite different in Buddhism and in Christianity. In Buddhism, it is the same type of enlightenment that leads a person to discover what he is and what the truth is. In this simultaneous enlightenment of oneself and the truth, one discovers in Buddhism that the self was only an illusion. In Christianity, these two types of truth obligation, the one concerned with access to light and the other concerned with discovering truth inside oneself, have always kept a relative autonomy – even after Luther and Protestantism.

I would also like to underline that the Christian discovery of the self does not reveal the self as an illusion. It gives place to a task that cannot be anything else but undefined. This task has two objectives. First, there is the task of clearing up all the illusions, temptations, and seductions that can occur in the mind and discovering the reality of what is going on – within ourselves. Second, one has to get free from any attachment to this self, not because the self is an illusion but because the self is much too real. The more we discover the truth about ourselves, the more we have to renounce ourselves; and the more we want to renounce ourselves, the more we need to bring to light the reality of ourselves. That is what we could call the spiral of truth formulation and reality renouncement, which is at the heart of the Christian techniques of the self.

Professor Peter Brown told me recently that what we have to understand is why it is that sexuality became, in Christian cultures, the seismograph of our subjectivity. It is a fact, a mysterious fact, that in this indefinite spiral of truth and reality in the self, sexuality has been of major importance since the first centuries of our era. It has become more and more important. Why is there such a fundamental connection among sexuality, subjectivity, and truth obligation? Then I met Richard Sennett's work.

Michel Foucault and Richard Sennett

Our point of departure in the seminar has been a passage of St. François de Sales. Here is the text in a translation made in the beginning of the seventeenth century:

> I will tell you a point of the elephant's honesty. An elephant never changes his mate. He loves her tenderly. With her he couples not, but from three years to three years. And that only for five days, and so secretly that he is never seen in the act. But the sixth day, he shows himself abroad again, and the first thing he does is to go directly to some river and wash his body, not willing to return to his troupe of companions till he is purified. Be not these goodly and honest qualities in a beast by which he teaches married folk not to be given too much to sensual and carnal pleasures?

Everybody may recognize here the pattern of decent sexual behavior: monogamy, faithfulness, and procreation as the main, or maybe the single, justification of sexual acts – sexual acts that remain, even in such conditions, intrinsically impure. Most of us are inclined, I think, to attribute this pattern either to Christianity or to modern Christian society as it developed under the influence of capitalist or so-called bourgeois morality. But what struck me when I started studying this pattern is that one can find it also in Latin and even Hellenistic literature. One finds the same ideas, the same words, and eventually the same reference to the elephant. It is a fact that the pagan philosophers in the first centuries before and after the death of Christ proposed a sexual ethics that was partly new but was very similar to the alleged Christian ethics. In our seminar, it was very convincingly stressed that this philosophical pattern of sexual behavior, this elephant pattern, was not at that time the only one to be.

During this period there was an evolution toward the nuclear family, real monogamy, faithfulness between married people, and distress about sexual acts. The philosophical campaign in favor of the elephant pattern was both an effect and an adjunct of this transformation. If these assumptions are correct, we have to concede that Christianity did not invent this code of sexual behavior. Christianity accepted it, reinforced it, and gave to it a much larger and more widespread strength than it had had before. But the so-called Christian morality is nothing more than a piece of pagan ethics inserted into Christianity. Shall we say then that Christianity did not change the state of things? The thesis I proposed in our discussions was that early Christians introduced important changes, if not in the sexual code itself, at least in the relationships everyone has to one's own sexual activity. Christianity proposed a new type of experience of oneself as a sexual being.

Sexuality and solitude

To make things clearer, I will compare two texts. One was written by Artemidorus, a pagan philosopher of the third century, and the other is the well-known fourteenth book of *The City of God* by Augustine. Artemidorus wrote a book about the interpretation of dreams in the third century after the death of Christ. He was a pagan; three chapters of this book are devoted to sexual dreams. What is the meaning, or, more precisely, what is the prognostic value, of a sexual dream? It is significant that Artemidorus interpreted dreams in a way contrary to Freud and interpreted sexual dreams in terms of economics, social relations, and success and reverses in political activity and everyday life. For instance, if a person dreams that he has sex with his mother, that means he will succeed as a magistrate, since his mother is obviously the symbol of his city or country.

It is also significant that the social value of the dream does not depend on the nature of the sexual act, but mainly on the social status of the partners. For instance, for Artemidorus, it was not important whether one had sex with a girl or with a boy in a dream. The problem was to know if the partner was rich or poor, young or old, slave or free, married or not. Of course, Artemidorus took into account the question of the sexual act, but he saw it only from the male viewpoint. The only act he knew or recognized as sexual was penetration, which was for him not only a sexual act but a part of the social role of a man in a city. I would say that for Artemidorus, sexuality was relational and that sexual relations could not be dissociated from social relations.

Now let us turn to Augustine's text, whose meaning is the point at which we want to arrive in our analysis. In *The City of God*, and later on in the *Contra Julian*, Augustine gives a rather horrifying description of the sexual act. He saw the sexual act as a kind of spasm. All the body is shaken by terrible jerks. One entirely loses control. "This sexual act takes such a complete and passionate possession of the whole man, both physically and emotionally, that what results is the keenest of all pleasures on the level of sensations, and at the crisis of excitement it practically paralyses all power of deliberate thought." It is worthwhile to note that this description is not an invention of Augustine: one can find the same in the medical and pagan literature of the previous century. Moreover, Augustine's text is almost the exact transcription of a passage written by a well-known pagan philosopher, Cicero in Hortensius.

The surprising point is not that Augustine would give such a classical description of the sexual act but that, having given such a horrible description, he then admits that sexual relations could have taken place in Paradise before the Fall. This is all the more remarkable because Augustine is one of the first Christian fathers to admit this possibility. Of course, sex in Paradise could not have the epileptic form we unfortunately know now. Before the Fall, Adam's body, every part of it, was perfectly obedient to the soul and the will. If Adam wanted to procreate in Paradise, he could do it in the same way and with the same control as he could, for instance, sow seeds in the earth. He was not involuntarily excited. Every part of his body was like the fingers, which one can control in all their gestures. Sex was a kind of hand gently sowing the seed. But what happened with the Fall? Adam rose up against God with the first sin. Adam tried to escape God's will and to acquire a will of his own, ignoring the fact that the existence of his own will depended entirely on the will of God. As a punishment of this revolt and as a consequence of this determination to will independently from God, Adam lost control of himself. He wanted to acquire an autonomous will, and he lost the ontological support for that will. That then became mixed in an indissociable way with involuntary movements, and this weakening of Adam's will had a disastrous effect. His body, and parts of his body, stopped obeying his commands, revolted against him, and the sexual parts of his body were the first to rise up in this disobedience. The famous gesture of Adam covering his genitals with a fig leaf is, according to Augustine, not due to the simple fact that Adam was ashamed of their presence, but to the fact that his sexual organs were moving by themselves without his consent. Sex in erection is the image of man revolted against God. The arrogance of sex is the punishment and consequence of the arrogance of man. His uncontrolled sex is exactly the same as what he himself has been toward God – a rebel.

Why have I insisted so much on what may be nothing more than one of those exegetic fantasies of which Christian literature has been so prodigal? I think this text bears witness to the new type of relationship that Christianity established between sex and subjectivity. Augustine's conception is still dominated by the theme and form of male sexuality. But the main question is not, as it was in Artemidorus, the problem of penetration: It is the problem of erection. As a result, it is not the problem of a relationship to other people, but the problem of the relationship of oneself to oneself, or, more precisely, the relationship between one's will and involuntary assertions.

The principle of autonomous movements of sexual organs is called libido by Augustine. The problem of libido, of its strength, origin, and effect, thus becomes the main issue of one's will. It is not an external obstacle to the will. It is a part, an internal component, of the will. And it is not the manifestation of petty desires. Libido is the result of one's will when it goes beyond the limits God originally set for it. As a consequence, the means of the spiritual struggle against libido do not consist, as with Plato, in turning one's eyes upward and memorizing the reality one has previously known and forgotten. The spiritual struggle consists, on the contrary, in turning one's eyes continuously downward or inward in order to decipher, among the movements of the soul, which ones come from the libido. The task is at first indefinite, since libido and will can never be substantially dissociated from one another. And this task is not only an issue of mastership but also a question of diagnosis of truth and illusion. It requires a permanent hermeneutics of oneself.

In such a perspective, sexual ethics imply very strict truth obligations. These consist not only in learning the rules of a moral sexual behavior but also in constantly scrutinizing ourselves as libidinal beings. Shall we say that after Augustine we experience our sex in the head? Let us say at least that in Augustine's analysis, we witness a real libidinization of sex. Augustine's moral theology is, to a certain extent, a systematization of a lot of previous speculation, but it is also an ensemble of spiritual techniques. The techniques were developed mainly in the ascetic milieu and in monastic institutions, and those relayed by the Augustinian theory of libido had, I think, a huge influence on Western technologies of the self. I shall be very brief about those spiritual techniques.

When one reads the ascetic and monastic literature of the fourth and fifth centuries, one cannot help noting that these techniques are not directly concerned with the effective control of sexual behavior. There is very little mention of homosexual relations, even though most ascetics lived in permanent and numerous communities. The techniques were mainly concerned with the stream of thoughts flowing into consciousness, disturbing, by their multiplicity, the necessary unity of contemplation and secretly conveying images or suggestions from Satan. The monk's task was not the philosopher's task: to acquire mastership over oneself by the definitive victory of the will. It was to control perpetually one's thoughts, examining them to see if they were pure, whether something dangerous was not hiding in or behind them, if they were not conveying something other than what primarily appeared, if they were not a form of illusion and seduction. Such data always have to be considered with suspicion; they need to be scrutinized and tested. According to Cassian, for instance, one has to be toward oneself as a moneychanger who has to try the coins he receives. Real purity is not acquired when one can lie down with a young and beautiful boy without even touching him, as Socrates did with Alcibiades. Rather, a monk was really chaste when no impure image occurred in his mind, even during the night, even during dreams. The criterion of purity does not consist in keeping control of oneself even in the presence of the most desirable people; it consists in discovering the truth in oneself and defeating the illusions in oneself, in cutting out the images and thoughts one's mind continuously produces. Hence the axis of the spiritual struggle against impurity. The main question of sexual ethics has moved from the relations to people, and from the penetration model to the relation to oneself and to the erection problem: I mean to the set of internal movements that develop from the first and nearly imperceptible thought to the final but still solitary pollution, through those ascetic techniques, as through the Augustinian theology. However different and eventually contradictory they were, a common effect was elicited. Sexuality, subjectivity, and truth were strongly linked together. This, I think, is the religious framework in which the masturbation problem – which was nearly ignored or at least neglected by the Greeks, who considered masturbation a thing for slaves and satyrs but not for free citizens – emerged in our society as one of the main issues of sexual life.

RICHARD SENNETT

In concluding, I wish to show how certain Christian ideas of confronting oneself through confronting one's sexuality have reappeared in modern society. I shall do this by tracing some of the history of ideas about masturbation from the middle of the eighteenth to the end of the nineteenth century.

In setting out this theme, I use the word *reappear* on purpose. At the opening of the eighteenth century, autoeroticism was not of much interest to medical and educational authorities. Of course, onanism was a sin, but there was a gap between the Christian rule and the medical diagnosis of it. Autoeroticism was simply grouped as one of a number of disorders that would occur if a person were sexually overindulgent. In Boerhaave's *Institutes of Medicine,* published in 1708, the general diagnosis of sexual overindulgence is given as follows: "The semen discharged too lavishly occasions a weariness, weakness, indisposition of motion, convulsions, leanness, dryness, heat and pains in the membranes of the brain, with a dullness of the senses, more especially of the sight, a *tabes dorsalis* foolishness and disorders of the like kind." By the time Krafft-

Sexuality and solitude

Ebing's *Psychopathology of Sexuality* appeared in 1887, these symptoms were confined to masturbation. Moreover, the cause of these symptoms was no longer "too lavish a performance of the sexual act," but sexual desire. Sexual desire, when experienced alone and continually, will lead to masturbation, then to homosexuality, and finally to madness. From the time of Boerhaave to Krafft-Ebing, sexuality was displaced from how a person behaves to how he or she feels.

Perhaps the single most critical medical document in this shift is the work of French-Swiss physician S. A. D. Tissot, *Onania, or a Treatise upon the Disorders Produced by Masturbation*, published in Lausanne in 1758. Tissot's was not the first book on this subject in the eighteenth century: That dubious honor belongs to the anonymous Englishman who published a work also called *Onania* in 1716. The Englishman asserted, for the first time, that masturbation was a special disease with a special clinical profile; but his assertions were made in so lurid and loose a way that, although the book had a success among collectors of erotica, it was not taken seriously by the scientific public. Tissot's book was, however: He set out to explain why, physiologically, masturbation should lead to insanity.

Tissot asserted that masturbation was the most powerful physiological sexual experience a person could have. More than any other sexual act, it pumped blood to the brain. "This increase of blood," he wrote, "explains how these excesses produce insanity... The quantity of blood distending the nerves weakens them; and they are less able to resist impressions, whereby they are enfeebled." Given the theories of blood/nerve relations current at the time, this seemed perfectly logical. What was new, shocking, and seemingly scientifically certified by Tissot's theory was that the pleasure a person can give himself or herself is more erotically powerful than the pleasure he or she can derive from intercourse with a member of the opposite sex. Without social restraints, left alone to follow the purest dictates of pleasure, everyone was in danger of being consumed by autoeroticism and so eventually driven insane.

In his text, Tissot argues against the clinical profile established a half-century earlier by Boerhaave. Tissot adduces eight reasons why masturbation is more dangerous than sexual excesses committed with women. The last and strongest is psychological. The masturbator is overcome with "shame and shocking remorse" as no Don Juan is. This inner psychological recognition pumps so much blood to the brain that a veritable flood of the nerves occurs. Again, the physiological explanation made sense to his contemporaries, and the shocking fact it seemed to prove was that the psyche can literally drive itself mad through unrestrained desire. The notion of driving oneself mad as an internal process first appears with Tissot. A wholly inner system of desire, recognition, and destruction is set up; Tissot defined the boundaries of a terrifying, enclosed, inner erotic life more passionate, more important, more dangerous than any other form of erotic experience. We must rescue man, Tissot said, from this solitude.

It is significant in Tissot's text that he applies his Calvinist puritanism to this particular sexual phenomenon. He distinguishes between the dispassionate, scientific attitude the doctor must have about other forms of sexual disease, like overindulgence, and the moral attitude the doctor must take toward masturbation. Masturbation is a "crime" that "more justly entitles" the masturbator to "the contempt than pity of his fellow creatures." Boerhaave fought to establish a scientific discourse about sexuality free of Christian morality. Tissot brought it back in, but selectively: Only autoeroticism is worthy – if that is the right word – of Christian censure.

Tissot set in motion three attitudes about autoeroticism that profoundly influenced medical and educational opinion later in the eighteenth and throughout the nineteenth century: Sexuality in solitude is, first, profoundly arousing; autoeroticism is, second, the condition in which one is most aware of oneself. To be alone and both sexually aroused and self-aware is, third, dangerous; the body is on the road to madness and the soul on the road to perdition. What is important about Tissot's legacy, and about the phenomenon of autoeroticism generally in the nineteenth century, is that through the prism of autoeroticism, authorities attempted to understand eroticism itself. Armed with these three assumptions, researchers set out to try to understand sexuality. Rather than considering people making love together as a domain of knowledge about which the doctor would learn, the notion was to separate individuals and to study them by themselves, because it was in isolation that persons felt their sexuality most strongly. This assumption that a person was to be considered as an isolated individual was an application to the study of sex of other forms of nineteenth-century individualism.

I wish to trace this effort to understand eroticism through autoeroticism, and therefore I shall not say much about the history of the idea that masturbation causes insanity – though it should perhaps be noted that after this idea appeared in the writings of Benjamin Rush, who was working in the Philadelphia Institute of Medicine, in 1812, and in those of Esquirol in 1816, it became a firmly entrenched medical opinion that masturbation led automatically to insanity. This belief lasted until the last fifteen years of the nineteenth century, when it was challenged increasingly.

The Tissot approach to autoeroticism became a method of conceiving of sexuality itself during the nineteenth century in the following ways. First, because of their beliefs about autoeroticism, doctors and educators became accustomed to thinking that sexual desire existed prior to, and was separable from, sexual attraction. Desire was thought to be normally experienced as a secret. That is, if desire belongs to the body in and of itself, it is something prior to desiring anyone else, and it is strongest when kept a secret. This sexual desire belongs to the individual: It is satisfied rather than created by the attraction to another human being. The problem for the doctor or teacher was to find out about this desire, since it was hidden within the individual. Remember the bizarre symptoms Victorian medicine had to invent for the masturbator: hair suddenly growing on the palms of the masturbating hand, the tongue swelling up, the eyes distending, and, in women, the radically distended clitoris. Victorian doctors had a reason for inventing these symptoms: Because sexual desire itself was secret, hidden within the individual, the doctor or other authority could get control over the individual only by creating symptoms that would give sexual desire away. The extreme of this fantasy-invention appeared in 1876 in a text by Pouillet on female masturbation, one of the first texts in the medical literature on the subject. The invariable signs that a woman has been masturbating were peevishness, surliness toward strangers, and lying. Finally, says Pouillet, "There is a certain aspect, a *je ne sais quoi*, easier to recognise than to express in words." Tissot had maintained that autoeroticism drew the offender into an inner, self-contained world. By the time of Pouillet, the very idea of sexual desire had become privately enclosed. Someone else can obtain power over this desire only by somehow finding signs on the body that betray its presence. It has to be something perceptible if that power relation is to be exercised.

The second way autoeroticism became a prism for understanding eroticism concerns the relation between sexual desire and the imagination. It will be recalled that Tissot believed autoerotic experience to be the most powerful sexual experience a person could have. In the nineteenth century, this was extended to the sexual imagination. It was believed that the sexual desires of a person in isolation went wild. In solitude, wrote Lallemand in 1842, a person invents an erotic life the world can never sufficiently fulfill. The evil force in character, causing desire to be more powerful than sexual intercourse, is the imagination. The doctor or other authority must tamp down the fires of sexual desire by externally repressive measures. According to Lallemand, marital sex was seen as the great chastizer of desire. What is aimed at in these external, social technologies of control is the counteracting of the influence of imagination. There is a basic antagonism between fantasy and social order.

Finally and crucially, the lesson of autoeroticism was that sexuality itself could be a barometer for measuring human character. In the course of the nineteenth century, the physiological view of Tissot fell by the wayside, but his connection of autoeroticism to the moral character of an individual grew even stonger. Here is how a popular "sex hygiene" guide for young people put the matter in 1917 (it is Robert Willson's *The Education of the Young in Sex Hygiene*): "The boy who can look his father and mother fully and laughingly in the eye, who can throw his shoulders back and breathe deep, that boy who regards his father as his comrade and his mother as his best friend, does not masturbate." By the time of Willson's manual, this kind of connection between character and sexuality had been generalized. Such matters as loyalty, reliability, and, above all, truthfulness were measured in terms of personality, and that is what is of interest about this quotation. The boy Willson admires can look his parents fully and laughingly in the eye because he has nothing to hide: He has no private, solitary secret about sex. This way of thinking becomes more general. Truthfulness with other people will depend on how a person has managed his or her own sexuality. What makes this management difficult is that sexuality has come to be seen as an innerdrawing, powerful, enclosed experience of desire. The problem in telling the truth about sex thus becomes enmeshed in telling the truth about a self that resists revelation.

This brief sketch of how autoeroticism became the vehicle by which sexuality and self-knowledge were joined during the last century may suggest, I hope, how certain Christian formulas reappear in secular discourse. Augustine believed that the definition of sexuality revolved around the question of feeling, rather than on questions of action or social position, as did Artemidorus. That is also the case here. Sexuality is the architecture of the whole realm of inner desire. And the medical and the Christian texts share the notion that confronting what one desires rather than what one does is what really constitutes self-knowledge.

Sexuality and solitude

There is a power relationship implicated in this knot of truthfulness, sexuality, and personal self-knowledge. The knot is tied in so complicated a way that an outside authority is necessary for the person to unravel it: Christians confess to the priest, the secular go to the doctor. It was not in its advocacy of sexual repression that Victorian medicine returned to the Christian roots of the culture, but in the psychological importance it assigned to knowledge of oneself through the counsel and control of another, more knowing human being.

This analysis of Tissot's legacy may be related to the issue of difference, which I raised at the outset. Sexuality is something every human being experiences, yet our inheritance from the medical and educational theories of the last century is that by understanding our sexuality we believe we will understand what is distinctive and individual about ourselves. The universal is used to define the particular. If there is one element in the Victorian heritage that makes this process confusing, it is the definition of sexuality in terms of desire rather than of activity. "Everyone makes love," said one of Krafft-Ebing's subjects, "but each person is thinking of something special when they do." It is difficult, if not impossible, to deduce from private sexual desires a person's capacity for loyalty, courage, or truthfulness with others. That these thoughts, these desires, these fantasies should be seen as privileged, as of importance in defining the whole of an individual personality, is what creates such a mystery about individual difference. The privilege accorded to desire is a Christian heritage. We are today far from being able to cope with what we have inherited.

JEAN STAROBINSKI

A short history of body consciousness

TRANSLATED BY SARAH MATTHEWS

In one of his *Cahiers*, Paul Valéry has the note:
> Somatism (heresy of the end of time),
> Adoration, cult of the machine for living.[1]

Have we come to the end of time? The heresy anticipated by Valéry has almost become the official religion. Everything is related to the body, as if it had just been rediscovered after being long forgotten; body image, body language, body consciousness, liberation of the body are the passwords. Historians, prey to the same infection, have begun inquiring into what previous cultures have done with the body, in the way of tattooing, mutilation, celebration, and all the rituals related to the various bodily functions.[2] Past writers from Rabelais to Flaubert are ransacked for evidence, and immediately it becomes apparent that we are far from being the first discoverers of bodily reality. That reality was the first knowledge to enter human understanding: "They knew that they were naked" (Genesis 3:7). From then on, it has been impossible to ignore the body.

Nevertheless, body consciousness, as it is practiced and spoken of in our society, does have certain new and original aspects that it is important to bring out and whose antecedents it would be useful to set in order in sound genetic fashion. But so as to not let myself be led astray (and because I believe that the most fruitful generalizations are those arising from fairly precise studies of limited topics), I will confine myself to a somewhat circumscribed area: the internal perception of our own bodies – *cenesthesia* – which is undeniably a component of our contemporary "sensibility," whether among philosophers or writers, or in certain psychotherapeutic practices ("autogenic training" [Schulz], relaxation, "body contacts"), or, finally, in psychoanalytic thinking.

A short history of body consciousness

We shall not dwell on the theories developed by the ancients, however fascinating they might be; but let us recall a few stages of earlier thinking, before pausing a little longer over the discussions that prevailed at the end of the nineteenth century and Freud's response to them.

In antiquity, the disciples of Aristippus of Cyrene spoke of an "internal contact" – *tactus intimus* in Cicero's translation.[3] Montaigne, quoting Cicero, reminds us that "the Cyrenaics... maintain that nothing external to themselves is perceptible, and that the only things that they do perceive are the sensations due to internal contact, for example pain and pleasure."[4]

For a long while, pain and pleasure were not attributed to a specific sensory system: They were called "bodily passions," whereas the traditional term, *internal sense* (*sensus internus*), referred to the conscious activities that the mind developed in and of itself (reason, memory, and imagination) on the basis of information provided by the *external senses* (sight, hearing, taste, touch, and smell). According to Aristotelian doctrine, the information provided by the external senses reached the internal sense only after having been unified by the *common sense* (*sensorium commune, koinon otistheterion*).[5] The body was in no way forgotten; but as long as Galenian medicine prevailed, it was principally by way of the humors, and not through nervous information, that the body was capable of modifying the activity of the souls and, in turn, of being modified by the soul.

In his treatise *The Passions of the Soul*, Descartes put forward a clear distinction between three different categories of perception: "that which relates to objects external to us" (art. 23), "that which refers to our body" (art. 24), and "that which refers to our soul" (art. 25). Bodily sensations were of many kinds:

> The cognisings we refer to our body, or to certain of its parts, are those we have of hunger, thirst, and of our other natural appetites – to which may be added pain, heat and the other affections which we sense as in our limbs, not as in external objects.[6]

Descartes thus analyzes and classes sensory activities as belonging to three specific areas – the body, the world, and the consciousness – daily experience of which leads us to an awareness of how they coincide and are superimposed one upon the other. But Descartes' influence in this regard was not particularly great among eighteenth-century doctors. Some of them, particularly in Montpellier, were more taken by Stahl's ideas, which conferred on the viscera a sort of relative autonomy and

JEAN STAROBINSKI

independent sensibility. Nonetheless, some philosophers, such as Lignac, Turgot, or d'Alembert, spoke with precision of a "sense of coexistence with our bodies," of an "internal touch," and so on.[7] Some of them (for instance, Bordeu, Lacaze, and Diderot) came to pick out a phrenic or diaphragmatic center, whose role merged with that of the splanchnic nexus of the sympathetic nerve. Cabanis, in 1800, attributed great importance to the "organic sensations" that ended in certain centers of reaction, the most important of which was, obviously, the brain. Thus the instincts were the transformation, at the level of behavior, of the most longstanding and most persistent of organic sensations. Instinct thus could be seen as the motor branch of a sensorimotor connection, the sensory branch of which was made up of "organic sensations."

It was in 1794, in Halle, in the title of a doctoral thesis at which Johann Christian Reil presided and of which he was the inspiration, that the word *coenesthesis* was used for the first time. The term was equivalent to the German *Gemeingefühl,* for which the French equivalent subsequently became on some occasions *sensibilité générale* (general sensibility) and on others *cénethésie* (cenesthesia).[8]

Reil (through the medium of his disciple Hübner) returned, without mentioning Descartes, to the tripartite division that we have already seen in *The Passions of the Soul*:

We encounter in the soul three sorts of representations, which differ in relation to the objects represented:
1) Its own intellectual state, its powers, its actions, its representations and concepts; it distinguishes these things itself, and in this way becomes conscious of itself.
2) It represents to itself its external state or the relations of the whole man to the world.
3) Finally, it represents to itself its own bodily state.
Each of these sorts of ideas, by which man is represented according to the three different types of state, is sited in the body in its own particular organic apparatus:
1) *Cenesthesia,* by means of which the soul is informed of the state of its body, which occurs by means of the nerves generally distributed throughout the body.
2) Sensation (sensatio externa). This is excited by the senses and represents the world to the soul.
3) Finally, the activities which originate and are carried out integrally within the organ of the soul. [*Organ der Seele* is the term Reil uses to designate the brain.]
By means of these (that is to say, by the *internal sense)* imagination and judgment are formed; the soul receives the representation of its powers, its ideas and its concepts, and is thus rendered conscious of itself.[9]

A short history of body consciousness

This distinction between three specific organic apparatuses can be found again, at the beginning of our own century, but without any direct reference to Reil, in Carl Weinecke. He proposed, as is well known, a model of psychic life that involved collaboration between an *allopsyche* (in relation to external objects), a *somatopsyche* (in relation to corporeal existence), and an *autopsyche* (in relation to its own system of representations).[10] In Reil (as in Weinecke), this functional distinction formed the basis for a pathogenic classification. Reil not only envisaged changes in cenesthesia due to general disorders, but he allowed there to be idiopathic disorders of the cenesthesia: There were in fact cases in which the effects of the disease were limited to the nervous apparatus involved in transmitting the somatic information – free of any effect on the visceral organs or on the brain itself. A distortion (the anatomo-pathological substratum of which Reil was entirely incapable of indicating) then sent a misleading message to the brain about the body's condition. A bodily illusion occurred – giving rise to a belief in a tumor or an abdominal parasite, despite the lack of any objective evidence. Up to a certain point, judgment could correct this false impression. But when the impression managed to take a hold, it created a state of madness. A good hundred years before the concept of *cenestopathy* appeared in France (with Dupré and Camus), Reil included in his psychiatric nosology a class of ailments characterized by a primary disturbance of bodily representations. This very extensive class contained the classic examples that had occurred for the previous two or three centuries in chapters on melancholia or hypochondria: people who believed themselves to be made of glass and liable to shatter at the slightest blow and who had lost the feeling of being present within their actual bodies. Reil had no difficulty adding disorders of the humors, or derangement of the instincts or the appetites, such as pica, bulimia, and polydipsia on the one hand, and nymphomania and lubricity on the other.

"Romantic" thought readily welcomed the concept of cenesthesia. From a genetic point of view, Reil had already accorded it priority in the order of sensory activities: It was the first that appeared in the fetus. Evolutionist speculation, right up to physiologists like Purkinje, could propose the notion of a primary bodily sense from which all the other sensory activities could be seen as being differentiated developments. As the first vital sensation, cenesthesia could be considered, by some, to be the source of all psychic life, insofar as that life was made up of sensory differences. What came to prevail, among scholars or philosophers claiming to be determinist or monist, was a "sensualist" conception of mental life, which opened the way for a sort of imperialism of cenesthesia. If mental life was determined by sensory activity, and if all sensory activity was made up of derivatives of cenesthesia, then one could finish by asserting, as Ribot did in 1884, in *The Diseases of the Personality*, that our personality resided entirely in the messages, partially unconscious, that derived from bodily life.

The fifteen French editions of Ribot's *Diseases of the Personality* (published between 1883 and 1914) bear witness to the immense influence exerted by this book and justify a fairly close examination of the theories propounded in it.

A first assertion was based on physiology: "Its [consciousness'] production is always associated with some activity of the nervous system."[11] In accord with the physiologists, however, Ribot allowed that a significant part of nervous activity might remain unconscious: "All nervous activity does by no means imply psychic activity – nervous activity being far more extended than psychic activity. Consciousness, accordingly, is something superadded."[12] It was an improvement, but it was doomed to *intermission*. (Ribot underlines the term, a term to which, as one knows, Proust was to attach great importance.) The personality was thus a variable kaleidoscopic phenomenon, by very reason of the incessant fluctuation of bodily states:

If, accordingly, we admit that the organic sensations proceeding from all the tissues, organs and movements produced – in a word, from all the states of the body – are in some degree and form represented in the *sensorium*; and if the physical personality be only their sum total, it follows that personality must vary as they vary, and that these variations admit of all possible degrees, from simple distemper to the total metamorphosis of the individual. Instances of "double personality" . . . are but an extreme case. . . We should find in mental pathology enough observations to establish a progression, or rather a continuous regression from the most transient change, to the most complete alteration of the ego. . . The ego exists only on the condition of continually changing.[13]

Following Ribot, Sollier proposed an interpretation of hysteria as the result of changes in cenesthesia; Séglas attributed to this same "peripheral" mechanism states of depersonalization and melancholic deliria of negation.

One would have no difficulty in demonstrating that what one is dealing with here is an entirely theoretical construction, supported in large part by an entirely *metaphorical* method of argumentation. The fundamental assumption is of a causality that operates on the basis of elementary materials, in which complex phenomena are *built up* from simple units. Ribot refers to Taine, who himself refers to Dr. Krishaber to maintain: "The Ego, the moral person, is a product of which sensations are the prime factors."[14] To this neosensualism are added curious political metaphors, which could have flowed only from the pen of a convinced democrat. Thus, after having declared that "in every animal the basis of its psychic individuality is the organic sense," he adds:

> But, in man and with the higher animals, the turbulent world of desires, passions, perceptions, images, and ideas covers up this silent back-ground. Except at given intervals, it is forgotten, from the fact that it is not known. Here the same takes place as in the order of social facts. The millions of human beings, making up a large nation, as regards itself and others, are reduced to a few thousand men, who constitute its clear consciousness, and who represent its social activity in all its aspects, its politics, its industry, its commerce, and its intellectual culture. And yet these millions of unknown human beings, – limited as to manner and place of existence, quietly living and quietly passing away – make up all the rest; without them there would be nothing[15]

Ribot, in the closing sentences of the book, introduces terms like *consensus* and *solidarity*, which have an equally clear social resonance:

> The unity of the ego, in a psychological sense, is, therefore, the cohesion, during a given time, of a certain number of clear states of consciousness, accompanied by others less clear, and by a multitude of physiological states which without being accompanied by consciousness like the others, yet operate as much and even more than the former. Unity, in fact, means co-ordination. The conclusion to be drawn from the above remarks is namely this, that the consensus of consciousness being subordinate to the consensus of the organism, the problem of the unity of the ego is, in its ultimate form, a biological problem. To biology pertains the task of explaining, if it can, the genesis of organisms and the solidarity of their component parts. Psychological interpretation can only follow in its wake.[16]

What this radical biologism lacked, without yet having at its disposal the more recent concept of the genome, was any apparatus of clinical experiments and proofs. It was hardly surprising, then, that after a brief moment of glory, this "peripheral" theory of the constitution of the ego, and above all the interpretation it suggested of disturbances of the personality, became the object of lively criticism. Ribot was the first to admit its shortcomings[17] and recognized latterly that in attributing so great an importance to somatic sensory information, he had neglected the motor components of psychic activity. Pierre Janet[18] observed that in all the cases of depersonalization he had examined, he had never been able to demonstrate any kind of peripheral sensory disturbance, and, as a corollary, that when dealing with tabetics whose bodily perceptions were seriously upset, he had not noted any psychic disturbances. To allege a disturbance in "corporeal sensoriality" was, according to him, to remain trapped in a "metaphysical" hypothesis. Psychopathological phenomena, such as depersonalization or a sense of emptiness, should be considered as a lack of action (or lack of the psychic energy available for action) and not as a disturbance in sensory receptivity. "Scientific psychology must consider psychological facts as actions and express them in terms of action. A sense of emptiness is a disturbance of action and not of the sensibility nor of a poorly understood consciousness."[19] This led Janet to introduce a distinction between what he called "primary actions" and "secondary actions." Primary action takes its cue from sensory stimuli, whether internal or external, and reacts directly to them; secondary action brings to primary action the reinforcement of a *belief*, an integrating device effective in the circumstances experienced. Pathological disturbance, in depersonalization, affects the secondary action, which can break down without the primary action showing the slightest anomaly. It is in the "relation to the real" that the real disturbance is to be found.

The affirmation of the primacy of the *active* response over somatic information was also characteristic of Freud's thinking. But before lingering more closely over a few significant pages of Freud, it would be appropriate to devote a moment to the theory put forward by Charles Blondel in *La Conscience Morbide* (1914). (Both a doctor and a philosopher, Blondel began as a careful follower of the teachings of Durkheim and Bergson; after the war, he wrote one of the first important studies of Proust and composed a hasty and disappointing work on psychoanalysis.) In *La Conscience Morbide*, Blondel opposed to the "peripheral theory" an active force – and this active force was language. It was not that the cenesthetic message was nonexistent, but it was not its supposed disruption that explained the disturbances of the sick mind. According to Blondel, a purely physiological theory was incapable of explaining the phenomena observed by the clinician. The "cenesthetic masses" (which he also called "pure psychology") did not by themselves determine mental illness: The "morbid" factor lay entirely in the insufficiency of the verbal response to the bodily perceptions – a response worked out by the individual in the act of thinking according to the linguistic tools he has received from society. Noting, as Dupré had done in his studies on cenestopaths, that the mentally ill had recourse to a wealth of metaphorical formulas with which to describe their symptoms,[20] Blondel sited the

A short history of body consciousness

anomaly not in the (supposedly neutral) bodily nervous information but in a fault in the "eliminatory action" that should have resulted from a successful intervention of language. The normal mind, according to Blondel, eliminates the idiosyncratically individual, the "pure psychology," by putting into effect the interpretative tools and concepts provided by the system of collective representations. The law of language, which is the result of social training, has as its function the *impersonalization* of the expression that we give to our individual states. Blondel quoted in this respect a revealing passage from Durkheim:

> There really is a part of ourselves which is not placed in immediate dependence upon the organic factor: this is all that which represents society in us. The general ideas which religion or science fix in our minds, the mental operations which these ideas suppose, the beliefs and sentiments which are at the basis of our moral life, and all these superior forms of psychic activity which society awakens in us, these do not follow in the trail of our bodily states, as our sensations and our general bodily consciousness do... This is because the world of representations in which social life passes is superimposed upon its material substratum, far from arising from it.[21]

Blondel concluded from this that the normal mind was a mind in which the cenesthetic factor was dominated and controlled by the impersonal system of socialized discourse. While believing himself to be asserting his *ego*, the rational individual was in fact affirming the triumph of collective norms. The disturbed mind, incapable of manipulating language according to these collective dictates, was a mind embroiled in the individual cenesthetic experience – in the nonverbal or the preverbal, which even the most daring play of metaphor was incapable of expressing. Blondel did not fail to remark the poetic nature of these attempts, which tended to imply that poetry was deviant from the social norms, that it was sited on the side of "pure psychology," that it had something in common with the "sick mind."

It was thus not the body that imposed its law on the mind. It was society that, through the intermediacy of language, took the commands of the mind and imposed its law on the body. Blondel's theory tended to dispose of the body as cause in order to return to it later as the agent of the *expressive* intentions that the individual imposed on it under the dictates of the collective consciousness. Thus we can see interest shifting from the body as physiological object (primarily the producer of internal information destined to be filtered by language) to the body according to society (primarily carrying out messages bearing *meaning*, according to the collective codes and rules). Social prescriptions not only dictated language, but also nonverbal bodily manifestations; there is nothing, in the passage that follows, that could not be quoted with approval by any of the sociologists or "paralinguists" of today who talk to us of "the body as a medium of expression":[22]

In order to find the motor or vaso-motor expression of our states of mind, we are dumbly preoccupied in seeking the right note, of finding the mime, regulated and defined by custom and propriety, corresponding to the emotion-standard to which our own emotion refers. From this point of view mime seems, so to speak, to have received its morphology and its syntax from the collective... If one thinks about it hard, it becomes apparent that there is not a single one of our motor manifestations which is not thus more or less stringently defined and with regard to which there does not exist a collective model, that is to say, a motor concept, to which it has to conform.[23]

In writing the *Traumdeutung*, Freud began by running up against the generally held late-nineteenth-century theories that dream activity of struggle or liberation, during sleep, derives from peripheral or visceral sensory excitation. Ribot, in *The Diseases of the Personality*, had formulated in passing a theory of the dream that was in perfect accord with the rest of his theory of the primacy of cenesthesia:

Constantly active [the physical bases of the personality], they make up by their continuity for their weakness as psychic elements. Hence, as soon as the higher forms of mental life disappear, they pass to the front rank. A clear example of this exists in dreams (whether pleasant or painful) aroused by organic sensations; as night-mares, erotic dreams, etc. In these dreams, even with a certain degree of precision, we may assign to each organ the part that belongs to it.[24]

Freud, well aware of the vast body of literature that, even before Ribot, tended in the same direction, consecrated several pages of his historic Introduction to *Leibreiztheorie* (he used the term *Gemeingefühl* more rarely) and concluded that "the theory of somatic stimulation has not succeeded in completely doing away with the apparent absence of determination in the choice of what dream-images are to be produced."[25] He returned to the question again in Chapter V ("The Material and Sources of Dreams"), section (C), ("The Somatic Sources of Dreams").

Freud did not deny that "organic impressions" played their part in the production of dreams. But he did not allow that they could be a sufficient condition and the only cause: It was not enough to invoke them to be free of the need to provide any other explanation. Like Janet, Freud was opposed to a purely physiological theory, the more so to one that might be unifactorial or unicausal, according to which dreams were

A short history of body consciousness

seen as being merely the cerebral propagation, through loose associations, of visceral sensory stimuli. He noted that these stimuli were not always efficient; organic sensations, by definition, are never interrupted, whereas dreams are intermittent: "These stimuli are present at all times, and... it is difficult to understand, then, why the mind does not dream continuously all through the night."[26] In a number of cases, a dream may derive solely from psychic sources. And even when the presence of somatic sensations can be admitted with a certain degree of probability, they can be seen as being simply the *material* to which *work* is then applied from quite another quarter, and that alone gives it meaning. In relation to its somatic sources, the dream is a "reaction," an interpretative working out, and our scientific attention should be directed to that reaction; our interpretation should be of the act of interpretation carried out by the dreamer:

There can be no doubt that physical cenesthesia... is among the internal somatic stimuli which can dictate the content of dreams. It can do so, not in the sense that it can provide the dream's content, but in the sense that it can force upon the dream-thoughts a choice of the material to be represented... The cenesthetic feelings left over from the preceding day link themselves up, no doubt, with the psychical residues which have such an important influence on dreams. This general mood may persist unchanged in the dream or it may be mastered, and thus, if it is unpleasurable, may be changed into its opposite.

Thus, in my opinion, somatic sources of stimulation during sleep (that is to say, sensations during sleep), unless they are of unusual intensity, play a similar part in the formation of dreams to that played by recent but indifferent impressions left over from the previous day. I believe, that is, that they are brought in to help in the formation of a dream if they fit in appropriately with the ideational content derived from the dream's psychical sources, but otherwise not. They are treated like some cheap material always ready to hand, which is employed whenever it is needed, in contrast to a precious material which prescribes the way in which it is to be employed. If, to take a simile, a patron of the arts brings an artist some rare stone, such as a piece of onyx, and asks him to create a work of art from it, then the size of the stone, its colour and markings, help to decide what head or what scene shall be represented in it. Whereas in the case of a uniform and plentiful material such as marble or sandstone, the artist merely follows some idea that is present in his own mind.[27]

All that the somatic sources do, then, is provide one of the commonest materials, of which the mind of the dreamer, working from other sources, will make something of its own. Freud, in his turn, has recourse to metaphors; the image of the sculptor brings us back to Aristotelian notions of causality. In Aristotelian terms, the somatic source is, in the best sense, the material cause of the dream. But the neurophysiological actuality is not simply a neutral and anonymous substratum. The dream has meaning because of the *form* imposed on this substratum. This setting into form is the result of an intention, of which the active agent is called the "spirit," the "wish," "dream-work." Freud assigned a double aim to the dream: to protect sleep and to fulfill a wish. In both cases, the dream works according to its own ends, *against* the somatic sensation – either to neutralize it or to transform it. Accepting these postulates entails an important consequence for anyone wishing to achieve an adequate understanding of dreams. It is vain to trace dreams back to their physiological source and to invoke a particular visceral disturbance, which could be measured in terms of the strength of the painful stimuli or in variations in the cardiac rate. What one now has to understand is the new language, the original form in which this material – in itself unimportant – has been interpreted and recast by the dream. Analysis is an exegesis of the final cause of the dream: It seeks to understand what the wish is aiming for, and why.

In other words, dream analysis can be seen as the "informed" interpretation of a "naive" interpretation, which has itself been reworked at the moment of narrating the dream. But this formula is still too simple; for the somatic stimulus is the starting point for a double translation. First, it gives rise to the deployment of *latent thoughts*, in which the wish can express itself without reserve; then it transports itself – through the distortions and puzzles of which Freud so carefully established the vocabulary – in the *manifest* dream. The "somatic source," the material cause, was in addition only an occasional cause, a pretext. Freud did not fail to recognize this, but he felt it unnecessary to reiterate it. This meant in effect reworking the definition of the unconscious. Despite what is fairly widely believed today, it was quite usual to speak of the unconscious before Freud's time, but it was an unconscious associated with the obscure murmurings of visceral functions, from which would emerge, intermittently, conscious acts. For Freud, the unconscious was the first interpretation of visceral stimuli, it was the *latent thoughts of the dream*, and the process that gave form to the manifest dream. Freud's original contribution was not to have spoken first of the unconscious but to have, so to speak, lifted the monopoly held on it by organic life and to have installed it within the psychic apparatus itself. It was thus at the price of abandoning the body (in which it was definable only in terms of weakness or strength, whether organic or "nervous") that the unconscious became the custodian of a language and the producer of palimpsests or puzzles that were then open to being

A short history of body consciousness

deciphered. Having ceased to have the life of the body as its exclusive source, the unconscious then escaped from the exclusive competence of a medical approach and became dependent on hermeneutics.

Thus, before Durkheim and Blondel opposed to cenesthesia the conceptual categories of language set up by the collective consciousness, Freud, in 1900, opposed to cenesthesia, to "organic stimuli," the operation of language, but a language in which the social norms were only partially represented – by censorship and interdictions. Another similarity – apart from any questions of priority – is worth noting: Though the body might see itself being refused any sort of importance as a causal source of psychic disturbance, it found a crucial role for itself as the *place* or *scene* in which this disturbance manifested itself. In a vision that placed in the background the sensory information being provided by the body, and that emphasized the reaction manifested in the act and in language, the body came to appear as the primary object of the act and as the primary signification worked out in the language. Just as Durkheim and Blondel, after having rejected the hypothesis of a cenesthetic source of psychosis, reestablished the importance of the body as bearer or enactor of manifestations of a gestural code of social origin, so Freud equally returned to the body, no longer considering it as explanatory *source* but as the place in which were carried out the expressive *aims* of the wish. Breuer and Freud had already taken this direction in their studies of hysteria. The case of the dream was equally clear; and among the different types of dream, the nightmare provided a typical example.[28]

Received medical opinion held that nightmares were the representational transposition of a purely somatic oppression. According to Freud, such a case was the exception; the greatest number of somatic sufferings felt in dreams were, on the contrary, the representation of a censored wish loaded with suffering: What could not be denied was that the suffering then *expressed* itself in the language of the body, though the "source" should be sought in the psyche. The inquiry should turn from the disturbed body to the affect that was at once revealed and hidden in the somatic register. The body was the wrong turning, the dead end taken by energy originating from the psyche, and to which the term *intention* was more appropriate than *excitation*.

At this point, it seems that in marking a radical difference between psychological explanation and physiological explanation, in "dephysiologizing" psychology, Freud was "desomatizing" the causal system commonly accepted by his predecessors. There is, in Freud's explanations, less body and more language than in the majority of his contemporaries; this explains the dissension that was to grow, at least for a while, between psychoanalysts and neurophysiologists. Freud took care never to sever the links with biology (which is far from being the case with some of those who, subsequently, claimed to be his followers). To be sure, what Freud retained of biology did not consist of experimentally measurable mechanism but, rather, of general schemes and of supposedly permanent laws of the nervous system and living matter. If Freudian psychology became detached, to some extent, from the physiological body, *metapsychology*, in compensation, showed itself to be a return to physiology and to the body in an intuitive and imaginative manner, but guided by phenomena that had been established sufficiently securely by experimental physiology to serve as *models*. One of the most illuminating texts in this regard is the 1915 study entitled *Instincts and Their Vicissitudes*. The physiological model on which Freud's thinking was based was that of stimulus and response, the sensorimotor reflex arc. To this was added another physiological assumption: "The nervous system is an apparatus which has the function of getting rid of the stimuli that reach it, or of reducing them to the lowest possible level; or which, if it were feasible, would maintain itself in an altogether unstimulated condition."[29]

On the basis of these assumptions, Freud established a distinction (a distinction already largely foreshadowed in the writings of nineteenth-century physiologists on instincts and passions) between external excitation, which is usually unique and momentary, and internal excitation, of somatic origin, which acts "as a constant force," whose effect is translated as "need," and whose satisfaction, whose "mastery," can only be carried out according to a single muscular response, such as flight, which would constitute the adequate response to the external excitation. Not only does the instinct derive from a somatic source, but its satisfaction can be obtained only by an action directed *toward* the exterior. The individual must bring into play a series of complex behavior patterns, the aim of which is to modify (to reduce) "the internal source of excitation."

Where the dream was concerned, the "somatic source" was optional. Where instincts were concerned, there was no question of its central role. But Freud, while conceding it precedence by right, by the status of a necessary condition and a material cause, in fact declared it to be irrelevant to the psychological investigation. At this level, physiology would have been in command had it not been (provisionally? definitively?) disarmed; as for psychology, it remained speechless:

> By the source of an instinct is meant the somatic process which occurs in an organ or part of the body and whose stimulus is represented in mental life by an instinct. We do not know whether this process is invariably of a chemical nature or whether it may also correspond to the release of other, e.g. mechanical, forces. The study of the sources of instincts lies outside the scope of psychology. Although instincts are wholly determined by their origin in a somatic source, in mental life we know them only by their aims. An exact knowledge of the sources of an instinct is not invariably necessary for purposes of psychological investigation; sometimes its source may be inferred from its aim.[30]

First remark: The transition from somatic to psychic, in the case of the instinct, is not the perceptive order; the instinct is not simply the cry of the organ echoed and recorded. At least, Freud does not lay any emphasis on this element, which would immediately raise the question of its more or less conscious character. The concept he used was that of *representation* (*repräsentieren*), which implies an operation of a "semiotic" nature. This foreshadows the "second topic," in which the id can be seen to take on a good part of this representative function.

Second remark: Contrary to what happened with the dream, the somatic source is regained at the end of the instinctual activity, since the *aim* of the instinct is a modification in the source of excitation. But this aim, at first held to be invariable, can have others substituted for it. This is the "physiological" return to the somatic source that does not take place and that, displacing the *site* of satisfaction, creates to some extent an illusory body in which the true (organic) body has no place:

> The aim of an instinct is in every instance satisfaction, which can only be obtained by removing the state of stimulation at the source of the instinct. But although the ultimate aim of each instinct remains unchangeable, there may yet be different paths leading to the same ultimate aim; so that an instinct may be found to have various nearer or intermediate aims, which are combined or interchanged with one another. Experience permits us also to speak of instincts which are "inhibited in their aim," in the case of processes which are allowed to make some advance towards instinctual satisfaction but are then inhibited or deflected. We may suppose that even processes of this kind involve a partial satisfaction.[31]

If "inhibition in their aim" implies a relative desertion of the body, a sidetracking or diversion in relation to the necessary "modification of the source," consideration of the *object* of the instinct brings up a number of possibilities, among which our "own body" is called upon to play a major role:

JEAN STAROBINSKI

The object of an instinct is the thing in regard to which or through which the instinct is able to achieve its aim. It is what is most variable about an instinct and is not originally connected with it, but becomes assigned to it only in consequence of being peculiarly fitted to make satisfaction possible. The object is not necessarily something extraneous: it may equally well be a part of the subject's own body. It may be changed any number of times in the course of the vicissitudes which the instinct undergoes during its existence; and highly important parts are played by this displacement of instinct.[32]

Our "own body" thus reappears, in the wide-open repertoire of places (that *in which*) or of means (that *by means of which*) that the instinct can choose in order to obtain its aim and on which it can on occasion become *fixated*. That is the case when there occurs – as in narcissism or masochism – a "turning round of an instinct upon the subject's own self."

Thus there appears a new role for the body; I was almost about to say a new body – the body as support for fixation or investment. And there is nothing to stop a new representation, prolonging or transforming that in which the somatic excitation has already been prolonged or transformed. We have not left the body. But if it is true that there persisted, for Freud, a distant analogy between the simple reflex arc and the way in which instincts work, then one could say that the body-object, the body of investment, corresponds to a *motor* effect, which seeks immediate confirmation in the order of perceptions, without being able to avoid getting mixed up in a whole imaginary or symbolic projection. When Schilder[33] came to study the image of the body, he paid very little attention to the primary bodily schema, as derives from the different kinesthetic or somesthetic apparatuses; he was much more concerned with the image, in part fantasized, that accompanies the different types of libidinal investment. What Freud established, through a system of representations taking over one from the other, was a circuit that could renew itself virtually infinitely: from the body as the source of the instinct to the body as aim, site, or means of "satisfaction."

All that I have done here is to recall, in a very simplified form, the essential characteristics that make it possible to place Freud's thinking in the history of ideas about cenesthesia and body consciousness. His contribution was considerable: Before him, cenesethesia was the first stage of a system of sensory information, from which sprang the personality, fully armed. Whether conscious or unconscious, these physiological data exercised their full power straightaway. All that remained to the higher centers was to submit to their law, or to respond as best they could; the traditional model included two terms, in relation to reciprocity. Traditional medical thinking used to be able to make only this simple account, reiterated in innumerable nineteenth-century works, which started in visceral irritation and ended in, for instance, mania (or vice versa), or started in a break in the apparatus of the somatic sensibilities and ended in depersonalization. In Freud, instincts had a goal and gave rise to much longer and more circumstantial accounts, as he pursued their migrations, their substitutions, and the meshing of different aims or objects. It was now a complex circuit that had to be considered, and no longer a simple short shuttling between "action" and "reaction." The feeling of depersonalization, for instance, is a loss that occurs at the end of a long process; *Mourning and Melancholia* traces the various stages, in which the first false step is the choice of a narcissistic object. It has no relation to the primary organic and sensory dysfunction that Ribot thought to discern.

At the beginning of this essay, I almost suggested a synonymity between *cenesthesia* and *awareness of the body*. But after our rapid rereading of Freud, and recalling what he said about the "turning round of an instinct upon the subject's own self" in narcissism and masochism, there is a question that cannot be avoided: Where do we draw the line between cenesthesia, which must be a basic assumption of every human existence, and *body awareness*, which would be the hypochondriacal or perverse consequence of a narcissistic or autoerotic investment?

Sartre (who is, through Dumas, so close to Ribot's ideas) would answer without a moment's hesitation that the manner in which we "exist our contingency" reveals itself to us in cenesthesia:

> When no pain, no specific satisfaction or dissatisfaction is "existed" by consciousness, the for-itself does not thereby cease to project itself beyond a contingency which is pure and so to speak unqualified. Consciousness does not cease "to have" a body. Cenesthetic affectivity is then a pure, non-positional apprehension of a contingency without color, a pure apprehension of the self as a factual existence. This perpetual apprehension on the part of my for-itself of an *insipid* taste which I cannot place, which accompanies me even in my efforts to get away from it, and which is *my* taste – this is what we have described elsewhere under the name of Nausea. A dull and inescapable nausea reveals my body to my consciousness.[34]

As for Merleau-Ponty, the discussion of the notion of the bodily schema leads him to assert that "one's own body is the third term, always tacitly understood, in the figure-background structure, and every figure stands out against the double horizon of external and bodily space."[35] But if to this inevitable and naive presence of the body – a "non-positional" (Sartre), "tacit" (Merleau-Ponty) presence – is added an intentional *awareness*, it is then appropriate to ask, with Freud, whether this interest presupposes a regressive or narcissistic libidinal investment. What I devote to an awareness of the body, I subtract from my presence in the world, from my investments in the *other*. In a conscious awareness of the body, the *aesthetic* element of cenesthesia is in the nature of an instinctual satisfaction undeniably confused with primary physiological information. It is a variation on "turning round upon the subject's own self." There is nothing very bold in drawing the only superficially banal conclusion that the present infatuation with the different modes of body consciousness is a symptom of the considerable narcissistic component characteristic of contemporary Western culture. I am, I know, far from being the first to say so. The so-called Chicago school, Richard Sennett,[36] and a variety of others have made such a declaration, based on other premises, a recurrent motif in their critical thought. Perhaps one could also enter a plea on behalf of Narcissus (or at least invoke extenuating circumstances in his favor). In a world in which technological mastery has made such rapid strides, can one not understand that the desire to feel – and to feel *oneself* – should arise as a compensation, necessary, even in its excesses, to our psychic survival?

NOTES

1 Paul Valéry, *Cahiers* (Paris: Pléiade, 1973), I, 1126.
2 Cf. Robert Brain, *The Decorated Body* (New York: Harper & Row, 1979); Victoria Ebin, *The Body Decorated* (Thames and Hudson, 1979).
3 Cicero, *Academia*, II, xxiv.
4 Montaigne, *Essais* (Paris: PUF, 1965), p. 587.
5 Aristotle, *De anima*, III, ii.
6 Descartes, *Traité des passions de l'ame*, in *Descartes' Philosophical Writings*, trans. Norman Kemp Smith (London: Macmillan, 1953), p. 290.
7 Cf. Georges Gasdorf, *Naissance de la conscience romantique au siècle des lumières* (Paris, 1976), pp. 285–316.
8 "Coenaesthesis, dissertatio (...) quam praeside J. C. Reil, pro gradu doctoris defendit Chr. Friedr. Hübner" (Halle, 1794).
9 On the history of the concept of cenesthesia in the nineteenth century, cf. Jean Starobinski, "Le Concept de cénesthésie et les idées neuropsychologiques de Moritz Schiff," *Gesnerus*, 34 (1977), fasc. 1/2, pp. 2–20.
10 Carl Weinecke, *Grundriss der Psychiatrie*, 2nd ed. (Leipzig, 1906).
11 Ribot, *The Diseases of the Personality* (Chicago, 1891), p. 5.
12 Ibid., pp. 5–6.

A short history of body consciousness

13 Ibid., p. 30.
14 Hippolyte Taine, *De l'Intelligence*, 12th ed. (Paris, 1911), II, 474.
15 Ribot, *Diseases*, pp. 19-20.
16 Ibid., p. 157.
17 Notably in *Problèmes de psychologie affective* (Paris, 1906), p. 26.
18 Pierre Janet, *De l'Angoisse à l'extase*, 2 vols. (1926; new ed. Paris, 1975), vol. II, ch. 1, 2.
19 Janet, *De L'Angoisse à l'extase*, vol. II, ch. II, §8, p. 71.
20 Ernest Dupré, *Pathologie de l'imagination et de l'émotivité* (Paris, 1925), pp. 289-304.
21 Charles Blondel, *La Conscience morbide* (Paris, 1914), p. 264. The quotation refers back to Durkheim, *The Elementary Forms of the Religious Life*, trans. J. W. Swain (London, 1915), p. 271.
22 See, among others, Ted Polhemus, ed., *Social Aspects of the Human Body* (London: Penguin, 1978); Jonathan Benthall and Ted Polhemus, eds., *The Body as a Medium of Expression* (London: Allen Lane/Penguin Books, 1975).
23 Blondel, *La Conscience morbide*, pp. 259-60.
24 Ribot, *Diseases*, p. 25.
25 Sigmund Freud, *The Interpretation of Dreams*, trans. J. Strachey (London, 1955), p. 39.
26 Ibid., p. 226.
27 Ibid., p. 237.
28 Ibid., p. 236.
29 Sigmund Freud, *Instincts and Their Vicissitudes*, in *The Standard Edition of the Complete Psychological Works of Sigmund Freud*, trans. J. Strachey (London, 1964), XIV, 120.
30 Ibid., p. 123.
31 Ibid., p. 122.
32 Ibid., pp. 122-3.
33 Paul Schilder, *L'Image du corps*, trans. F. Gantheret and P. Truffert (Paris: Gallimard, 1968).
34 Jean-Paul Sartre, *Being and Nothingness*, trans. Hazel E. Barnes (London: Methuen, 1967), p. 338.
35 Maurice Merleau-Ponty, *Phenomenology of Perception*, trans. Colin Smith (London: Routledge & Kegan Paul, 1962), p. 101.
36 Richard Sennett, "Le Narcissisme et la culture moderne," in *Former l'Homme*, Rencontres Internationales de Genève, Neuchâtel, La Baconnière, 1979, pp. 187-203.

NATALIE ZEMON DAVIS

The sacred and the body social in sixteenth-century Lyon

Where is the sacred in the sixteenth-century French city? We think readily of church towers and spires, which in the old engravings give the town its characteristic profile. We hear the bells ring for terce and nones and other hours of the priest's day, which mark the sacrifice of the mass, which announce the feast's arrival, the neighbor's death, and the funeral's passage. We visualize the penitential processions winding through the streets with their relics, statues, and great crosses, to appease God's wrath at a time of famine or an act of sacrilege. We see the confraternities' processions, more joyous perhaps, banners flying, drums beating, blessed bread held high, all to the devotion of their patron saint. We see the city's poor, in queues or clumps, waiting for their alms of bread in courtyards, at doors and gates. We see Protestant worshippers, dressed in sober clothes, singing the Psalms of David as they move through the town to their preachers; Protestant crowds, breaking idols in the cathedral, mocking the host and threatening the priests; Catholic crowds, throwing themselves on those who have dared affront the body of Jesus Christ and insult his holy mother.

Such scenes are familiar ones, and historians have used them for a variety of purposes: to ascertain whether religious behavior is or is not bringing people spiritual security and tranquility, is or is not living up to standards of Erasmian or Lutheran piety. They have been used to describe the conflict between clergy and laity - an important perspective[1] - and to characterize the religious style of different social groups, such as the merchants. But despite a growing documentation on urban piety in the sixteenth century, on urban charitable institutions, on the events of the Protestant and Catholic Reformations in individual cities, and on urban witchcraft and possession, we have come to few conclusions on the ways in which religion formed and gave expression to urban values and mentality in that period.

The sacred and the body social in Lyon

Why should this be so? In my view, because historians have been limited in their thinking about the roles that religion can play in an urban environment and about the resources available to study them. As for roles, we have considered, say, how religion can mobilize city dwellers during the catastrophe of a plague or of a famine, but much less the question posed by Ernst Troeltsch, Max Weber, and Bernd Moeller: How can religion continuously shape a sense of urban community, of urban solidarity?[2] We have considered how religion can facilitate class differentiation (as with the workings of the Calvinist doctrine of providence) but much less the other kinds of social divisions (such as those between native and foreigner or between male and female) that religion can foster. For many, the early modern city has been either the source of "rational," ethical religion or of laicization, fragmentation, and anonymity. Only these developments are seen to mesh well with a business economy. In such a view, the sacred appears as a residue from the village or from the tradition-bound premodern town; and lower-class millenarianism, if it develops, is seen as a defense *against* the city. Why not reconsider the evolutionary view of urban secularization and look for a wider set of possible religious responses to the city?[3]

As for resources available for the study of religion, historians of the sixteenth century have somewhat neglected its symbolic aspects – that is, have not considered as deeply as they might the meanings of metaphors used in religious material or implied by ecclesiastical organization; and have examined doctrine and the social and ethical teachings of the churches much more than liturgy and other forms of worship, supplication, and sacrifice. Symbolic analysis has its perils – sometimes a maypole is just a maypole, a colleague reminds me – but recent historical work on royal ceremonial shows how much this technique can teach us about social relationships and deeply held beliefs.[4]

In this essay I would like to make such an inquiry about the role of the sacred in the city of Lyon, especially in the years from 1550 to 1580, when Calvinism had emerged as an organized movement in active conflict with Catholicism for control of the town. I shall not be considering here the origins of the Reformation, though some of the material presented has a bearing on that. Nor shall I be looking at the relation of the city to the king, important though that question may be, because I want to focus for the moment on social interaction within the town walls.

I am going to approach Protestantism and Catholicism as two languages that among many uses, could describe, mark, and interpret

41

urban life, and in particular urban space, urban time, and the urban community. They shared some of the same vocabulary and metaphors – such as that of the human body – and at least in the 1530s they could find common terms for talking about the burning issue of poor relief. By mid-century, however, it was evident that their grammars were distinct. For both languages, there were areas of human experience about which they fell silent or could respond only in expletives. Yet both could be adequate to some of the needs and complexities of a sixteenth-century city. I shall be building on and reformulating Max Weber's view of the positive and novel connections between Calvinism and capitalism, suggesting that Catholicism too could have positive connections with a changing urban life and economy, while Calvinism could sometimes be powerless before the city. That is to say, I shall be reformulating Max Weber's notion of the potentiality of traditional–magical religion and of the "rationality" of Calvinism.

I

Let us begin with a look at the major features of Lyonnais life in the sixteenth century. Lyon was a town growing rapidly to be the second largest city in France, and larger than any in Germany; between 1530 and 1555 its resident population increased by a third, from around 45,000 people to 65,000. One of the financial and commercial capitals of Europe, its fairs, started up in the fifteenth century, and its new industries (printing, silk, metallurgy) drew young men from nearby villages and far-away towns. At mid-century (according to all the marriage contracts remaining in the archives for the four years from 1557 to 1560) over 60 percent of the men and about a third of the women living in Lyon were born elsewhere. It was a town whose social structure had changed since "la république des clercs" of the mid-fifteenth century. Now rich merchants were taking their places along with the lawyers and doctors of law on the city council. The artisans were enjoying a little more prestige than before, relative to the merchants, especially those in printing, in the goldsmith's art, and in silk-making. Even their journeymen had a higher rate of literacy than before: In the book and metal trades, for instance, more than 70 percent of the men knew how to sign their names. Finally, the social structure had changed its shape somewhat at the bottom – or at least, so it seemed to the *gens du bien*, the "respectable people," who worried a great deal about the vagabonds and poor beggars who were multiplying at Lyon. A new municipal welfare organization, the Aumône-Générale, had been set up to deal with them.[5]

From this brief sketch I want to single out two elements important to my analysis: the fairs and the foreigners. They were both essential for the existence, for the survival of this town with its advanced economy. But at the same time they seemed to threaten its moral health and to put a heavy strain on the bonds of trust that held together the body social. Consider the fairs. Four times a year for about two weeks the town breathed, opened, lowered its guard, so that people and merchandise "from every country of the world" could penetrate its gates and disembark at its ports. Every part of the city was *en foire*, became a fairground; there was no limiting it, as the Lyonnais had recently tried to limit the plague to the new quarantine hospital of St. Laurent, just outside the town walls. The days themselves were privileged: Merchants from enemy countries could come to Lyon with a safe conduct; commercial disputes were judged by a special court, rapid and efficient. Everything was up for sale, every currency was put in exchange; and it all had to move with the ease of a river – and not with the languor of the Saône but with the swiftness of the Rhône. The organization of artisanal work was almost as free as that of commerce. Apart from the trades of the surgeons, the goldsmiths, and the locksmiths, there were no "sworn crafts" at Lyon in the sixteenth century or any fully developed guilds. Anyone with money or credit could come and set himself up as a printer or a fustian manufacturer or a pewterer.[6]

And what of these foreigners? Not those who left after the fairs, but that large percentage of males, not natives of Lyon, who lived within its walls. Of all adult males residing in the city at mid-century, about 19 percent came from outside the kingdom of France. The most notable were *Messieurs des Nations* – the Florentine, Genoese, and Lucchese merchants, who controlled the money market at the fairs and who had taught the Lyonnais the techniques of international trade. *Messieurs des Nations* had their own political institutions in Lyon and their own places of honor in municipal parades; they gave generously to the new Aumône-Générale; they mounted extravagant festivals, mummeries, and costumed games, thereby dazzling the *Enfants de la Ville* (the native patrician youth), who had not yet thought of dressing up as African queens or as Roman soldiers, or of putting on a mock battle with oranges. Certain of the wealthy Italians were quite ready to become naturalized citizens of France, to Frenchify their names and to wed a Lyonnaise. But most of these families remained apart, sometimes for generations, speaking Italian and marrying among themselves while keeping close contact with their town of origin and with their relatives in commercial branches in Antwerp and in Spain.[7]

As for the other foreigners in Lyon – the numerous Savoyard traders and artisans, the Italian silkmakers, the Germans, the Flemish, and those Frenchmen from neighboring and distant provinces (for anyone not from the Lyonnais was considered an *étranger*) – only the German bankers had special civic institutions like those of the Italian merchants. The other newcomers adapted themselves to the city more or less slowly, making use of contacts among their compatriots, their relatives, and their fellow workers and then often taking a Lyonnaise as wife.[8]

The fairs and the foreigners were necessary and prized. But why were they at the same time dangerous? Because people feared that this opulence, this freedom of exchange, would burst the dams controlling the human appetites. What disorders could come about when the apertures of the body social were so open? What "a boiling up of contrary humours" when "true and natural citizens," "peaceful and obedient," were mixed with "people from every corner of the earth"? What enmities could one expect in a city that was like "a great park, enclosing an infinite number of animals, all different and contrary in their nature"? "Lyon," the saying went, "is as spotted and fragmented as a leopard skin." So the humanist Symphorien Champier remarked: "Better twenty sous among one's own kind than golden ducats among strangers." A Protestant man of letters longed for the old days when everyone wore wool: "Then there was no question of a simple butcher or Lyon artisan going about every feast-day in an outfit costing thirty crowns to tailor, not to mention the fabric." It was the fault of the current trade in silk cloth, in the hands of foreign bankers, who "by this sweet poison are drawing off all the money in the kingdom." How can you trust men, asked the Catholic town lawyer, who have forgotten "their natural country" and have no other tie to Lyon but "their ambition and avarice"? "We confess," said a Catholic song of prayer:

> We confess that usury
> Still endures
> That pride and lubricity
> And greed hold sway
> Undermine us
> And arouse thy wrath.

A Protestant eclogue asserted that:

The sacred and the body social in Lyon

> Userers at Lyon are too welcome by far...
> Haven't I seen the Italian burning
> For profit, whether going or coming?
> Near the Saône bridge, to make some gain
> He'll have God's honour in contempt and disdain.[9]

I want to stress that these sentiments did not emanate from groups that hoped to suppress the fairs and expel the foreigners from Lyon. In fact a xenophobic movement had appeared at Lyon at the beginning of the sixteenth century, when master pinmakers and saddlers and furriers and the like had tried to establish "sworn trades" under pretext of confraternity. It was a practical effort to limit the free-work system and competition, and it failed.[10] Here it is a question rather of ambivalence. The Protestant speaking against bankers was himself a foreigner from the Franche-Comté; there were velvet manufacturers among the elders of the Reformed consistory; and the Huguenot regime in Lyon in 1562–3 tried hard to keep the great fairs in the city. The Catholic lawyer reproving the avarice and ambition of the foreigners was himself married to an Italian and was willing elsewhere to celebrate the city's commerce, the charitable acts of *Messieurs des Nations*, and the excellent manufactures that came from the "conferring and communication" among artisans from so many places.[11]

We shall return later to this ambivalence and see how it was expressed in Calvinist and Catholic attitudes toward the city. But first let us look at the social composition of the two religions in the middle decades of the sixteenth century, and especially of those milieus that influenced liturgical style and devotion.

The Huguenot movement, at its apogee in 1562, never involved more than a third of the population in Lyon. (My description of it is based on an analysis of about 2,300 men who were Protestants between 1550 and 1575).[12] It drew men from the patriciate, from the middle-rank notables, and the *menu peuple* ("little people") in numbers roughly proportional to their distribution in the urban population at large. There was only the floating world of the unskilled day laborer and the very poor who were not represented. At each social level, however, the Protestants tended to come from occupations that were more skilled, or in process of being transformed, or more recently introduced to Lyon. On the city council they were drawn especially from the entrepreneurs and merchant-publishers, and much less from the doctors of law and judicial officers, already established in control in the fifteenth century. (That is, we are seeing a conflict among lay élites about how power is to be used, not a

NATALIE ZEMON DAVIS

conflict between a lay group with power and one without power.) In the little world of notaries, attorneys, and writing masters, on the other hand, Protestants were more numerous. Almost all the printers and barber-surgeons, poor journeymen as well as prosperous masters, followed the religion of the Gospel for a time anyway, and there was important representation from the silk industry and from the metal trades, such as clockmaking and cannon and gun manufacture. By

Table 1. *Geographical origin of males residing in Lyon and of Protestant males in Lyon*

Place of birth	Geographical origin of males residing in Lyon and marrying Easter 1557–Easter 1561[a]		Geographical origin of Protestant males in Lyon 1550–75[b]	
	Number	Percentage of known origin	Number	Percentage of known origin
Lyon	140	38	345	32
Elsewhere in the Lyonnais	75	20	71	7
Other French provinces	87	23	318	29
Outside France	70	19	350	32
Unknown	157[c]	—	1,232[d]	—
Totals	529		2,316	

[a] Based on an analysis of all marriage contracts remaining in the Archives départementales du Rhône from Easter 1557 to Easter 1561. All relevant registers were examined in Series B and 3E and contracts were found in B (*Insinuations*), Donations, vols. xi–xxv, and in 3E 349, 366, 374, 538–40, 565, 608–9, 666, 3227–8, 3848, 3851, 3930–3, 3947–50, 4735, 4482–3, 4497, 5295, 5300–1, 5304, 6942, 7167–70, 7176, 7183–5, 7598.
[b] Based on an analysis of the origins of all Protestant males of known occupation residing in Lyon 1550–75. Information has been extracted especially from Archives municipales de Lyon, BB, CC, EE, GG; Archives départmentales du Rhône, B, 3E, G, H; Archives de la Charité de Lyon, E; Archives de l'Hôtel-Dieu de Lyon, E; Archives d'État de Genève, Livre des habitants, Registres du consistoire, Notaires (J. Rageau, J. Jovenon), Procès criminels.
[c] As likely as not to be from Lyon in origin, as verified by checking persons of known origin, whose place of birth is not given in the contract.
[d] More likely not from Lyon, as a very wide range of local documents has been checked, not only for the individual name but for the family name.

The sacred and the body social in Lyon

contrast the provisioning trades, a very large and not highly literate group at Lyon, remained quite faithful to the mass, with one exception: the tavernkeepers and hotelkeepers, that is, men who were almost all able to read and were central to communications in the city. The Protestant women came from a similar range of families and, though their literacy rate as a whole was much lower than that of the males, the leaders among them included female innkeepers and printers – again, people in a position central to the communicative economy of the town.[13]

There was a second important characteristic of Protestant men in Lyon – their geographical origin (see Table 1). About 68 percent of the Reformed males had been born outside Lyon. Whereas in the urban population as a whole roughly 20 percent of the inhabitants had been born in the nearby Lyonnais, Beaujolais, or Forez, this group contributed only 7 percent of the Protestants. Male supporters of the new religion came from a wide geographical range, including the Île-de-France and Normandy. Furthermore the percentage of men in the Reformed movement born outside the kingdom of France was one and two-thirds times as many as in the city population at large. And what of *Messieurs des Nations*? Did these merchant bankers abandon the mother church? Only a few, and these especially among the Germans, the Lucchese, and the Genoese rather than among the Florentines.[14] The multitude of foreign Protestants in Lyon were the Italian, Piedmontese, Savoyard, German, and Flemish *not* associated with the particular civic institutions of "national" identity and were, I think, more ready to follow the path of assimilation.

The religious and political direction of the Huguenot movement in Lyon, then, was an alliance – a holy alliance – among foreigners, people from France, and a certain number of families originating in Lyon. The ministers, who presided over the Reformed consistory, had a similar range in social background, and almost all of them had come to the city on the Rhône from elsewhere. Pierre Viret, for instance, the most important Reformed preacher in Lyon in the 1560s, had been born in a village in Switzerland.[15]

These were the people who in the late 1550s hoped through God's aid to change the social structure of the city by eliminating the clerical class. They would silence the clergy's lies, banish their "charms," "monkey-shines," and "Moorish dances" from the temples; and break up their "detestable" monopoly over spiritual things – these be "terryble marchauntes ... their occupyenge conteyneth a whole world"; and would send them and their concubines packing. (See Plate 1.) Organized first in rather fluid conventicles, then making use of informal networks of almsgiving and of the urban militia, finally united in an all-city consistory, God's church would put an end to Catholic divisiveness and papist monarchy. Lyon might then be "a holy and free community" of families, linked by worship and charity.[16]

Plate 1. Catholic clerics fishing for souls and trafficking in sacred things.

The sacred and the body social in Lyon

Within the Catholic majority, there were three groups with a major role in the shaping of public piety: the clergy, the confraternities, and the parishes. The clergy had at its head the canon-counts of the Cathedral of St. Jean, all the sons of very old noble families of the Lyonnais and other adjacent areas. Some of them, such as Gabriel de Saconay, resided in Lyon, bringing to the cloister their strong and particular sense of the geographical region, of the archdiocese of Lyon and its past. The rest of the secular clergy were mostly natives of the city: the sons of lawyers, canons at St. Paul; the sons of merchants, canons at St. Nizier; the brother of a cloth dyer, the parish priest at St. Sorlin. By contrast the male religious orders were the domain of newcomers and foreigners: Over at the Franciscan convent, for instance, three-quarters of the brothers were from Burgundy, Dauphiné, Paris, even from Savoy. When the Jesuits arrived in Lyon in 1561 their most gifted preachers were Emond Auger, son of a peasant from Champagne, and the Italian Antonio Possevino.[17]

As for the confraternities, there were at least sixty-eight of them in Lyon during the sixteenth century; and despite a serious decline in membership between 1550 and 1565 they contributed much to the religious style of laymen. Rather closed in character, their brotherhood tended to be limited to men of the same vocation or of the same social stratum. Here are three examples that can suggest the social and psychological foundations of Catholic reform. First, the Confraternity of the Florentine Nation at Lyon – that is to say, of the great merchant-bankers, who bestowed on the Dominican convent dedicated to Our Lady sumptuous organs, silver reliquaries, damask chasubles, and flowered altar cloths, and who had the right (perhaps unique in the city) to place two religious relics "of the Italian language and nation" in the convent. A second type was the Confraternity of the Holy Cross, which united rich merchants and important lawyers from both sides of the Saône and which maintained a cemetery for the poor and for themselves at the Hôtel-Dieu, that is, the poor hospital. And finally, there was the Confraternity of the Pilgrims of St. James of Compostella, which grouped together butchers, pastrymakers, carters, and other men in retail trades, who were devoted to this old shrine in Spain. For a thirty-year period, from the 1560s to the 1580s, this confraternity fought with the canons of St. Nizier for the possession of the keys to their Chapel of St. Jacquême, a chapel that interestingly enough, was closely associated with the earliest political history of the commune of Lyon.[18]

Catholic reform also had an important base in the organization of certain parishes. For instance, in 1572 the parishioners of St. George, a little neighborhood of fishermen and artisans, complained by petition to the Official of the Church of Lyon because neither their curate nor his vicar was saying parish mass, and that every time they needed one of them they had to go and fetch him from a scandalous brothel outside the parish. Some years later everything was calm; the curate was residing in the parish, and during the feast days for St. George, Our Lady of Mid-August (Assumption), and St. Eulalie, a "kingdom" was organized in the parish – enabling the parishioners to elect a king, queen, dauphin, and dauphine and the church to receive generous gifts of wax for candles.[19]

This review of the composition and structure of two religious movements at Lyon prepares us for their differing interpretations of urban space, time, and community. The Catholic movement included foreigners but had more roots in the milieus of Lyon and the Lyonnais than did the Protestant. Both included persons from advanced sectors of the economy, but manufacturers were more numerous among the Calvinists, and bankers more numerous among the Catholics.[20] Furthermore the Catholic movement took in more people in traditional crafts. From what I have said about the organization of the two movements, the reader may already have some inkling of what I shall say about their differing self-perception – that of the Protestants a rather symmetrical communication network linking family units, that of the Catholics an organic combination of diverse groups.

II

The space of the Catholic city was not all homogeneous or symmetrical. The nine parishes, established for centuries and with well-known boundaries, bore no relationship to the distribution of population. The huge parish of St. Nizier, in the heart of the artisanal quarter, had 22,000 communicants at Easter, so it was said in 1534, while the parish of St. Pierre-le-Vieux and St. Romain embraced only a little circle of families. Catholic space was full of special places and sacred spots (see map). The presence of relics – the jaw of St. John the Baptist at the cathedral and the bodies of St. Irénée (the second bishop of Lyon) at the church on the hill of Fourvière, of St. Bonaventure at the Franciscan church, of St. Ennemond (a seventh-century bishop of the city) at St. Nizier, of one St. Reine, "who did miracles for the health," at the cloister of the Carmelites, among many others – intensified the sanctity

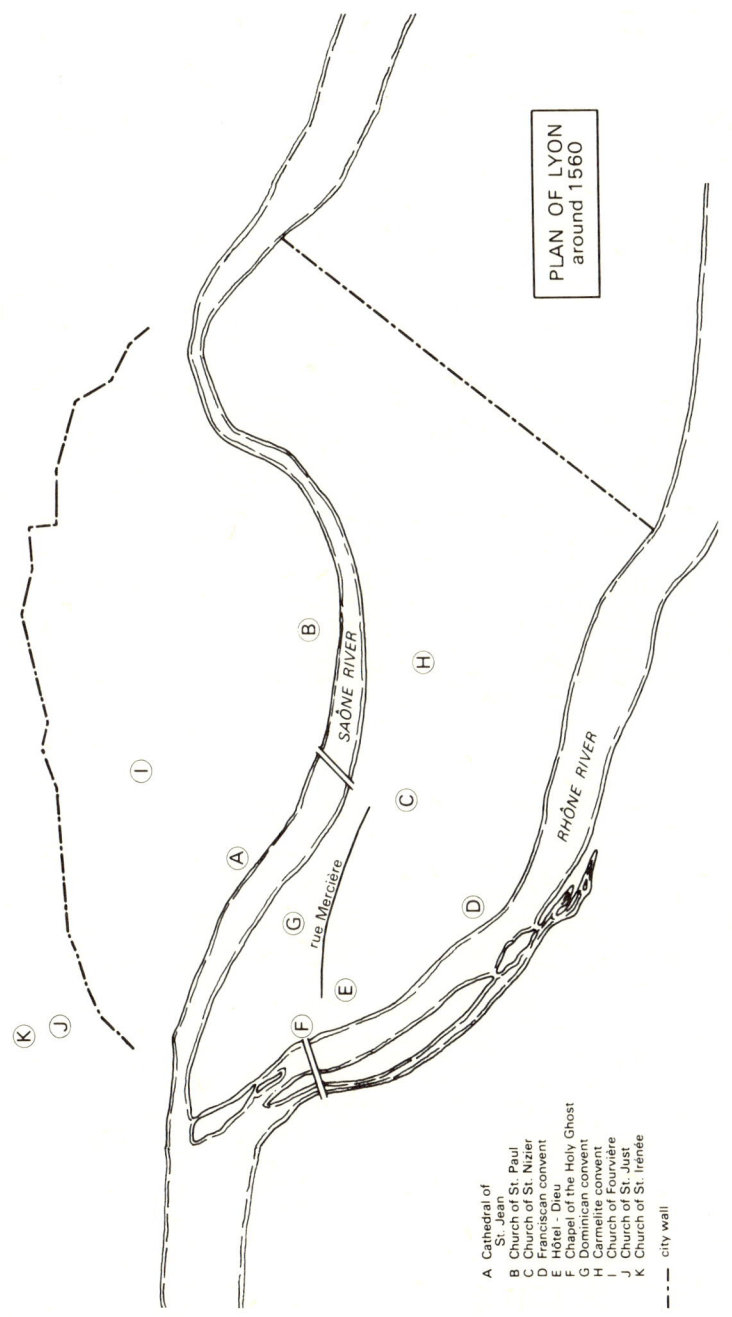

Huiusdem? Regnum dinisum permanet ay ne?
Non fuit Unquam Visum tempus durius isto
Tu Licet ipse Legas antiqua Volumma cuncta.

Singula quid memorem? cecinunt in tristia tantum,
Euersum templum diui sub nomine Justi,
Ecclesia facies nulla, hic vbi terra Virescit:
Hic depascit ouis, confecta plena ruina
Terra est, multum denotus hocus altamen olim,
Ac quoqz sanctus, quo toto non sanctior orbe.
Ignis Sulphureus positus consumpsit id omne.

Plate 2. Calvinist destruction of churches on the hill of Fourvière as portrayed by a Catholic artist. "De tristibus galliae" (1567): Bibliothèque municipale de Lyon, Fonds ancien, MS. 156.
(Photo by courtesy of the Bibliothèque municipale de Lyon.)

The sacred and the body social in Lyon

of certain locations. Catholic devotion to this sense of space was, if anything, strengthened by the Calvinist iconoclasm of 1562–3 (see Plate 2); they hastened to purify buildings and to locate and verify relics (such as St. Irénée's head, miraculously preserved among the ruins for ten years) and put them on display.[21]

Catholic ceremonial was also very sensitive to the natural features of the urban environment – the hill of Fourvière, which dominated the city, and the rivers. (See Plates 3 and 4.) Processions of the clergy climbed up at least twice a year to the little Chapel of Our Lady of Fourvière, and

Plate 3. View of the hill of Fourvière overlooking the cathedral and the Saône. Detail of an engraving attributed to Bernard Salomon, from G. Guéroult, *Epitome de la corographie* (Lyon, 1553). *(Photo by courtesy of the Houghton Library, Harvard University.)*

Plate 4. The meeting of the Saône and the Rhône. Detail of a seventeenth-century copy by Tardieu of the *Plan scénographique de Lyon* (circa 1560): Archives municipales de Lyon. (*Photo by courtesy of the Archives municipales de Lyon.*)

The sacred and the body social in Lyon

for most of the sixteenth century a "Kingdom" of the newly wed made a pilgrimage there on Assumption Day. The choirboys of the cathedral, dressed up as adult canon-counts, went up the hill after Christmas to the heights of St. Just, received a blessing from their boy bishop, and paid their respects to the bones of one of the Innocents slaughtered by Herod. The hill was viewed as a source of protection and help for the city. Often yielding ruins from its Roman past, discovered by gardeners and treasured by wealthy townsmen and humanists, it also contained the blood and bones of the early Christian founders and martyrs.[22]

The slow-moving feminine Saône – the characterization is theirs – was the place for joyous festivals, sacred and popular. In the fourteenth century, in the days before the fairs when the Saône was the central artery of the city, a Feast of Marvels had been celebrated on the river in June, in honor of St. Pothin, first bishop of Lyon, and his comrades. The entire clergy of the city was afloat, praying and singing on the Saône, accompanied by officers, notable citizens and artisans; enormous boats performed a complicated ritual, which started at a rock at the north of the city, centered on the Saône bridge, and moved down to the point where the Saône flowed into the Rhône. This festival had ended in the fourteenth century, but there still existed on Ascension Day a colorful pilgrimage by boat of laity and clergy up to Our Lady of Île-Barbe, north of the city. In addition to mass at the ancient abbey, which was near the border between France and Savoy, the master of the ports at Lyon and his aides took down the escutcheon of the duke of Savoy and replaced it with the arms of France. On Sundays and feast days during the summer, the boatmen of the parishes of St. George and St. Vincent on either side of the Saône marked their common boundary by jousting on the river. On the eve of the major feast of St. John the Baptist, it was from the Saône bridge that the consulate set off the fireworks.[23]

The Rhône, by contrast, was a powerful, masculine (again their characterization), and dangerous river. As sixteenth-century people still remembered, the building of the bridge over it had initially been commanded by the Lord himself in a miraculous message to a shepherd boy in the mid-thirteenth century. Its difficult construction had had to be preached like a crusade and financed by the many indulgences that penitents could purchase through visiting the Chapel of the Holy Ghost at the Lyon end of the bridge. It was finally completed only at the beginning of the sixteenth century, and people still feared it would collapse – and with reason, for the strong currents often swept away some of its stanchions. As for the Rhône itself, there was constant worry not only that it would be too high or too low for the navigation essential to the fairs, but also that it would overflow. The flood of 1570 was so furious that Catholics claimed that "the water had wished to purge the filth... scattered about by Calvinians"; Protestants claimed it as a judgment of God against the Catholics for their persecution of his church. In any case, now that the Rhône was so important to Lyon life, Catholic ceremonial took increased note of it and many processions passed by the little chapel on the bridge, especially at Pentecost, the festival of the Holy Ghost. As with the Saône, there were associated popular festivals: At Pentecost young men dressed themselves as horses (more precisely as *chevaux fous*, or horse fools) and danced through the streets from the end of the peninsula, where the Rhône and Saône "embraced," up to the Rhône bridge. (See Plate 4.) This custom, which exists elsewhere in France and which has been interpreted variously as a fertility cult and a male initiation rite, was thought by some sixteenth-century Lyonnais to signify escape and uncontrollability. In this case, wild horses might well dance and jump toward a barely tamed river.[24]

Catholic processions did not serve only to visit the border points of Lyon, such as the Rhône bridge and the Île-Barbe, but also to unite the two parts of the city cut by the Saône – the Church of Lyon with the king's men at the Palais de Roanne; and the bankers on the side of the hill of Fourvière (Côte de Fourvière) with the town hall, merchants, and artisans of the St. Nizier side (Côte de St. Nizier). For example, a general procession of the parishes for Corpus Christi Day or a procession of the Confraternity of the Holy Cross for its feast on 3 May assembled at the Cathedral of St. Jean with their monstrances for the holy wafer, their crosses, banners, bells, candles, and torches; went north to St. Paul; crossed the Saône bridge to St. Nizier, over to the Franciscans along the Rhône at St. Bonaventure; down to the Rhône bridge hospital, across to the Dominicans at Nôtre Dame du Confort in the midst of the printing quarter; and then, taking the rue Mercière (the main commercial route in the city), returned to St. Jean.[25] (See map.)

Can we conceive of this fashion of moving through and marking urban space as significant for, as functional in, the economic and social life of Lyon? For the most part, yes. These processions could dramatize the city's identity and give protection to the body of the town, and this effect could last in fair-time and outside fair-time (*en foire et hors foire*). And note that these were not rites to give a sense of closure to Lyon (as did rural processions on Rogation days, when among other activities the parish bounds were beaten and sprinkled with holy water); these

The sacred and the body social in Lyon

processions did *not* go around the enlarged town fortifications constructed in the 1520s. Rather, one visited the Rhône bridge to keep it open.[26]

Furthermore, with the exception of a newly established house of mendicants on the hill of Fourvière, who protested the bellowing of animals at the cattle market across the road, the church objected rather little in the sixteenth century to the proximity of commerce to sacred things. Vintners and candlemakers hawked their wares outside the cathedral door to supply the needs of pilgrims on the feast day of St. John the Baptist. People selling food came there at other times as well, and the canon-counts made only halfhearted efforts to stop them. Especially illustrative is the quarrel that broke out over the mercers and petty traders who surrounded the church of St. Nizier. The canons had no desire to expel them, so long as they left enough room in front of the doors and four feet between their stalls and the church (canon law prescribed thirty feet, but who cared?). The quarrel of 1559 was between the canons and the city council: Who was going to collect the rent for those stalls? The church won, and the tradespeople remained (in fact, they are there to this day).[27]

With the Protestants, who (as we have seen) were in large part not natives of Lyon or even of the region, this orientation toward urban space changed. As for hills, rivers, gates, bridges, and geographical boundaries, it would be an abuse to seek their protection regularly by prayer. The streets through which the dark-clad Calvinists marched singing their Psalms were not sacred routes but avenues for the expression of the believer's faith, a message of communion to other Christians and of reproof to the canon-counts. That the sacred could be enclosed in a thing – in a host, in a bone, in a building, in a piece of land – was a notion smacking of idolatry. With zeal, in 1562, the Calvinist crowds purged the Catholic holy places; with thoroughness they then inventoried and melted down reliquaries, whitened church walls, and put in simple windows where before there had been stained-glass pictures. Crosses were smashed at crossroads; old but still used hermitages were razed. Public squares were built on top of cemeteries; and through the ruins of cloisters with a thoroughness that went well beyond the urbanist efforts of the city council some years before, new streets were built to facilitate the circulation of carts and artillery. A butcher's shop was set up on the chapter house of St. Paul; a draper's shop in the ancient Chapel of St. Jacquême; a clockmaker's establishment in the Chapel of Our Lady of the Rue Neuve; and in the cloister of the Dominicans, after the horses of the Calvinist captain, the baron des Adrets, were installed, even worse – married couples, that is, Reformed ministers and their wives.[28]

In short, Protestants were opening urban space and making it more uniform and available for exchange, traffic, and human communication. Significantly, the elders for their consistory were drawn not from the old parishes but from the more equally populated civic wards.[29] Were the Calvinists in the process, then, "of disenchanting the world," to use the phrase associated with Max Weber? Yes, in Weber's narrow sense that they were cutting back on the use of sacraments and magical ritual, that they were removing the sacred from specific crossroads and particular moments so as to provide a more general and fluid way of viewing the city. But no, in the sense that they did not simply put the holy into another transcendent realm, did not simply move the pointer over on a preexisting scale of holiness, with immanence at one end and transcendence at the other.[30] Rather they thought in terms of a new measure, redefining how the holy should be present in the world. Through their ideas on consecration and pollution they set limits to what they could do to space and objects. "A thing which is consecrated," explained a Reformed minister, "is dedicated to a holy and sacred usage... A house is consecrated to God when it is assigned and ordained to some holy use, such as preaching the Word of God... or for public prayer." Concomitantly, if a house or a town were employed for usury, gaming, masking, or licentiousness, then it was polluted, "a dissolute Corinth."[31] If for the Catholics urban space had its hot points and cold points, for the Calvinists the environment was – well, not lukewarm, for that would have to be spewed forth – but held together by a middling tension, by listening and by watchfulness.

In cutting the tie between the sacred and place, the Calvinists were facilitating the possibility of a city *en foire permanente* – a city that was a permanent market – a form of commercial organization more like that of seventeenth-century Amsterdam. On the other hand, in redefining the tie between the sacred and usage, between the sacred and assigned purpose, they were rendering themselves and their sense of vocation in the world more conscious than ever of the moral dangers of the fairs. Here is the expression of the Reformed ambivalence about the Lyon economy, which we noted above. At the same time that a Protestant eclogue about the Calvinist-administered city of 1562 was celebrating "profitable fairs" in a "purified Lyon," a Reformed synod was condemning usury and permitting only "some mediocre profit" to bankers.

The sacred and the body social in Lyon

The Reformed regime was defeated in Lyon in 1563, but one wonders how, if it had been more enduring, it would have accommodated itself to the inherited orgy of commerce four times a year. (Perhaps the moderates among the Huguenot leaders would have tried to change things in a way that, to Calvin, would have looked suspiciously like Spiritual Libertinism.) The Catholic church of St. Nizier did not worry itself about the mercers and retailers at its walls; perhaps they even helped clarify the wonder of the mass being performed within. The Reformed temple of St. Nizier, a draper's shop already in its Chapel of St. Jacquême, was more vulnerable to the temptations of nonascetic worldliness. The traders were banished from the environs of the temple, lest the noise of their transactions interrupt the Psalms and prayers of the faithful.[32]

A similar contrast existed between the Catholic and Calvinist ordering of urban time in Lyon. Catholic ceremonial time was complex, bunched, and irregular. Any parish or neighborhood might have special rhythms of its own; in the area around the cathedral, for instance, from May to mid-August, at least six local feasts were held – for young law clerks, or for the furriers, or in honor of St. Christopher and St. Roch – and this quite apart from the major holidays that fell within those weeks. But the festive calendar for the city as a whole was not homogeneous either. It expanded and contracted, like the diets of the devout, who moved from eating to fasting; like the spirits of the penitent, who moved from carnival to Lent. Putting together the events of the church's liturgical calendar with those initiated by the city council (a procession and mass on Trinity Sunday up to the municipal College of the Trinity; a procession and mass on the Sunday after Easter, of all the poor receiving aid from the municipal charity, and the like) and with those events initiated by parishioners (such as streetdancing at Pentecost), we have periods of high activity in late December and early January; carnival and early Lent; Easter; May and June, a time of intense ceremonial life; and August. Autumn and Advent were the relatively quiet times.[33]

The Catholic city breathed in and out as did the commercial and manufacturing city. How did the rhythms relate? The peak of May and June was not matched by a peak of economic busyness; but apart from that, the festive calendar clustered around three of the four fairs: the Fair of Kings, the Easter Fair, and the August Fair. Only the Hallowmas Fair in November, following fast on the somber Day of the Dead, had rather little liturgical build-up or follow-up. Whereas in pre-

Reformation Coventry, a small town, Charles Phythian-Adams has shown that the ceremonial and work calendars were concentrated in different half-years and alternated, like responses, in Lyon the ceremonial life often intensified the economic life, like counterpoint.[34]

The Calvinist ordering of liturgical time was more simple, even, and uniform. Early Protestants in Lyon had considered the idea of having no special hours, no special times at all: "We pray when the Spirit of the Lord pushes us to it, and with all the more feeling when urgent necessity requires it." Then with the institutionalization of the Reformed church, as Pastor Viret pointed out, it was convenient to have certain hours for public prayer, and it was well to agree upon Sunday, since many working people could not assemble every day. It was not as though they were making a "narrow religion," a "spiritual mystery," out of Sunday, another minister commented; an arranged time was simply necessary to keep "good order" in the church. During the Calvinist regime of 1562–3, both Sundays and Wednesdays were set aside for preaching and public prayer throughout the city (as they had been in Geneva); and although catechism classes and preaching were offered on other days of the week as well, there was nothing analogous to the variations in Catholic ceremonial time. As the temperate Christian should not follow Moses' uncommon fast of forty days, but rather eat soberly at all meals (public fasts were promulgated at most twice a year, and usually less often), and just as the God-fearing Christian should not experience wild changes of mood but hold himself or herself in steady vigilance and at attention, so time would move evenly from work to prayer. Four days a year had great solemnity and were prepared for with care: the communion of the Lord's Supper, spaced out at Christmas, Easter, Pentecost, and September ("like the fairs of Lyon," a canon-count noted with malice). The Reformed calendar did not breathe, however, but alertly watched (to quote a Calvinist entrepreneur) for a slow, steady increase in faith, a slow, steady increase in material blessings, and feared the diabolic leap to great riches, inevitably to be followed by ruin in very little time.[35]

There were also differences between the two religions in their conceptions of the Christian community. These surfaced most clearly after 1559, when the start of economic difficulties and the religious wars broke asunder the cooperation among religious moderates symbolized by the Aumône-Générale thirty years before. With the Catholics, the traditional image of the human body was still at the center of their symbolism and their social reflection.[36] If processional life had been

The sacred and the body social in Lyon

ready, as we have seen, to keep open the entries and exits of Lyon, liturgical and polemical life thought increasingly of expelling the heretic, of sealing the apertures of the body social, and keeping all its members in good order. Here was the Catholic expression of ambivalence toward the urban economy. A popular poem provides an epitaph for "The Tomb of Calvinism" at Lyon:

> His father was Pride
> Avarice his mother
> Dispute his sister
> His wife War. . . .

A rhymer from the Celestine convent insists that the people of Lyon must live "conjoined by faith and perfect alliance":

> It's not permitted to all that be
> To interpret Divine Scripture by his fantasy.
> The priest without doubt holds the sense so true.
> Listen then . . .
> If by pride someone swells with great breath
> And obeys not the priest at holy church
> Let him be judged and condemned to death.

According to Gabriel de Saconay, a canon-count at St. Jean, the Huguenots are "Germans and other strangers," who in 1562 "chased out an infinite number of natural citizens of Lyon." They wanted "to set themselves up as a canton like those of Geneva," added the town lawyer, and then he prescribed for the restoration of Lyon "hatred" of traitors and of all those who preached a Gospel other than obedience. It was this image of the body social with its definite boundaries that Catholic crowds expressed at Lyon in their bloody anti-Huguenot riots. Observing such an uprising in late 1567, Gabriel de Saconay remarked: "In an instant the Catholics were united and conforming, so that one could finally say that in such a town, composed of so many sorts of nations, there was only one heart, one will and one head."[37]

Having protected the exterior of the body social, Catholic preachers, such as the Jesuit Emond Auger, insisted strongly on the communion and sacred alliance within. Through the mass and the sacrament of the Eucharist, where Christ is really present and ingested, we are joined tightly to our brothers. The fruits of the mass and the prayers accompanying it are numerous, even if the Christian cannot understand the words: One can help the dead, one can help children, one can help those who are absent, the governors of the city and the kingdom, and many others. Auricular confession and the sacrament of Penitence also had social advantages. "How many evil projects," said Auger, "how many domestic conspiracies have been halted by this sacrament! How many enemies have been reconciled!"[38]

The liturgical event that gave the best expression to this Catholic image of community was the rite of conjuration and exorcism. The one that took place in 1582 at the Franciscan convent can serve as our example. The victim was Pernette Pinay, a fifty-seven-year-old widow from a village near Lyon. Through the evildoing of a witch in her village, she had been possessed by seven devils. Six of them she had forced out of herself by a pilgrimage and by prayers to Mary; now there was left a single devil named Frappan. Pernette had a holy soul and she had struggled with Frappan, so that he had been able to take over only her body. The exorcism, led by the preacher and theologian Jean Benedicti, lasted several days before a large audience. Frappan shouted a great deal, insulted people, and stammered over the name of Jesus Christ. Everyone in the gathering purified herself or himself by prayers, fasts, confession, and communion. Everyone prayed for Pernette and vowed to make a pilgrimage to Our Lady at Île-Barbe. Twice during the rite a fountain appeared, distilled from the tears of all the spectators. Finally, Frappan departed during the mass. At that very instant a citizen on the Rhône bridge saw a great flash of fire above the Franciscan church. Thus were refuted the lies of the Calvinists about the mass; thus were demonstrated the power of the priest, the virtue of widows, and the direct aid that Christian can give to Christian. Indeed, one could nourish another person spiritually, as the liver and heart nourished the body with blood, natural spirits, and vital spirits.[39]

The Reformers had a very different idea of social alliance. They too made use of the traditional Pauline metaphor of the human body, especially in justifying the existence of officers who had a special vocation in the church. As Pastor Viret said, Jesus Christ is the head of the church; the ministers and the *surveillants* (the laymen supervisors, as the elders of the consistory were initially called) were the eyes, ears, nose, and mouth; and the hands, belly, and legs of the church must not be jealous of them. But Viret offered another biological image of the Christian community, which he pulled out and separated from the older metaphor of the body and which, in my opinion, expressed more authentically the Calvinist urban vision – that of the ligaments, the nerves, and the senses. "The discipline of the church," he commented,

The sacred and the body social in Lyon

"is like the ligaments and the nerves in a body. Without these, you have just a confused jumble of vices and of vicious persons – a synagogue – rather than a church of God and a holy company assembled in the name of Jesus Christ." The holy company was a human communication network, the senses, the voice, the ligaments, the muscles, the nerves, with God as its animator. The Protestant service, *La forme des prière ecclésiastiques*, was a communication in which the pastor was described variously as the "mouth" of the Lord talking to the attentive ear of the faithful, and as the "mouth" of the congregation talking to the Lord.[40]

This image accords better than that of the whole body to other Reformed ideas about the structure of their religious organization. A body has qualitatively different organs in it. But the Reformed church of Lyon had rid itself of special confraternities and convents, and was a linkage of families and wards in an all-city consistory. A body has limits, well marked. But the Reformed consistory was so preoccupied in those decades with the purification of the visible church that one could not see its boundaries very distinctly. There was the outer circle of people whom the consistory had excommunicated; the circle of people temporarily forbidden to take communion at the Lord's Supper; and a circle of hypocrites present at the Lord's Supper, but warned by the pastor that they really ought not to pollute and contaminate the sacred food (such as persons secretly rebellious to their parents, secretly avaricious, gluttons, and many others). Indeed the pastor gave a general excommunication of all such sinners, secret or public, before the bread and chalice were offered.[41] By contrast the priest was to let the hypocrites worry about their damnable state themselves and was not to deny the sacrament to a parishioner because he knew of some unresolved secret sin. The categories of persons forbidden to take communion at the Catholic rite and to whom the priest must deny it were less numerous, and the people in them easier to identify by external sign (for example, manifest heretics, public prostitutes and usurers, someone not from the parish, someone who had not made prior confession).[42]

Furthermore the image of a network of human communication – of the animal spirits sending their messages from the brain to the senses, the nerves, and muscles – corresponds well to the Calvinist conception of the assistance that Christians can give each other. One can pray for other people among the living, though not, of course, for the dead. One can "move each other more deeply" by praying together and singing the Psalms together. One can teach another. The bravery of a martyr's death can encourage others. One can, in fact one ought to, give each other charitable aid in money and goods: "Charity makes of several hearts one, of several souls one," said a clandestine preacher. But one could not fast for another, or make a promise that would help another. And as Pastor Mainardo said in his *Anatomy of the Mass*, one could no more take communion for another person (as the priest did in the mass) than one could eat food for another person. "We are not nourished by the faith of another," echoed Pastor Viret. "We cannot communicate in the spiritual goods which are in him. We are not like the child fed in the womb of the mother."[43]

Evidently, in the spiritual economy of holy mother church, one could sometimes eat for another person. The Reformed believer, by contrast, was fed by Christ alone. If the boundary around the Calvinist body social was still fuzzy, that around the individual body was clear (even the preferred Reformed silhouette was close in to the body, as ministers inveighed against farthingales and elaborate hairstyles). One could be penetrated, alas, by devils, but not by other men, not even by those with whom one was conjoined by faith, prayer, and hymn.[44]

On this note, let me try to sum up my conclusions about the relations of our two "languages," our two religions, to the city. First, I have suggested that if each "language" was structured in part by doctrine and by the social-spiritual relations between laity and clergy, it was in part inflected and colored by the distinctive experience of the people who used it. That is, I have argued that the geographical mobility of the Calvinists and their presence in skilled crafts and advanced industries and at nodes of oral and printed communication interacted with Reformed belief and ritual to give a distinctive view of urban space, time, and social alliance. With the Catholics I have pointed to their deep regional roots; their connection with a wide range of occupations, from banking to baking; and their location in traditional collective organization as the elements of experience that interacting with Catholic doctrine and ritual, perpetuated another sense of place, rhythm, and community in the city.

Second, I have tried to reformulate the relation of both religions to commercial capitalism and early manufacture. Sixteenth-century Catholicism could adapt its magic and ceremony readily to the varying character and risks of commercial and banking life in Lyon and could tolerate business practice up to its very walls. On the other hand, the Catholic ambivalence toward the foreigner, expressed in religious efforts both to keep the gates of the city open to him and exclude him as heretic,

The sacred and the body social in Lyon

was to have negative consequences at the end of the century, if not for the rapidity of commercial exchange at Lyon, then at least for its quantity. Calvinism cleared space and time for multiple uses and marshaled human energy and attention for steady, productive work. On the other hand, its commitment to consecrated ends for all activity put a limit on, introduced a contradiction into, the so-called "rational" pursuit of economic goals. Each religion represents a possible urban style; in each the sacred remains somewhat in tension with strict economic goals.

Finally, let us consider how well each religion functioned as a source of safety and solidarity in the city. The Catholic images and rituals were not at all innovative in regard to the integration of foreigners in Lyon. The solution of the confraternity, so successful for the Florentine bankers, was not adequate for many of the newcomers. They still had to make their Easter confession in a language they did not know well, and in the large parishes may hardly have known who the priest was. Further, the celebration of killing as a means to create "one heart, one soul" was hardly a long-term answer to mistrust within the city. But these matters apart, Catholicism had some resources to assist the integration of the different quarters and social groups in Lyon (in a curious way, which I have not had time to consider here, it even had resources to provide multiple arenas for tolerable social conflict).[45] It could add sanctity to some of the familiar features of the environment and could try to pacify the dangerous ones. For a city with walls, which housed a population that ran from nobles to day laborers, and an advanced economy as well as traditional economies – for such a city, perhaps this body social, with its changing physical states, its particular organs, its hierarchical order, its arteries, veins, and umbilical cords of aid, made some sense.

The metaphor of the network of human communication was more creative, as was also the organization of the Reformed consistory, which untied rather trustfully the Lyonnais, the French, the Italians, and the Germans around a common urban piety and common vernaculars.[46] The network image could give a plausible interpretation of social intercourse to people who had left local gods and fathers behind them, who were highly skilled in technical crafts and innovating entrepreneurs, who were publishers and tavernkeepers, who resented the dependence of the child in the womb and of the pupil on the schoolmaster.[47] And a network is flexible: One can tighten it in times of trouble; one can extend it easily, especially, when one ignores the natural features of the environment. So the Reformers created synods to spread through a whole country. So enterprising Lyon Calvinists hoped to plant the seeds

NATALIE ZEMON DAVIS

of industry and the seeds of the Gospel in landscapes that had been denuded of their shrines and sanctuaries.[48]

But a network cannot cover everything, at least not with the technology and the techniques of watching, listening, talking, and controlling available in the the sixteenth century. There was much space in Lyon, many people, a heavy need for charitable exchange, and frequent occasion for pollution. The vision and the vulnerability of the Calvinists are suggested by an engraving of the 1560s (see Plate 5), the work of a Lyon artist Pierre Cruche, alias Eskrich, himself of German extraction, a native of Paris, and frequent visitor to Geneva. Next to a dangerous river full of teeth, Protestant pastors are trying to break down the walls of the wicked papal city. Their weapons are books and manuscripts, and in the engraving the walls are tumbling down.[49] The Reformed consistory flourished in the great market city of seventeenth-century Amsterdam partly because it relinquished some of that heroic hope and was forced to tolerate the existence of other religious styles. In sixteenth-century Geneva, a city that had just undergone a political revolution, a city with a population mixed with foreign refugees but with a simpler economy and only a quarter of the size of Lyon, the consistory had a splendid but comprehensible success. In a city like Lyon – for a year and a half one of the largest Calvinist cities in Europe – such a success would have been a miracle. At Geneva, Calvinism conquered the Rhône; but

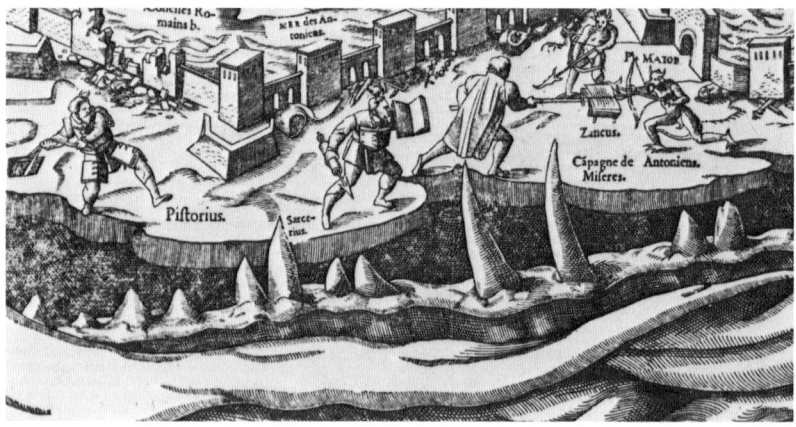

Plate 5. Protestant pastors breaking down the walls of the papal city with books. Details from an engraving by Pierre Eskrich in *Histoire de la mappemonde papistique...* [Geneva, 1567]. *Photo by courtesy of the Bibliothèque publique et universitaire de Genève.*)

The sacred and the body social in Lyon

at Lyon, at the massacres of St. Bartholomew's Day, it was the other way around; it was the Rhône that received the bodies of the Calvinists.

NOTES

World Copyright: The Past and Present Society, Corpus Christi College, Oxford, England. This article is reprinted with the permission of the Society and the author from *Past and Present: a journal of historical studies*, no. 90 (Feb. 1981).

For support in the preparation of this essay, I am grateful to the Humanities Research Council of the University of California, Berkeley, the Institute for Advanced Study, and the Committee on Research in the Humanities and Social Sciences of Princeton University. Among many colleagues who have given me helpful criticism on this material, I want especially to thank Clifford Geertz, Claudia Koonz, and James K. McConica.

The following abbreviations will be used: A.N. (Archives nationales, Paris); A.D.R. (Archives départementales du Rhône); A.M.L. (Archives municipales de Lyon); A.Ch.L. (Archives de la Charité de Lyon); A.H.D.L. (Archives de l'Hôtel-Dieu de Lyon); A.E.G. (Archives d'État de Genève).

1 The Reformation as emerging out of a conflict between laity and clergy is especially well described in the valuable book of Steven E. Ozment, *The Reformation in the Cities: The Appeal of Protestantism to Sixteenth-Century Germany and Switzerland* (New Haven, Conn., 1975).

2 Ernst Troeltsch, *The Social Teachings of the Christian Churches*, trans. O. Wyon, 2 vols. (London, 1950); Max Weber, *The Sociology of Religion*, trans. E. Fischoff (Boston, Mass., 1963), esp. ch. 13; Bernd Moeller, *Reichsstadt und Reformation* (Verein für Reformationsgeschichte, xlix, Gütersloh, 1962), trans. H.C. Erik Midelfort and Mark U. Edwards Jr., as *Imperial Cities and the Reformation* (Philadelphia, 1972), esp. pp. 69-90.

3 Gideon Sjoberg, *The Preindustrial City Past and Present* (New York, 1960), ch. 9; Harvey Cox, *The Secular City* (New York, 1965); Peter L. Berger, *The Sacred Canopy: Elements of a Sociological Theory of Religion* (New York, 1969), ch. 5; Gerhard Lenski, *The Religious Factor: A Sociologist's Inquiry* (New York, 1961); Robert Bellah, *Beyond Belief* (New York, 1970), ch. 2, "Religious Evolution"; Max Weber, *The Protestant Ethic and the Spirit of Capitalism*, trans. Talcott Parsons (New York, 1958), ch. 2; S.N. Eisenstadt (ed.), *The Protestant Ethic and Modernization* (New York, 1968), esp. S.N. Eisenstadt (ed.), "The Protestant Ethic Thesis in an Analytical and Comparative Framework," pp. 3-45. For an effort to rethink the possibilities of religion in an urban setting, see Paul Tillich, "The Strange and the Familiar in the Metropolis," in Robert M. Fisher (ed.), *The Metropolis in Modern Life* (New York, 1955), pp. 347-8; Max L. Stackhouse, *Ethics and the Urban Ethos: An Essay in Social Theory and Theological Reconstruction* (Boston, Mass., 1972).

4 For a thoughtful discussion of some of the problems in interpreting ritual symbols, see Ronald Grimes, *Symbol and Conquest: Public Ritual and Drama in Santa Fe, New Mexico* (Ithaca, N.Y., 1976), pp. 43-6; Ernst H. Kantorowicz, *The King's Two Bodies: A Study in Medieval Political Theology* (Princeton, 1957); Ralph Giesey, *The Royal Funeral Ceremony in Renaissance France* (Geneva, 1960); Frances Yates, *Astrea: The Imperial Theme in the Sixteenth Century*

NATALIE ZEMON DAVIS

(London, 1975). Some important works by historians sensitive to the nature of religious symbolism and the relation of the sacred to social life are Peter Brown, *The World of Late Antiquity* (London, 1971); Peter Brown, "Society and the Supernatural: A Medieval Change," *Daedalus* [Special issue on *Wisdom, Revelation and Doubt: Perspectives on the First Millennium B.C.*] (1975), pp. 133–51; John Bossy, "Blood and Baptism: Kinship, Community and Christianity in Western Europe from the Fourteenth to the Seventeenth Centuries," in D. Baker (ed.), *Sanctity and Secularity: The Church and the World* (Studies in Church Hist., x, Oxford, 1973), pp. 129–43; John Bossy, "The Social History of Confession in the Age of the Reformation," 5th ser., xxv (1975), pp. 21–38; Richard Trexler, "Florentine Religious Experience: The Sacred Image," *Studies in the Renaissance*, xix (1972), pp. 7–41; Richard Trexler, "Ritual Behavior in Renaissance Florence: The Setting," *Medievalia et Humanistica*, iv (1973), pp. 125–44; Richard Trexler, "Ritual in Florence: Adolescence and Salvation in the Renaissance," in C. Trinkaus and H.A. Oberman (eds.), *The Pursuit of Holiness in Late Medieval and Renaissance Religion* (Leiden, 1974), pp. 200–64; Richard Trexler, *Public Life in Renaissance Florence* (New York, 1980). See also *Local Religion in Sixteenth-Century Spain* by the anthropologist William Christian Jr. (Princeton, 1981).

A particularly helpful perspective on the modernizing features of both the Catholic and Protestant Reformations is found in Jean Delumeau, *Naissance et affirmation de la Réforme* (Paris, 1965), and his *Le catholicisme entre Luther et Voltaire* (Paris, 1971).

5 On sixteenth-century Lyon, see Richard Gascon, *Grand commerce et vie urbaine au XVIe siècle: Lyon et ses marchands* (Paris, 1971); Jean-Pierre Gutton, *La société et les pauvres: l'exemple de la généralité de Lyon, 1534–1789* (Paris, 1969); N.Z. Davis, *Society and Culture in Early Modern France* (Stanford, 1975), chs. 1–3,7 (which includes material on rates of literacy). The "république des clercs" of the fifteenth century has been treated by René Fedou, *Les hommes de loi lyonnais à la fin du moyen âge: étude sur les origines de la classe de robe* (Paris, 1964).

For the geographical origins of men and women residing in Lyon, I have examined all marriage contracts in A.D.R., Series 3E and Series B (*Insinuations*) for the years from Easter 1557 to Easter 1561 (that is, to the end of 1560 by the old reckoning). A quarter of the 529 women contracting marriage were already widows, which suggests the range of age in the sample. Of the 529 grooms, 61 percent were artisans, which suggests the social range of the sample. This has seemed a better source than the records of entries into the Hôtel-Dieu used by Richard Gascon in his "Immigration et croissance urbaine au XVIe siècle," *Annales. E.S.C.*, xxv (1970), pp. 988–1001. The hospital records concern only the poorest strata of the population and mix travelers and residents indiscriminately.

6 Guillaume Paradin, *Memoires de l'histoire de Lyon* (Lyon, 1573), pp. 1, 305–6; Claude de Rubys, *Les privileges, franchises et immunitez octroyees par les roys treschrestiens, aux consuls, eschevins, manans et habitans de la ville de Lyon* (Lyon, 1574), pp. 48–9; Nicolas de Nicolay, *Généralle description de l'antique et célèbre cité de Lyon* (manuscript at Bibliothèque nationale, 1573), edn. Société de topographie historique de Lyon (Lyon, 1881), chs. 18–20. In addition to

The sacred and the body social in Lyon

Gascon, there are the older works by Marc Brésard, *Les foires de Lyon aux XVe et XVIe siècles* (Lyon, 1914); Natalis Rondot, *L'ancien régime du travail à Lyon* (Lyon, 1897); Henri Hauser, *Ouvriers du temps passé*, 5th edn. (Paris, 1927), ch. 7. The apothecaries became a fourth "sworn trade" in Lyon in 1588.

7 Gascon, *Grand commerce et vie urbaine*, pp. 357-69, and passim. There is also much material on the Italians in Lyon in E. Picot, "Les italiens en France au seizième siècle," *Bulletin italien*, i (1901), pp. 92-137, 269-94; ii (1902), pp. 23-53, 108-45; iv (1904), pp. 294-315; xvii (1917), pp. 160-84; xviii (1918), pp. 28-36. *La magnificence de la superbe et triumphante entree de la noble et antique cité de Lyon faicte au treschrestien roy de France Henry deuxiesme de ce nom... MDXLVIII* (Lyon, 1549), ed. Georges Guigue (Lyon, 1927), pp. 11-12, 63-4; *La chronique lyonnaise de Jean Guéraud, 1536-1562*, ed. Jean Tricou (Lyon, 1929), pp. 66-7, 71-82, 89-93, 114; Jean Tricou, *Les enfants de la ville* (Lyon, 1938); A.M.L., BB55, fos. 36^r, 92^v-93^r.

Of the fourteen Florentine merchants representing the Florentine Nation residing at Lyon in the 1541 contract with the Dominican friars (A.D.R., 3H40, 1 May 1541), only three became naturalized citizens of France: Palla Strozzi (A.D.R., BP3640, fo. 67^{r-v}), Leonard Spini, and Pierre Orlandini (A.N., JJ249^1, fos. 3^r, 34^{r-v}). Several of those present, such as Jehan Bonguillaume and Nicolas Manelli, had representatives of their families already residing in Lyon in 1502, if not earlier: Gascon, *Grand commerce et vie urbaine*, p. 907.

8 A.M.L., BB55, fos. 92^{v-r}; *La magnificence de la superbe... entrée de... Henry deuxiesme*, p. 12. Of all the nonnative artisans marrying in Lyon in the years 1557-60, only one-tenth married women from their own province or country; 57 percent married girls native to Lyon, another 13 percent married widows established in Lyon, and a quarter married women living in Lyon, but born in the Lyonnais or in other regions. This distribution cannot be explained only by the differential between male and female immigration to Lyon: 80 percent of the immigrant women married men either native to Lyon or from regions other than those in which they had been born.

9 Symphorien Champier, *Sensuyt ung petit traicte de la noblesse et anciennete de la ville de Lyon: ensemble de la rebeine ou rebellion du populaire de la dicte ville* (Paris, 1529), fo. viii^{r-v}; Symphorien Champier, *Cy commence ung petit livre du royaulme des Allobroges*, in P. Allut, *Étude biographique et bibliographique sur Symphorien Champier* (Lyon, 1859), p. 396. Champier's exact phrase is: "Mieulx vault ung escu entre les siens, que ung noble avec les estranges et differens de meurs et conditions." A noble was an English coin dating from the reign of Edward III, which was worth more than the French écu. Paradin, *Mémoires de l'histoire de Lyon*, fos 2^v-3^r, pp. 282-3, 372; Antoine du Pinet, *Plantz, pourtraitz et descriptions de plusieurs villes et forteresses, tant de l'Europe, Asie et Afrique, que des Indes et terres neuves* (Lyon, 1564), pp. 35-6; de Rubys, *Privileges, franchises et immunitez de Lyon*, pp. 53-5, 57; [Gabriel de Saconay], *Cantique d'oraison pour le peuple de Lyon: le tombeau du Calvinisme, renay en l'an 1517, mort et r'enterré l'an 1568* (Lyon, 1568), fo. q2^r; *Eglogue de deux bergers, demonstrant comme la ville de Lyon a esté reduite à la religion vrayement chrestienne* (Lyon, 1564), fo. A3^v.

10 A.M.L. (inventaire-sommaire), AA151; *Documents relatifs à l'histoire de l'industrie et du commerce en France*, ed. G. Fagniez, 2 vols. (Collection de textes pour servir à l'enseignement de l'histoire, xxii, xxxi, Paris, 1898-1900), ii, pp. 279-84; André Bassard, "La querelle de consuls et des artisans à Lyon 1515-1521," *Revue d'histoire de Lyon*, viii (1909), pp. 3 ff.

11 On Antoine du Pinet, native of Besançon in Franche-Comté, see Antoine du Pinet, *La conformité des eglises reformees de France, et de l'eglise primitive en police et ceremonies* (n.p., 1564), pp. 9-14, dedication to the seigneurs of the government of Besançon from Lyon, 18 Apr. 1564; François de La Croix Du Maine, *Premier volume de la bibliotheque* (Paris, 1584), pp. 19-20; Eugénie Droz, "Antoine Pinet, traducteur de Bucer," in her *Chemins de l'hérésie: textes et documents*, 4 vols. (Geneva, 1970-6), ii, pp. 55-146.

Men in the silk trade on the Reformed consistory in the period 1562-4 include Claude Gousset, alias Luguin, *veloutier* (velvetmaker); Jean Darut, a silk entrepreneur and native of Franche-Comté; Gabriel Veny, *marchand de draps de soie* (silk cloth merchant); and Jean-Pierre Grand, a silk dyer and native of Verona: A.M.L., GG84, act of 13 Nov. 1564; A.M.L., GG84, *liasse* 107, *pièce* 2; Nicolay, *Génralle description de Lyon*, p. 160; A.E.G., Notaries, Jovenon, iii, fos. 291^r-294^v, will of Jean Pierre Grand. *Ordonnance du roy et de Monseigneur de Soubize, commandant pour le service de dieu et dudit sieur roy a Lyon... pour la seureté et protection des manans et habitans de ladite ville, et autres frequentans et negocians en icelle, tant en foire que hors foire* (Lyon, 1562); A.M.L., BB83, fos. 105^v-106^r.

De Rubys, *Privileges, franchises et immunitez de Lyon*, pp. 30, 49, 71. De Rubys was married to Diamante de La Volpe, native of Padua, who sought letters of naturalization in December 1577: A.D.R., BP3645, fo. 126^{r-v}.

12 I am giving full treatment to this material in my forthcoming book *Society and Salvation at Lyon*.

13 On Protestants in publishing in Lyon and among Lyon women, see Davis, *Society and Culture in Early Modern France*, chs. I, 3; on literacy rates, see ibid., pp. 72-3, 209-10. On females in tavernkeeping and printing, see my "Women in the *arts mécaniques* in Sixteenth-Century Lyon," in *Lyon et l'Europe, hommes et sociétés: mélanges d'histoire offerts a Richard Gascon*, 2 vols. (Univ. de Lyon II, Centre Pierre-Léon, Lyon, 1980), i, pp. 139-67.

14 The most important of the Reformed merchants or merchant bankers from outside the kingdom were men like George Obrecht, native of Strasbourg; Christophe Neythart (Neidhart), native of Augsburg; Jean Baptist Balian (Giovanni Battista Imperiali Baliani) of Genoa, an elder of the consistory in 1564 (A.M.L., GG87, *liasse 1, pièce 1*); and Julien Calendrin (Giuliano Calandrini) of Lucca, one of the initial organizers of the consistory in 1558-9. Among the Florentines, Bonacorsi Bonacorsi (Buonaccorsi) was a Protestant for a while (A.M.L., BB83, fo. 59^r, and CC 1110, fo. 362^{r-v}); but he was not from one of the great families, serving rather as an agent for a Milanese house and as a bank courier.

15 Of thirty-three ministers preaching in Lyon from 1560 to 1572, two were natives of Lyon and both of them (the surgeon Antoine Royet and the master printer François Gaillard) served only for a short time: A.D.R., 3E4061, 16 Nov. 1566; A. Ch. L., E 19, p. 491; A.D.R., 3E8030, 26 Oct.

The sacred and the body social in Lyon

1565, and 3E4542, 15 July 1566. The geographical origin of the other ministers is as follows: Auvergne 1, Berry 1, Burgundy 2, Dauphiné 2, Île-de-France 2, Languedoc 3, Normandy 5, Provence 4, Switzerland 3, unknown 6. On Pierre Viret, see Jean Barnaud, *Pierre Viret, sa vie et son oeuvre* (St.-Amans, 1911); Robert D. Linder, *The Political Ideas of Pierre Viret* (Geneva, 1964).

16 Pierre Viret, *Les cauteles et canon de la messe* (Lyon, 1563), pp. 113–16, 118–20, 151–3, 166–8; Pierre Viret, *Du vray usage de la salutation faite par l'ange à la vierge Marie* ([Geneva], 1556), pp. 15, 37; Antoine de Marcourt, *The Boke of Marchauntes, Right Necessarye unto All Folkes* (London, 1534, S.T.C. 17313.3), fos. A iii^v–A vii^r, Biii^{r-v} (a translation of the most important tract to emerge from the early Protestant movement in Lyon: Antoine de Marcourt, *Le livre des marchans, fort utile a toutes gens* ([Neuchâtel, 1533]); [Nicolas Barnaud], *Le cabinet du roy de France* (n.p., 1582), pp. 19 ff. (on the concubines of the church of Lyon); E.P.D., "Epigramme du dieu des papistes," in *Discours de la vermine et prestraille de Lyon, dechassé par le bras fort du seigneur* (n.p., 1562; copy in the Bibliothèque Méjanes, Aix): "charmes, signes, singeries et mines;" *La polymachie des marmitons, ou la gendarmerie du pape* (Lyon, 1563). Plates 1 and 5 are from the engraving to *Histoire de la mappemonde papistique... Composee par M. Frangidelphe Escorche-Messes. Imprimee en la ville de Luce Nouvelle, par Brifaud Chasse-diables*, 1567 ([Geneva], 1567; copy at the Bibliothèque publique et universitaire de Genève). These engravings were designed and executed by Pierre Cruche, alias Eskrich, an artist working in Lyon who made frequent visits to Geneva. See note 49 for further information on Eskrich.

"Saincte et franche communaute," from Pierre Viret, *Instruction chrestienne en la doctrine de la loy et de l'evangile, et en la vraye philosophie et theologie*, 2 vols. (Geneva, 1564), i, p. 86.

17 On the canon-counts of St. Jean, see J. Beyssac, *Les chanoines de l'Eglise de Lyon* (Lyon, 1914). Gabriel de Saconay, from an old family of the Lyonnais, became a canon in 1528 and held a series of important offices at the cathedral until his death in 1580. Information on the social and geographical origins of the canons at St. Paul's and St. Nizier is taken from A.D.R., 13G13 and 15G22-9. Guillaume Pignot, priest and vicar of the parish of St. Sorlin from 1539 to the 1560s, was the brother of a *teinturier* (dyer) and uncle of a velvetmaker and of printers: A.D.R., 3E7595, 30 Mar. 1538/9, 2 Sept 1539; 3E7184, fo. 249^{r-v}; 3E3908, fos. 29^r-32^r; 27H408, 17 May 1550. On the origins of the Franciscan friars at St. Bonaventure, see A.D.R., 4H27, 12 Aug. 1576. On Emond Auger, see A. de Backer and C. Sommervogel, *Bibliothèque de la Compagnie de Jésus*, new edn., 12 vols. (Brussels, 1890–1932), i, 631–42; Frances A. Yates, *The French Academies of the Sixteenth Century* (London, 1968), pp. 165-7; A. Lynn Martin, *Henry III and the Jesuit Politicians* (Geneva, 1973). I shall give full details of the social and geographical origins of the Lyon clergy in my *Society and Salvation at Lyon*.

18 A.D.R., 3H40, 1 May 1541, 1 Apr. 1588; 3H52, 11 Aug. 1517. The Germans founded a confraternity at the Dominican house in 1491 (A.D.R., 3H39), while the Lucchese merchants had a confraternity at the convent of the Observantine Franciscans just outside the city walls on the Saône side

(A.D.R., 3E4494, fo 219^r). These confraternities were much less active than that of the Florentines. On the Confraternity of the Holy Cross, see A.D.R., 10G3623, 10G3626, fos. 7^r, 49^r, and 3E346, fos. 208^r-219^v; J.B. Vanel, "L'abbé Joseph Courbon, 1748-1823: le custode de Saint Croix," *Bulletin historique du diocèse de Lyon*, i (1922), p. 59. On the Confraternity of St. Jacques, see A.D.R., 15G25, fos. 158^v-159^r; 15G157; 3E7184, fo. 203^{r-v}; A.M.L., CC684, fo. 3^v. On the chapel of St. Jacquême, see Paradin, *Memoires de l'histoire de Lyon*, p. 266; A. Kleinclausz (ed.), *Lyon des origines à nos jours* (Lyon, 1925), p. 16. One of the demands of the artisans who wanted to reform the fiscal and political structure of Lyon in 1517-20 was the holding of consular elections in the Chapel of St. Jacquême, rather than in the city hall, Claude de Rubys, *Histoire veritable de la ville de Lyon* (Lyon, 1604), p. 360.

19 A.D.R., 4G22, 24 June 1572; A.M.L., GG528-9.
20 The majority of the merchant-publishers and important master printers were supporters of the Reformed movement in the 1560s. So was Jean Tricaud, who had introduced fustian manufacture to Lyon; so were the successful silk manufacturers Claude Gapaillon and René Laurencin, among others. Virtually all the clockmakers in Lyon were Protestants; so was the merchant-armorer Jacques Buellstrat, a native of Brabant, and the canon and artillery manufacturer Robert de Chinon, a native of Brittany. By contrast most of the Florentine bankers remained Catholic; for the Protestant banker George Obrecht, see note 14.
21 *Procès de Baudichon de la Maisonneuve, accusé d'hérésie à Lyon*, ed. J.G. Baum (Geneva, 1873), p. 56; A.M.L., GG 1-3; GG269-70; L. Niepce, "Les trésors des églises de Lyon," *Revue lyonnaise*, vi (1883), pp. 425-8, 572-84; vii (1884), pp. 496-507; viii (1885), pp. 35-77; A.D.R., 15G109, 13 Aug. 1528, 25 Oct. 1575; 16G16, 11 June 1638; 3H52, 11 Aug. 1517; 27H402; A.M.L. (inventaire-sommaire), BB90, 1572; Champier, *Petit traicte de la noblesse et anciennete de Lyon*, fo. xxiii^v; de Rubys, *Privileges, franchises et immunitez de Lyon*, pp. 27-8; Jean de Saint-Aubin, *Histoire ecclesiastique de la ville de Lyon ancienne et moderne* (Lyon, 1666), pp. 69-78; J.-B. Martin, *Histoire des églises et chapelles de Lyon*, 2 vols. (Lyon, 1908), ii, p. 102; L.A. Pavy, *Les grands cordeliers de Lyon, ou l'église et le couvent de Saint-Bonaventure* (Lyon, 1835), pp. 72-4. Plate 2 is taken from "De tristibus galliae" (1567), an illustrated Latin poem about the religious wars and the Protestant destruction in Lyon: Bibliothèque municipale de Lyon, Fonds anciens, MS. 156; this scene shows the destruction of St. Just and St. Irénée on the hill of Fourvière by Huguenots with the heads of monkeys.
22 A.D.R., 10G3626, fo. 4^v; 16H1, fo. 2^r; 13G87, 23 Dec. 1610; Jean-Marie-H. Forest, *L'école cathédrale de Lyon* (Paris, 1885), pp. 170-7; Paradin, *Memoires de l'histoire de Lyon*, pp. 416-44, 47-8; Champier, *Petit traicte de la noblesse et anciennete de Lyon*, fo. ii^{r-v}.
23 *Du benefice de Iesuchrist crucifie, envers les chrestiens. Traduict de vulgaire Italien, en langage Francoys*, 2nd ed. (Paris, 1548), fo. 5', repr. by Salvatore Caponetto, in Benedette da Mantova, *Il beneficio di Cristo* (Corpus Reformatorum Italicorum, Florence, 1972), pp. 96, 506. The *Benefice* was first published in Lyon in 1545. Maurice Scève, *Saulsaye* (Lyon, 1547), p. 8; Nicolay, *Généralle*

The sacred and the body social in Lyon

description de Lyon, p. 16; Paradin, *Memoires de l'histoire de Lyon*, pp. 16-17, 200-2; Forest, *L'école cathédrale de Lyon*, pp. 155-61; Bonaventure Des Periers, "Du voyage de Lyon a Nostre Dame de L'isle, 1539," in *Recueil des oeuvres de feu Bonaventure des Periers*, ed. Antoine du Moulin (Lyon, 1544), p. 52; A.N., JJ251, fos. 93^v-94^r; de Rubys, *Histoire veritable de la ville de Lyon*, pp. 500-1; V.L. Saulnier, *Maurice Scève*, 2 vols. (Paris, 1948), i, pp. 194-201.

In an article forthcoming in the *Revue historique* on the "Cycle médiéval des fêtes lyonnaises," Jacques Rossiaud gives a critical examination of the Fête des Merveilles, showing that an alleged nautical joust between the youth of the Dauphiné and the youth of Lyon was a myth invented in the sixteenth century.

24 *Du benefice de Iesuchrist*, fo. 5^r; Paradin, *Memoires de l'histoire de Lyon*, pp. 2-4, 141-2; Scève, *Saulsaye*, p. 8; M.-C. Guigue, *Recherches sur Notre-Dame de Lyon* (Lyon, 1876); Kleinclausz, *Lyon des origines à nos jours*, pp. 14-16; A.M.L. (inventaire-sommaire), CC655, CC665, BB25, BB27; *Chronique lyonnaise de Jean Guéraud*, ed. Tricou, p. 115; A. Sachet, *Le pardon annuel de la Saint Jean et de la Saint Pierre*, 2 vols. (Lyon, 1918), i, pp. 391-2. On the Rhône flood of 1570, see *Discours sur l'espouvantable et merveilleux desbordement du Rosne* (Lyon, 1570), repr. in L. Cimber and F. Danjou (eds.), *Archives curieuses de l'histoire de France*, 24 vols. (Paris, 1834-40), vi, pp. 395-405; *De l'effroyable et merveilleux desbord de la riviere du Rhosne en 1570* (Paris, 1576), repr. by P.M. Gonon (Lyon, 1848), esp. p. 6; Paradin, *Memoires de l'histoire de Lyon*, pp. 386-9; de Rubys, *Privileges, franchises et immunitez de Lyon*, p. 29; [Jean Ricaud], *Discours du massacre de ceux de la religion Réformée par les catholiques romains... l'an 1572* (Lyon, 1574; repr. Lyon, 1848), p. 110. On the *cheval fol* of Pentecost, see de Rubys, *Histoire veritable de la ville de Lyon*, pp 502-3; [Louis Garon], *Stances sur l'ancienne confrairie du Saint Esprit fondee en la chapelle du pont du Rhosne a Lyon, avec l'origine du cheval fol et la resioussance des Lyonnois aux festes de la Pentecoste* (Lyon, 1609), repr. in *Revue du lyonnais*, v (1836), pp. 447-56. Cf. Jean Baumel, *Le "masque-cheval" et quelques autres animaux fantastiques: étude de folklore, d'ethnographie et d'histoire* (Paris, 1954); Jean-Claude Schmitt, "'Jeunes' et danse de chevaux des bois: le folklore méridional dans le littérature des 'exempla,'" in *La religion populaire en Languedoc du XIIIe siècle à la moitié du XIVe siècle* (Cahiers de Fanjeaux, xi, Toulouse, 1976), pp. 127-55.

Jacques Rossiaud is completing a *thèse d'état* on the Rhône and its economy and culture in the late Middle Ages. The Saône also flooded from time to time (see, for example, *Chronique lyonnaise de Jean Guéraud*, ed. Tricou, p. 88), but even though deaths could ensue, it was not feared in the same way that the Rhône floods were.

25 A.D.R., 10G3626, fo. 30^v; 10G3623. The route described here is that of a *general* procession on Corpus Christi day; the parishes often had internal processions on that *fête*. General processions on other occasions would also cover stations on both sides of the Saône.

26 Rogation day processions in Lyon went up the hill of Fourvière to visit St. Just and St. Irénée and to different stations at churches on either side of the Saône; they linked parts of the city rather than marking the boundary: A.D.R., 10G3626, fos. 6^v-7^r; 14G66, fos. 22^r, 29^r; *Liber sacerdotalis seu*

rituale, secundum usum primae Lugdunensis ecclesiae (Lyon, 1692), ch. on "Processions;" Forest, L'école cathédrale de Lyon, pp. 149 ff. On rural processions for Rogation days, see Arnold Van Gennep, Manuel de folklore français contemporain, 4 vols. (Paris, 1943-72), iii pp. 1640-9. On the social functions played by processions in European cities, see Samuel Berner "Florentine Society in the Late Sixteenth and Early Seventeenth Centuries," Studies in the Renaissance, xviii (1971), pp. 221-7; Claude Gauvin, "La fête-dieu et le théâtre en Angleterre au quinzième siècle," in J.J. Jacquot and E. Konigson (eds.), Les fêtes de la Renaissance, 3 vols. (Paris, 1956-75), pp. 440-9; and the works by Richard Trexler cited in n. 4. On Catholic processions as a symbolic conquest of urban space in contemporary Santa Fe, New Mexico, see Grimes, Symbol and Conquest, pp. 51-76.

27 On the conflict over the cattle market at the Croix de Colle opposite the convent of the Minimes, see A.D.R., 16H1, fos. 4^r, 100^r; 16H13. This mendicant order, founded in Italy by St. François de Paule, was established in Lyon in 1553: A.D.R., 10G588, Oct. 1497, Nov. 1544, Mar. 1577. On the tradesmen and shops around St. Nizier, see A.D.R., 15G95-6, 15G163. Compare the forthright action taken in 1554 by the rector of the Chapel of St. Côme and St. Damien, when the merchants Simon and Nicolas de Fert (both early Protestants) rented some old houses nearby, installed hammering artisans inside them, and especially built latrines and privies right next to the church walls. The latter were ordered to be demolished or another wall constructed: A.D.R., 27H440.

28 On the Reformed attitude toward the right and wrong uses of prayer, objects and processions, see [Antonio Mainardo], Anatomie de la messe et de messel ([Lyon], 1562), pp. 367, 396, 411-13; Pierre Viret, Du vray usage de la salutation faite par l'ange de la vierge Marie ([Geneva], 1556); Pierre Viret, Exposition familiere de l'oraison de nostre seigneur Iesus Christ (Geneva, 1551); Pierre Viret, De l'institution des heures canoniques et des temps determinez aux prieres des chrestiens (Lyon, 1564), pp. 13-19 (a procession was initially of military origin; it is necessary that "Christians be always on the watch [au guet]," p. 15); N.Z. Davis, "The Protestant Printing Workers of Lyon in 1551," in G. Berthoud et. al., Aspects de la propagande religieuse (Geneva, 1957), pp. 247-57; Pierre Viret, Disputations chrestiennes, touchant l'estat des trepassez, faites par dialogues (Geneva, 1552), p. 33. On Calvinist iconoclasm and rebuilding in 1562-3, see Chronique lyonnaise de Jean Guéraud, ed. Tricou, pp. 155-8; Gabriel de Saconay, Discours des premiers troubles advenus à Lyon (Lyon, 1569), pp. 284 ff., and passim; A.M.L. (inventaire-sommaire), AA46, BB83, 91, 95, 97, 111, 117, 129; A.D.R., 13G13, fos. 133^r-134^r; 15G24, fo. 29^r (a clockmaker in the Chapel of Nôtre Dame de Rue Neuve); 15G157, act of 1573 (a draper had set up shop in the Chapel of St. Jacquême); 2H35; 3H53 (Reformed inventory of the possessions of the Dominican convent; listing of ministers and their wives living there); 11H40; A.D.R., 3E566, 10 May 1562; 3E7179, fos. 411^v-421^r; A.M.L., GG77, pièce 1.

29 On the ways in which networks for traffic (transporting people and goods) and for communication (connecting human activities) give character to a commercial city, see the fascinating study by Sibyl Moholy-Nagy, Matrix of Man: An Illustrated History of Urban Environment (New York, 1968), ch. 5,

The sacred and the body social in Lyon

"Linear Merchant Cities." As Moholy-Nagy distinguishes these channels for communication from triumphal roads of various kinds, so one can distinguish the clearing of space in Protestant Lyon from the "construction of arrow-straight connecting roads between the seven principal pilgramage churches" in the Rome of Sixtus V (ibid., p. 143). Catholic Lyon is a mixed type by Moholy-Nagy's standards: a linear merchant city, with elements of the "geomorphic" and the "concentric" (concern both for geographical shape and for sacred place). Calvinist Lyon moved away from the geomorphic elements, generalized the symbolic features of the city, and intensified its linear character.

On the redrawing of urban parishes and especially the weakening of their powers in regard to all-city institutions in other Protestant areas, see Robert M. Kingdon, "Protestant Parishes in the Old World and the New: The Cases of Geneva and Boston," *Church Hist.*, xlviii (1979), pp. 290–304; Bernard Vogler, *Vie religieuse en pays rhénan dans la seconde moitié du XVIe siècle, 1556–1619*, 2 vols. (Lille, 1974), i, pp. 532–44.

30 See the valuable discussion of Weber's contrast between "traditional" and "rationalized" religions in Clifford Geertz, "'Internal Conversion' in Contemporary Bali," in his *The Interpretation of Cultures* (New York, 1973), pp. 171–5. I am trying here to recast the question of "immanence" in the Reformation, raised in the provocative but unconvincing book by Guy E. Swanson, *Religion and Regime: A Sociological Account of the Reformation* (Ann Arbor, Mich., 1967), ch. 1.

31 Mainardo, *Anatomie de la messe et de messel*, pp. 158–9, 161, 249ff., 367; Viret, *Disputations chrestiennes*, p. 33; Ricaud, *Discours du massacre*, 1572, p. 157.

32 *Eglogue de deux bergers*, fos. Aiii^v–Bi^r, Jean Aymon, *Tous les synodes nationaux des églises Réformées de France* (The Hague, 1710), p. 26; *Ordonnances du roy et de Monseigneur de Soubize... pour assister aux presches et prieres publiques: et ne tirer hacquebouzes ne sonner tabourins durant lesditz presches et aussi de n'user de blasphemes ny de ieux dissolus* (Lyon, 1562), fos. Aiii^v–Aiv^r: *revendeurs* and *revenderesses* were forbidden to set up stalls near temples before, during, and after services, especially next to St. Nizier, on pain of confiscation of merchandise at first offense, and prison and fine at second offense.

On the tensions introduced into a painting by the juxtaposition of markets and sacred buildings, see Keith P.F. Moxey, "The 'Humanist' Market Scenes of Joachim Beuckelaer: Moralizing Exempla or 'Slices of Life'?" *Koninklijk Museum voor Schone Kunsten-Antwerpen: Jaarboek* (1976), pp. 109–86. In seeking to understand the ways in which "profane" activities can sometimes underscore rather than threaten the sacredness of nearby religious activities, I have been much helped by conversations with Bruce Kapferer and Alfonso Ortiz.

For *later* developments in Counter-Reformation architecture, which give it a more general and uniform character and perhaps make it less tolerant of the profane at its walls, see Pierre Charpentrat, "L'architecture et son public: les églises de la Contre-Reforme," *Annales. E.S.C.*, xviii (1973), pp. 91–108.

33 3rd May, Invention of the Holy Cross (Confraternity of the Holy Cross); 22nd May, *fête* of St. Yves (Confraternities of the Bazoche and of royal

officers at the little Church of St. Alban near the cathedral); 22nd June, *fête* of St. Alban (celebration by the same confraternities); 24th June, *fête* of St. John the Baptist (Confraternity of the Furriers at the cathedral); 25th July, "Kingdom" of St. Christopher (celebrated at Ste. Croix); 16th August, "Kingdom" of St. Roch (celebrated at St. Pierre-le-Vieux). All of these churches are within a few minutes' walk of each other. M.C. and G. Guigue, *Bibliothèque historique du lyonnais* (Lyon, 1886), pp. 54–8; Sachet, *Le pardon annuel de la Saint Jean et de la Saint Pierre*, i pp. 321, 323, 535–6; A.D.R., 10G3626, fos. 7^r, 33^r, 47^v, 52^v; A.M.L., GG270, fo. 6^v; GG388, 22 May 1594; Martin, *Histoire des églises et chapelles de Lyon*, ii, p. 60. On *fêtes* organized by the consulate, see Paradin, *Memoires de l'histoire de Lyon*, pp. 301–3; de Rubys, *Histoire veritable de la ville de Lyon*, p. 501. For street dancing on St. Peter's Day and at Pentecost, see ibid., pp. 406, 502.

34 Charles Phythian-Adams, "Ceremony and the Citizen: The Communal Year at Coventry, 1450–1550," in Peter Clark and Paul Slack (eds.), *Crisis and Order in English Towns, 1500–1700* (Toronto, 1972), pp. 57–85. See also Mikhail Bakhtin, *Rabelais and his World*, trans. H. Iswolsky (Cambridge, Mass., 1968), p. 154: "Thus every year Lyon led for two months a life of fairs and carnivals, for even if there was no carnival, strictly speaking, its atmosphere reigned at every fair." I am suggesting here that sometimes the *temps de l'église* reinforces the *temps du marchand*, rather than being in tension with it; cf. J. Le Goff, "Temps de l'église et temps du marchand," *Annales. E.S.C.*, xv (1960), pp. 417–33; A.Y. Gourevitch, "Le temps comme problème d'histoire culturelle," in Paul Ricoeur (ed.), *Les cultures et le temps* (Paris, 1975), pp. 257–76.

35 Testimony of Claude Monier, 1551, in Jean Crespin, *Histoire des martyrs persecutez et mis à mort pour la verité de l'evangile*, ed. D. Benoît, 3 vols. (Toulouse, 1885–9), i, p. 553; Viret, *De l'institution des heures canoniques*, pp. 18–25; François Bourgoing, *Paraphrase ou briefve explication sur le catechisme* (Lyon, 1564), p. 416; *Ordonnances du roy et de Monseigneur de Soubize... pour assister aux presches*, fo. Aii^v; Jean Calvin, *Commentaire de M. Iean Calvin sur les cinq livres de Moyse* (Geneva, 1564), pp. 529–30; Théodore de Bèze, *Confession de la foy chrestienne* ([Geneva], 1559), pp. 167–9; *Discours catholique sur les causes et remedes des malheurs intentés au roy* (Lyon, 1568), pp. 69–70; A.E.G., MS., Jérome Desgouttes, "Recit de la maizon et origine des Goutes" (written by a Calvinist merchant and silk manufacturer about his family, which originated in St.-Symphorien-le-Chateau in the Lyonnais, and about his life in Lyon), fos. 12^v–13^r, 15^r, 18^v, 20^v–21^r.

36 Among valuable studies on the metaphor of the body and body symbolism, see Kantorowicz, *The King's Two Bodies*; Raymond Firth, *Symbols Public and Private* (London, 1973), chs. 8–9; Mary Douglas, *Purity and Danger* (London, 1966); Mary Douglas, *Natural Symbols: Explorations in Cosmology* (New York, 1970); John Blacking (ed.), *The Anthropology of the Body* (Assoc. Social Anthrop. Monograph, xv, London, 1977); Leonard Barkan, *Nature's Work of Art: The Human Body as Image of the World* (New Haven, Conn., 1975).

37 [De Saconay], *Cantique d'oraison pour le peuple de Lyon*; Anselme du Chastel, *Notables sentences de la Bible, tournees en quatrains* (Lyon, 1579), fos. 27^r, 30^r; De Saconay, *Discours des premiers troubles advenus à Lyon*, pp. 219, 222; de Rubys,

The sacred and the body social in Lyon

Privileges, franchises et immunitez de Lyon, pp. 16-17, 37; Claude de Rubys, *Oraison prononcee a Lyon a la creation des conseillers et eschevins de ladicte ville en l'église S. Nizier, le iour de la feste S. Thomas, 21 de Decembre 1567* (Lyon, 1568), fo. Bb 4^r; Gabriel de Saconay, *De la providence de dieu sur les roys de France treschrestiens, par laquelle la saincte religion catholique ne defaudra en leur royaume* (Lyon, 1568), p. 165. On Catholic riots, see "The Rites of Violence," in my *Society and Culture in Early Modern France,* ch. 6.

38 Emond Auger, *De la vraye, reale et corporelle presence de Iesus Christ au sainct sacrement de l'autel* (Paris, 1566), p. 225; Emond Auger, *Continuation de l'institution, verite et utilite du sacrifice de la messe* (Paris, 1566), pp. 108-10, 137; Emond Auger, *Du sacrament de penitence, livres III* (Paris, 1571), fo. Ci^r. See also Gabriel de Saconay, *Du vray corps de Iesu Christ au s. sacrament de l'autel* (Lyon, 1567), pp. 79-80, 109, 167.

39 Jean Benedicti, *La triomphante victoire de la vierge Marie sur sept malins esprits finalement chassés du corps d'une femme dans l'eglise des cordeliers de Lyon* (Lyon, 1583); Roland Antonioli, *Rabelais et la médecine* (Geneva, 1976), pp. 227-34 (on current medical theory about the role of the blood, heart, and liver in nourishing the body); François Rabelais, *Le tiers livre des faicts et dicts heroiques du bon Pantagruel,* chs. 3-4, in *Oeuvres complètes,* ed. J. Boulenger and L. Scheler (Paris, 1959).

40 Viret, *Instruction chrestienne,* pt. 2, pp. 360-3; Pierre Viret, *Response aux questions proposees par Iean Ropitel minime aux ministres de l'église Reformée de Lyon* (Lyon, 1565), p. 87. On the pastor as the "mouth" of the Lord and the "mouth" of the congregation, see Pierre Viret, *Du vray ministere de la vraye église de Iesus Christ, et des vrais sacremens d-icelle* ([Geneva], 1560), pp. 53-61; Pierre Viret, *Exposition familiere des principaux points du catechisme et de la doctrine chrestienne, faicte en forme de dialogue* ([Lyon], 1562), p. 170; Pierre Viret, *Le manuel, ou instruction des curez et vicaires, de l'église romaine* (Lyon, 1564), pp. 169-71. See also Bourgoing, *Paraphrase ou briefve explication sur le catechisme,* pp. 239-44, where the communication among members of the church and with Christ is compared not with the movement of the blood, but with the action of the soul: "Thus the members have their part in what the head communicates to them by the soul, which is spread throughout the whole body and which also gives life to all its members"; the original French reads "Ainsi que les membres ont leur part à ce que le chef leur communique par l'ame, qui est espandue par tout le corps, laquelle aussi baille vie à tous les membres d'iceluy."

The imagery of Viret and Bourgoing here went beyond that of Paul's Epistle to the Ephesians iv. 15-16: "But let us followe the trueth in love, and in all things growe up into him, which is the head, that is Christ, By whome all the bodie being coupled and knit together by everie joynt, for the furniture thereof (according to the effectuall power, which is in the measure of everie parte) receiveth increase of the bodie, unto the edifying of itself in love": *The Bible and Holy Scriptures* (Geneva, 1560); "Ains à fin que suyvans verité avec charité nous croissions en tout en celuy qui est le chef, à scavoir Christ Duquel tout le corps bien adiousté et serré ensemble par toutes les iointures du fournissement, prend accroissement de corps selon la vigueur qui est en la mesure de chacune partie pour l'edification de soy-mesme en

NATALIE ZEMON DAVIS

charité": *La Bible, qui est toute la saincte escriture* ([Geneva, 1565]).
41 Pierre Viret, *L'interim, fait par dialogues* (Lyon, 1565), pp. 59–60; du Pinet, *La conformité des églises Reformées de France*, pp. 85–98; *La forme des prieres et chantz ecclesiastiques, avec la maniere d'administrer les sacremens, et consacrer le mariage: selon la coustume de l'église ancienne* (Geneva, 1542; facsimile repr., Basel, 1959), fo. 17^v.
42 *La confession generale de Pasques* (n.p., n.d. [before 1500]; copy in A.H.D.L.), fo. a7^{r-v}; Jean Benedicti, *La somme des pechez, et le remede d'iceux* (Paris, 1595), p. 229; *Statuts et ordonnances synodales de l'église metropolitaine de Lyon* (Lyon, 1578), fo. 11^r.
43 R.E. Siegel, *Galen on Sense Perception* (Basel, 1970), p. 4; Rabelais, *Le tiers livre*, chs. 3–4; Viret, *De l'institution des heures canoniques* 9–20; Viret, *Disputations chrestiennes*, pp. 248–9; Claude Monier, in Crespin, *Histoire des martyrs*, i, p. 555. If we may judge from a sample of seventy Reformed wills, made by persons from artisanal or commercial backgrounds in the years 1562–80, Calvinists took the injunction to charity seriously: Fifty-two of the seventy persons made bequests either to the poor of the Reformed church or the Aumône-Générale or Hôtel-Dieu or to both civic and church charities: A.D.R., 3E 2810-12, 5296, 6942, 7170, 7184-5; A.E.G., Notaries, Jovenon, i, with wills taken in Lyon.

Mainardo, *Anatomie de la messe et de messel*, pp. 18–19, 233–4; Pierre Viret, *De la communication des fideles, qui cognoissent la verité de l'evangile, aux ceremonies des papistes* (n.p., 1560), pp. 91–3.
44 Viret, *Instruction chrestienne*, pt. I, pp. 564–5; *Le blason des basquines et vertugalles* (Lyon, 1563); Charlotte Arbaleste, *Mémoires de Madame de Mornay*, ed. Henriette de Witt, 2 vols. (Paris, 1869), ii, pp. 283–97.
45 For example, the encouragement of artisanal confraternities sometimes facilitated the existence of journeymen's organizations, which could be used for pressing claims against masters.
46 There was presumably some preaching in Italian, for one of the ministers, Jean-François Salluard, was a native of Piedmont, and the Florentine Francesco Giuntini preached in Italian for a while in 1561, before his reconversion to Catholicism. There was some concern about radical Protestant movements among the Italians: Henri Meylan, "Bèze et les italiens de Lyon," *Bibliothèque d'humanisme et renaissance*, xiv (1952), pp. 234–49. But common vernaculars replaced local dialects and languages as well as the clerical Latin. See Abner Cohen, *Two Dimensional Man: An Essay on the Anthropology of Power and Symbolism in Complex Society* (Berkeley, 1976), pp. 84–6, on "the problem of cultural heterogeneity": "a group which has effective functions of communication can afford to have less effective functions of distinctiveness."
47 "Wherefore the law was our schoolmaster to bring us unto Christ, that we might be justified by faith. But after that faith is come, we are no longer under a schoolmaster": Galatians iii. 24–5. This text played an important role in the preaching of Aimé Meigret, the first clerical convert to Protestantism in Lyon: Aimé Meigret, *Epistre en latin . . . à messeigneurs de parlement de Grenoble: plus un sermon en françois presché à Grenoble . . . l'an de grace mil cinq*

The sacred and the body social in Lyon

cens vingtquatre (n.p., 1524), fos. dvi^r-dviii^v; Henri Hours, "Procès d'hérésie contre Aimé Maigret, Lyon-Grenoble, 1524," *Bibliothèque d'humanisme et renaissance*, xix (1957), pp. 14-43.

48 On the effort to disseminate Protestant ideas in the Lyonnais, see A.D.R., B, Sénéchaussée, *Sentences*, 1556-9 (sentence of July 1559); *Ordonnances du roy et de Monseigneur de Soubize... pour assister aux presches: avec commandement à tous les lieux circonvoisins de ce pays de se pourvoir de pasteurs et ministres* (Lyon, 1562), fo. Bi^r. On the interest of Jérome Desgouttes and his cousin Symphorien Thelusson in rural manufacture in the Lyonnais, see Gascon, *Grand commerce et vie urbaine*, p. 526. Subsequently, in exile in Switzerland, Jérome tried to establish woollen manufacture in the rural lands of Berne, "in which place I pray God for the grace for me and my family to live so that He be glorified and we be good examples and edification for the inhabitants": A.E.G., MS., Desgouttes, "Recit de la maizon et origine des Gouttes," fo. II^v.

49 For full title of the edition, see note 16. Natalis Rondot, "Pierre Eskrich, peintre et tailleur d'histoires à Lyon au XVIe siècle," *Revue du lyonnais*, xxxi (1901), pp. 241-61, 321-50; Paul Chaix, *Recherches sur l'imprimerie à Genève de 1550 à 1564* (Geneva, 1954), p. 99; A. Cartier, *Bibliographie des editions des De Tournes, imprimeurs lyonnais* (Paris, n.d.), pp. 21, 105; A.M.L. (inventaire-sommaire), CC150, fo. 151, 1112, 1225; A.M.L., EE25, fo. 31^r.

II

The nature of acting

VICTOR TURNER

Acting in everyday life and everyday life in acting

Acting, like all "simple" Anglo-Saxon words, is ambiguous – it can mean doing things in everyday life or performing on the stage or in a temple. It can take place in ordinary time or in extraordinary time. It may be a way of working or moving, like a body's or machine's "action"; or it may be the art or occupation of performing in plays. It may be the essence of sincerity, such as the commitment of the self to a line of action for ethical motives; or it may be the essence of pretense, as when one "plays a part" in order to conceal or dissimulate. The former is the ideal of Jerzy Grotowski's Poor Theater; the latter happens every day "at work." A spy, a con-man, an *agent provocateur* – each of these has skill in "acting" and yet can "put on" an act or "act divinely." These opposites coincide in our common parlance; we speak of "playing a role" when we intend a reference to some civically serious activity, such as an advisory role to a president. On the other hand, we talk of "great acting" as the source of some of our deepest understandings of the human condition. Acting is therefore both work and play, solemn and ludicrous, our mundane trafficking and commerce and what we do or behold in ritual or theater. In both major senses it is indispensable to mental health; as William Blake said: "He who nourishes Desires but Acts not, breeds Pestilence," a doublet "Proverb of Hell" to, "Expect Poison from the standing Water." In Western languages, action has also the flavor of contestation. Action is agonistic. *Act, agón, agony,* and *agitate* are all derived from the same Indo-European base *ag-, "to drive," from which came the Latin *agere,* "to do," and the Greek *agein* ('ἄγειν), "to lead." In Western (Euro-American) culture, work and play both have this driving, conflictive character, which seems to antedate anything like a Protestant ethic. In genres of cultural performance that predated Greek theater – for example, myth recitation, ritual, oral epic or saga, and the telling and acting of lays and märchen – wars and feuds between groups of deities or clans and lineages headed by well-armed heroes, as well as competition for position, power, or scarce resources, men's conflict over women, and divisions between close kin, were clearly prominent. Phyllis Hartnoll (n.d.:8) writes of the development of Greek tragedy from the dithyramb (or unison hymn) sung round the altar of Dionysus during certain religious feasts. The dithyramb, originally in lyric form, a song of praise for Dionysus, came to deal with his life and mythos in much the same way as early medieval European liturgical plays about the birth, life, and resurrection of Christ (narratives loaded, of course, with conflict) grew from the lyrical portion of the Easter morning mass. The mass, the Eucharist, itself was, of course, a drama with a scriptural script long before it gave rise to Passion plays. The Greek dithyramb expanded to embrace not only Dionysian tales but also those of gods, demigods, and heroes, some of whom were regarded as the founding ancestors of the Hellenes and their Mediterranean neighbors. Writes Hartnoll:

> The deeds of these heroes, good or bad, their wars, feuds, marriages and adulteries, and the destinies of their children, who so often suffered for the sins of their parents, are a source of dramatic tension, and give rise to the essential element of conflict – between man and god, good and evil, child and parent, duty and inclination. This may lead to comprehension and reconciliation between the conflicting elements – since a Greek tragedy need not necessarily end unhappily – or to incomprehension and chaos. The plots of all Greek plays were already well known to the audience. They formed part of its religious and cultural heritage, for many of them dated from Homeric times. The interest for the spectator lay, therefore, not in the novelty of the story, but in seeing how the dramatist had chosen to deal with it, and no doubt, in assessing the quality of the acting, and the work of the chorus, both in singing and dancing, about which unfortunately we know very little. [pp. 8-9]

Hartnoll's summary is correct – as far as it goes. But it does not mention the important fact that the plays – the comedies of Aristophanes as much as the tragedies of Aeschylus and Sophocles – in Geertz's terms were social "metacommentaries" on contemporaneous Greek society; that is, whatever the nature of their plot, whether drawn from myths or reputed historical accounts, they were intensely reflexive. If they were "mirrors held up to nature" (or rather to society and culture), they were *active* (that propulsive word again!) mirrors, mirrors that probed and analyzed the axioms and assumptions of the social structure, isolated the building blocks of the culture and sometimes used them to construct novel edifices, Cloud Cuckoolands, or Persian courts that never were on land or sea but were, nevertheless, possible variants based on rules underlying the structures of familiar sociocultural life or experienced social reality (Geertz, 1980).

Theater is perhaps the most forceful, "active," if you like, genre of cultural performance, but there are many others, some of which I have mentioned. No society is without some mode of metacommentary. In the simpler preindustrial societies, there were often complex systems of ritual – initiatory, seasonal, curative, and divinatory – that acted, so to speak, not only as means of "reanimating sentiments of social solidarity," as an older generation of anthropologists would put it, but also as scanning devices whereby the difficulties and conflicts of the present were articulated and given meaning through contextualization in an abiding cosmological scheme. The anger of gods or ancestors may be proposed as the cause of present misfortune, anger aroused by some blatant or persistent transgression of customs handed down from high antiquity and vouched for by revered origin myths. In complex, large-scale societies, in which the sphere of leisure is clearly separated from that of work, innumerable genres of cultural performance arise in accordance with the principle of the division of labor. These may be labeled art, entertainment, sport, play, games, recreation, theater, light or serious reading. They may be collective or private, amateur or professional, slight or serious. Not all of them have the reflexive character of many Greek plays. Not all of them have universal reference, for many are limited to specific constituencies (men, women, children, rich, poor, intellectual, middlebrow, etc.). But in this prolixity of genres now given wider scope by the electronic media, some seem more effective than others in giving birth to self-regulatory or self-critical works, which catch the attention or fire the imagination of an entire society or even of an epoch, transcending national frontiers. In a complex culture it might be possible to regard the ensemble of performative and narrative genres as a hall of mirrors or, better, as magic mirrors, in which social problems, issues, and crises (from *causes célèbres* to changing categorial relations between the sexes and age groups) are pinpointed, evaluated, or diagnosed in works typical of each genre, then shifted to another genre better able to scrutinize certain of their aspects, until many facets of the problem have been illuminated and made accessible to conscious remedial action. In this hall of mirrors the reflections are multiple, some magnifying, some diminishing the faces peering into them, but in such a way as to provoke not merely thought,

VICTOR TURNER

but also powerful feelings and the will to modify everyday matters in the minds of the gazers. For no one likes to see oneself as ugly, ungainly, or dwarfish.

Theatre is perhaps closer to life than are most performative genres in that, despite its conventions and spatial restraints on physical possibility, it is, as Marjorie Boulton wrote in *The Anatomy of Drama* (1971:3), "literature that walks and talks before our eyes, meant to be performed, 'acted' we might say, rather than seen as marks on paper and sights, sounds, and actions in our heads." This proximity of theater to life makes it the form best fitted to comment or to metacomment on conflict, for life is conflict – "Without Contraries is no Progression," as Blake said, if only in the sense that Life and Death, Eros and Thanatos, are, in Freud's words, "immortal antagonists," which is, incidentally, another term in the *agere*, *agein*, *agón* family. Even when, in certain kinds of theater, in different cultures, conflict may appear to be muted or deflected or rendered as a playful or joyous struggle, it is not hard to detect threads of connection between elements of the play and sources of conflict in the sociocultural milieu. The very mufflings and evasions of scenes of discord speak eloquently to their real presence in society and might be regarded as a cultural defense mechanism against conflict rather than as a metacommentary.

I might be supposed to have an intellectual vested interest in conflict and in drama as conflict, since I have discussed social conflict as social drama in many of my publications since my first book, *Schism and Continuity*, which was written a quarter of a century ago. Indeed, I have had to defend myself against such critics as my former teachers Sir Raymond Firth and the late Max Gluckman, who accused me of unwarrantably introducing a model drawn from literature (they did not say *Western* literature, but clearly they had the Aristotelian model of tragedy in mind) to throw light on spontaneous social processes, which are not authored or set in conventions, but rather arise from clashes of interest or from incompatible social structural principles in the give-and-take of everyday life in a social group. Recently, I took heart from an article by Clifford Geertz, "Blurred Genres: The Refiguration of Social Thought" (1980), which not only suggests "that analogies drawn from the humanities are coming to play the kind of role in sociological understanding that analogies drawn from the crafts and technology have long played in physical understanding" (p. 165), but also gives qualified approval to the "drama analogy for social life" (p. 172). Geertz ascribes to me the role of a "proponent of the ritual theory of drama," as against "the symbolic action approach," which stresses "the affinities of theater and rhetoric – drama as persuasion, the platform as stage" (p. 172), associated with Kenneth Burke. His pithy formulation of my position saves me the task of repeating my own. Geertz's prose even makes it sound better, though it omits certain aspects I regard as important, and which I will shortly discuss. He writes:

For Turner, social dramas occur "on all levels of social organization from state to family." They arise out of conflict situations – a village falls into factions, a husband beats a wife, a region rises against the state – and proceed to their denouements through publicly performed conventionalized behavior. As the conflict swells to crisis and the excited fluidity of heightened emotion, where people feel at once more enclosed in a common mood and loosened from their social moorings, ritualized forms of authority – litigation, feud, sacrifice, prayer – are invoked to contain it and render it orderly. If they succeed, the breach is healed and the status quo, or something resembling it, is restored; if they do not, it is accepted as incapable of remedy and things fall apart into various sorts of unhappy endings: migrations, divorces, or murders in the cathedral. With differing degrees of strictness and detail, Turner and his followers have applied this schema to tribal passage rites, curing ceremonies, and judicial processes; to Mexican insurrections, Icelandic sagas, and Thomas Becket's difficulties with Henry II; to picaresque narrative, millenarian movements, Caribbean carnivals, and Indian peyote hunts; and to the political upheaval of the sixties. A form for all seasons. [p. 172]

This final shaft of wit was fired by Geertz's insistence in several of his writings that the social drama approach focuses too narrowly on "the *general* movement of things" (my italics) and neglects the multifarious cultural contents, the symbol systems that embody the ethos and eidos, the sentiments and values of *specific* cultures. He suggests that the "text analogy" (p. 175) can remedy this; that is, textual analysis attends to

how the inscription of action is brought about, what its vehicles are and how they work, and on what the fixation of meaning from the flow of events – history from what happened, thought from thinking, culture from behavior – implies for sociological interpretation. To see social institutions, social customs, social changes as in some sense "readable" is to alter our whole sense of what such interpretation is towards modes of thought rather more familiar to the translator, the exegete, or iconographer than to the test giver, the factor analyst, or the pollster. [pp. 175–6]

My answer to Geertz is simply that he has perhaps failed to read carefully enough the texts produced by many who have used the social drama approach. He mentions "ritualized forms of authority – litigation, feud, sacrifice, prayer" that are used "to contain [crisis] and render it orderly." Such forms crystallize the uniqueness of any culture.

Victor Turner

I have written books and articles that, in effect, treat the ritual and juridical symbol systems of the Ndembu of Western Zambia as text analogues. But I have tried to locate these texts in contexts of performance rather than to construe them as abstract, dominantly cognitive systems. Geertz does concede, however, that many anthropologists today, including himself, use both textual and dramatistic approaches, according to problem and context. Some of these misunderstandings and apparent contradictions can be resolved if we examine the relationship between the two modes of acting – in "real life" and "on stage" – considering them as components of a dynamic system of interdependence between social dramas and cultural performances. Both dramatistic and textual analogies then fall into place. Richard Schechner recently represented this relationship as a bisected figure eight laid on its side (see Figure 1). The two semicircles above the horizontal dividing line represent the manifest, visible public realm; those below it, the latent, hidden, perhaps even unconscious realm. The left loop represents social drama, divided into its four main phases, breach, crisis, redress, and positive or negative denouement. The right loop represents a genre of cultural performance – for our purposes, a stage of aesthetic drama. Note that the manifest social drama feeds into the latent realm of stage drama; that is, its characteristic form in a given culture, at a given time and place, unconsciously, or perhaps preconsciously, influences not only the form but also the content of the stage drama of which it is the active or "magic" mirror. The stage drama, when it is meant to do more than entertain – though entertainment is always one of its vital aims ("But that's all one, our play is done, And we'll strive to please you

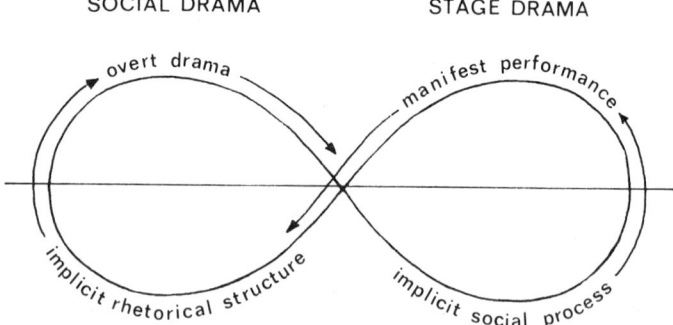

Figure 1. Diagram of Richard Schechner's description of the relationship between social dramas and cultural performances.

every day" [*Twelfth Night*]) - is a metacommentary, explicit or implicit, witting or unwitting, on the major social dramas of its social context (wars, revolutions, scandals, institutional changes). In addition, its message and its rhetoric feed back into the latent processual structure of the social drama and partly account for its ready ritualization. Life itself now becomes a mirror held up to art, for the protagonists of a social drama have been equipped by aesthetic drama with some of their most salient opinions and ideological perspectives. Neither mutual mirroring - life by art, art by life - is exact; at each exchange something new is added, something old is lost or discarded. Human beings learn through experience, though all too often they repress painful experience; and perhaps the deepest experience is through drama, not through social drama or stage drama (or its equivalent) alone, but in the circulatory process of their mutual and incessant modification.

If one were to guess at origins, my conjecture would be that all the genres of cultural performance, from tribal rituals to television specials, are potentially present in the third phase of the generic social drama - which like the mammalian condition we still have with us throughout all the radiation of mammalian forms to fill special niches - the phase of redressive processes. In a social drama, the first phase occurs when one or more social norms regarded as binding and as sustaining key relationships between persons or subgroups in a more or less bounded community are broken or are all too obviously disregarded. Often there is a symbolic act drawing public attention to the breach. Once this occurs, no group member can turn a blind eye to its implications. In the next phase, *crisis*, people take sides, supporting either the rule breaker or the target of his action. Factions, coalitions, cabals are formed, heated language is exchanged and actual violence may occur. Former allies are opposed, former foes united. Conflict is usually contagious: Old grudges are reanimated, old wounds opened, buried memories of victory or defeat disinterred. For no social drama is ever finally concluded: The terms of its ending are often the conditions under which a new drama will arise. The unity and continuity of the community may be menaced. All this may be "low key" or "high key," the weapons may be gestures, words, fisticuffs, or spears and firearms. When the community's integrality is thus threatened, those held responsible for its continuity and for the structural form of its continuity - the polity, in short - move to counteract the contagion of continuing breach and endeavor first to contain, then dispel, the crisis. These agents of redress may be chiefs, elders, lawmen, judges, members of the military, priests, shamans, diviners, fathers, mothers, grand juries, village panchayats – often they are the repositories and representatives of legitimacy, of conformity to established rules, standards, or principles. But the redressive agents and the instruments they have at their command, such as courts, parliaments, assemblies, councils, armies, police, negotiating tables, divining apparatuses, oracles, or powers to curse or bless, may lose their legitimacy or efficacy in the eyes of the group members. Then the response to crisis may emerge from a group intent on altering or restructuring the social order in some decisive way, from reformative to revolutionary. Such a clash between conserving and reforming parties may create a new crisis as the representatives of the *ancien* and *nouveau régimes* confront one another. Redress may then take the form of civil war, insurgency, or revolution.

Much depends upon the size and scale of the group and the degree to which its social–economic division of labor has advanced. Such factors determine what modes of redress are applied or devised. In state societies with hierarchical social structures, failure to resolve crisis at the local or regional levels may result in redressive action by the central political or judicial authorities operating through their courts and police. In simpler, preliterate, stateless societies, redressive machinery is often of two kinds: jural or ritual. Jural action may mean informal or formal arbitration by elders, the summoning of a chief's court with councillors and assessors, or recourse to blood vengeance or feud. What is of special interest to us here is ritual action. What Western cultural tradition distinguishes as social, moral, and natural orders are regarded in many small-scale societies as a single order with visible and invisible components. The term *supernatural*, like nature itself, is a Western concept. Thus, illness or bad luck in the community, whether personal or epidemic, may be conceived as resulting from the invisible action of ancestral spirits, offended by covert or overt malicious deeds (witchcraft or quarreling) among community members descended from them. Or it may be attributed to the hidden malice of living witches or sorcerers. If outbreaks of illness or successive untoward events (plagues, locusts, hurricanes, famine, drought, unexpected raids by outsiders) coincide with breaches of rules and relationships *within* the community, and no rational settlement of disputes appears possible in terms of customary law, recourse may be had to divination or oracles, procedures that detect the invisible causes of conflict and prescribe the appropriate type of ritual to propitiate or exorcise the afflicting spirit or witch's familiar.

Such rituals, which I called "rituals of affliction" in the Central

Acting in everyday life and everyday life in acting

African context, are found in many societies and often develop an elaborate symbolism. Sometimes they are associated with cosmogonic or cosmological myths that explain how death and disease came into the world of men and women. Ritual in such societies is seldom the rigid, obsessional behavior we think of as ritual after Freud. Rather it is an orchestration of symbolic actions and objects in all the sensory codes – visual, auditory, kinaesthetic, olfactory, gustatory – full of music and dancing and with interludes of play and entertainment. It may involve painting (including body painting), sculpture, wood carving, instrumental and choral music, systematic medical treatment (patients are given herbal potions and baths, steam inhalation, etc., as part of the ritual process), dramatic plotting (ritual officiants often enact the roles of gods, ancestors, or demons as described in myths), festal cuisine (certain kinds of food and drink are reserved for rites dedicated to specific gods or spirits), preaching and homiletic (rituals of these types allow a good deal of freedom for innovative verbal behavior, often regarded as messages from spirits through possessed mediums or shamans), psychological analysis (diviners seek to probe the hidden tensions and grudges in the community that are believed to be responsible for affliction), dance drama and choreography (according to set rules), and many more aesthetic and cognitive modes that later come to be specialized as para-ritual, quasi-secular, then fully secularized professions in more complex societies. Not only rituals of affliction but even life-crisis rituals (birth, puberty, marriage, funerary, etc.) and seasonal rituals (first fruits, harvest, solar solstice, etc.) have reference to conflict. Whereas rituals of affliction are sometimes a direct response to misfortune regarded as a manifest symptom of hidden conflict, the other main types may be viewed as prophylactic against conflict by vividly demonstrating the blessings of cooperation. For example, in my book *Forest of Symbols*, I examine the Ndembu and show how both the boys' circumcision ritual (*Mukanda*) and the girls' puberty ritual (*Nkang'a*) dramatize the characteristic divisions and oppositions between men and women. In this matrilineal society, such oppositions arise from custom itself: Group placement, inheritance, and succession are acquired through the mother's side; whereas power and authority, village headmanship and chieftainship are held by men and women who leave their mothers and siblings to reside in their husbands' villages after marriage. This structural conflict between female continuity and male authority is "the undying worm" of Ndembu culture, even though ritual, myth, and symbol proliferate to mask it, decorate it, palliate it, or explain it away.

VICTOR TURNER

Briefly, I am saying that the performative genres of complex, industrial societies, as well as many of their forensic and judicial institutions, the stage, and the law court, have their deep roots in the enduring human social drama, particularly in its redressive phase. This drama has its direct source in social structural conflict, but behind it perhaps is an endemic evolutionary restlessness. We seem to be a species that becomes easily bored with even its most advantageous cultural adaptations. From this perspective social dramas keep us alive, give us problems to solve, postpone ennui, guarantee the flow of our adrenaline, and provoke us into new, ingenious cultural formulations of our human condition and attempts to ameliorate it, even beautify it.

The social drama typical of cultures and social orders of the cyclical, repetitive type, however, differs radically from that found in rapidly changing societies, such as Western society. In the former, the full sequence of stages, breach, crisis, redress, and restoration of peace through reconciliation or mutual acceptance of schism can be more easily completed, because redress, whether legal or ritual, depends on wide, even general, agreement about values and on meaning. In complex, plural, class-, race-, age-, and gender-divided societies stressing competition, inventiveness, and innovation, general consensus is less likely to be obtained. Nevertheless, for the same reasons, it is highly likely that a multitude of models, utopian or otherwise, for social order and a multiplicity of religious, political, and philosophical systems for assigning meaning to the typical events of the epoch will be generated and will operate through a wide variety of rhetorics and other means of persuasion. And since the individual in general rather than the social persona (the bundle of statuses and roles comprising the social personality) is both the generator and ultimate audience of these narrated, dramatized, or otherwise aesthetically coded models – the final appellate court, so to speak – there is no surety that in any major crisis full agreement will be reached on the terms under which peace and order will be restored. Hence the contemporary paradox that in a world that respects learning, literacy, argument, negotiation, persuasion, and legality, many major social dramas are settled by armed force, "by cutting the Gordian knot" – the quick, simple solution to problems of any complexity or more than average perplexity. That is why so many nations are now under military rule. Where dissension reigns over meaning, consensus is replaced by force. Of course, the forceful seizers of power and settlers of issues then endeavor to socialize the young in

Acting in everyday life and everyday life in acting

terms of a single simplified belief system that defines legitimacy in such a way that social dramas will once more have agreed-on mechanisms of redress, heavily charged with secular ritual. In such societies, the genres of cultural performance that have replaced the rituals and jural processes of tribal and feudal societies, in the course of their complexification into industrialized, urbanized polities and international mercantile systems, fall under heavy political attack. The industrialized modes of retribalization on the scale of nations with which we have become familiar in this century, whether left, right, or center in political ideology, are united in their opposition to diversity in thought and in life-style, for diversity leads to the slow resolution of social dramas, wherever they may show up in the social process or on the national map, and may lead to a critique of the polity itself. Retribalization, it may be argued, on the scale of huge industrialized polities, is really in sharp dialectical contradiction to the modern mode of production, whose diversity and constant response to new technology (e.g., computers, miniaturization) demand equal diversity in the sphere of culture, especially in those aspects concerned with the redress, direct or indirect, of the social dramas constantly erupting from the new relations of production. Paradoxically, retribalization, "one Law for the Lion and the Ox," as Blake might have put it, is being carried on under the aegis of evolution to a "higher stage" of society. Retribalization, whether defined as "fascist," "socialist," "communist," or any other mode of authoritarian or totalitarian control, must seek to control crises of all types – not only by force but by reritualization of the third phase of all social dramas, that of redress. Thus, a contradiction arises between manifold and diverse forces and means of production, as individual human inventiveness penetrates the economic infrastructure and the monolithic state structures whose control of the means of production stifles productive creativeness.

Ritual, unlike theater, does not distinguish between audience and performers. Instead, there is a congregation whose leaders may be priests, party officials, or other religious or secular ritual specialists. All share the same set of beliefs and accept the same system of practices, the same rituals or liturgical actions. A congregation is there to affirm the theological or cosmological order, explicit or implicit, that all hold in common, to actualize it periodically for themselves and to inculcate the basic tenets of that order into their younger members, often in a graded series of life-crisis rituals: passages from birth to death, through puberty, marriage, initiation into prestigious secret societies, and so on. Theater – from the Greek *theasthai*, "to see, to view," is rather different. Richard Schechner (1977: 211) argues:

> Theater comes into existence when a *separation* occurs between audience and performers. The paradigmatic theatrical situation is a group of performers soliciting an audience who may or may not respond by attending. The audience is free to attend or stay away – and if they stay away it is the theater that suffers, not its would-be audience. In ritual staying-away means rejecting the congregation – or being rejected by it, as in excommunication, ostracism, or exile.

One might add that it is not a mortal sin if one fails to attend a play by Ibsen, Chekhov, Brecht, or Ionesco, but it used to be a mortal sin if one failed to attend Sunday mass. (In this case, one wonders whether the Catholic Church now sees itself as approaching the mode of theater, even as it calls for greater congregational participation.) In totalitarian states, it came to be regarded as an existential sin if one did not attend a local rally for nationally dominant political figures – the dissident became a scapegoat and was duly punished.

Now back to my original point that everyday life is intrinsically connected with acting and vice versa. It seems to me that tribalism and retribalization (however phony the latter may be in face of the movement of social reality) both stress the social structure and, with it, the roles, statuses, and positions that are its hierarchical components, at the expense of what social thinkers, from Durkheim to Kenelm Burridge, have called "the individual." The *person*, Burridge argues (1979: 4) is content with things as they are; the *individual* posits an alternative set of moral discriminations. "The individual" is a concept arising rather late in most complex human cultures. Burridge relates its earlier forms to what I have called, following Van Gennep, the *liminal period*, in rites of passage from one social state and status to another, at birth, puberty, marriage, death, and so on. The liminal period is that time and space betwixt and between one context of meaning and action and another. Characteristic of this liminal period is the appearance of marked ambiguity and inconsistency of meaning, and the emergence of liminal demonic and monstrous figures who represent within themselves ambiguities and inconsistencies. As ambiguous figures, they mediate between alternative or opposing contexts and thus are important in bringing about their transformation. In our society we might see the Theater of the Absurd of Ionesco, Arribal, and Becket as liminal, though I would prefer the term *limin*oid, as being at once akin to and perhaps following on the "liminal" of tribal and feudal rituals, and

Acting in everyday life and everyday life in acting

different from it as being the creation of individual and not collective inspiration and critical of rather than furthering the purposes of the existing social order. The incipient individual, in preliterate societies, does emerge, but often in veiled form. Burridge makes some interesting speculation about this proto- or ur-individual. He regards what he calls "the self" not as a static entity, but as "an inter" between the structural persona and the potentially antistructural individual. This enables him to write:

The liminal period becomes an introduction to, and test of, moral beings. Generally re-enacting the transformation from nature to culture, pubertal rites bring the components of being together and confront the cultural faculties with the oppositions and correspondences between animal, moral, and spiritual beings. To use another idiom, the initiand is asked to measure communitas and anti-structure – wherein human beings, stripped of their roles, statuses, memberships, and moralities, are in communion as human selves – against the demands of organization and structure.

In this situation, most initiands, responding to past pressures of kinsfolk and conformists, yield to the more obvious and overt side of the ritual. Some, intuitively grasping that symbols and symbolic activities contain a mysterium – a latency, a promissory note, an invitation to realize that which lies behind the obvious and overt – may perceive and order a truth which, because they cannot withstand conformist pressures, they will hold in their hearts all the years of their lives. Others lose themselves in the chaos, unable to bring it into order. A few persevere and are led into areas which the overtness of the cultural symbols hide from most. But while the affirmation of a truth discovered calls a halt, one negation breeds another and discovery becomes a continuing journey. Truth's center seems to grow more distant with each successive launch from closing peripheries. [Perhaps this is why so many millions, to this day, go on pilgrimage to the shrines of deities or saints.] Each arrival entails a further moral choice if it is to make a new point of departure, and each departure requires a further transformation of the self in relation to otherness. In Turner's phrase, man grows through antistructure, and conserves through structure. [1979: 146-7]

Elsewhere, and evidently thinking of the post-Renaissance "individual-in-general," Burridge writes of the individual as

the moral critic who envisages another kind of social or moral order, the creative spark poised and ready to change tradition. Yet if some people are wholly individuals and others are persons, it is a matter of common observation that most people are in some respects and most frequently persons, while in other respects and at other times they can appear as individuals. And this apparent oscillation or movement between person and individual – whether in a particular instance the movement is one-way or a return is made – may be identified as individuality. Or, individuality refers to the opportunity and capacity to move from person to individual and/or *vice versa*. [1979: 5-6]

Burridge presumably means that in a society already characterized by the possibility of making many choices, a biological individual can opt to be a persona *in extremis*, a "Southern colonel," "a Madam," "a great actor," "a Northern senator," "a dear old schoolmaster," "a motherly soul," even an "eccentric," or an individual who eschews identification with all available social personas.

Theater, in Western liberal–capitalist society, is a liminoid process, set in the liminoid time of leisure between the role-playing times of "work." It is, in a way, "play" or "entertainment" (which means, etymologically, "held in between," that is, it was a liminal or liminoid phenomenon). Originally, I supposed it to be one of the abstractions from the original pansocietal "ritual," which was part of the work as well as the play of the whole society before the division of labor and specialization split that great ensemble or gestalt into special professions and vocations. Theater was concerned initially, among other things, with resolving crises affecting everyone and assigning meaning to the apparently arbitrary and often seemingly cruel sequence of events following personal or social conflicts.

The simple point I am trying to make – and much research is needed to bring in the necessary supporting evidence – is that in the simpler preindustrial societies, acting a role and exemplifying a status was so much a part of everyday life that the ritual playing of a role, even if it was a different role from that played in mundane life, was of the same kind as one played as son, daughter, headman, shaman, mother, chief, or queen-sister. The difference between ordinary and ritual (or extraordinary) life was mainly a matter of framing and quantity, not of quality. In ritual, roles were separated from their embedment in the ongoing flow of social life and singled out for special attention, or else they were seen as points of entry and exit made during a continuous process (boy to man, girl to woman, commoner to chief, villager to member of hunting cult, ghost to ancestor), with some interesting transitional symbolism and the shadowy appearance of the lineaments of the antistructural individual at some places and times. But in these societies, acting was mainly role playing; the persona was the dominant criterion of individuality, of identity. Thus, the great collective that articulated personas in hierarchical or segmentary structures was the real protagonist, both in life and in ritual.

Against this symmetry of everyday life and its liminal double, ritual, we find the asymmetry of life vis-à-vis acting in post-Renaissance, pretotalitarian Western societies. But now we detect an interesting

Acting in everyday life and everyday life in acting

contrast, even a paradox. For Western theater has often posited, like Western art generally, a contrast between everyday life, whether work or that part of nonwork devoted to institutionalized concerns, membership of family, sports clubs, charity organizations, union locals, or secret societies (Elks, Masons, Knights of Columbus) and truly antistructural life (personal religion, taking part in the arts as creator or spectator, etc.). The persona works, the individual plays; the former is governed by economic necessity, the latter is entertained. The former is in the indicative mood of culture; the latter is in the subjunctive or optative moods, the moods of feeling and desire, as opposed to those that stress rational choice, full (if reluctant) acceptance of cause and effect, calculation of probable outcomes of action, and awareness of realistic limitation on action. But though it has abandoned its former ritual and claims to be a means of communication with invisible powers and ultimate reality, theater can still assert, particularly since the rise of depth psychology, that it represents the reality behind the role-playing masks, that even its masks, so to speak, are "negations of the negation." They mask the false face in order to portray the possibility of a true face.

Theater has, in fact, become the domain of the individual-in-general, of what post-Renaissance man and woman would call "the real self," or William Blake "the individual" with his "Definite and Determinate Outline" as distinct from the "General, Abstract Selfhood." In anthropology, this position is partly represented by Paul Radin, who regarded history as the agency for revealing the nature of human beings. This view, of course, opposes Kroeber's notion of the superorganic and his consequent lack of interest in the individual in history, his sweeping efforts to classify whole civilizations by configurations and traits affirmed by a combination of intuitive and quantitative means, and his insistence on ethnology as a "natural science" – that is, as having a subject matter composed of discrete, isolable, and objectively determinable elements that can be traced and categorized on their own terms. All this did violence to Radin's focus on the individual as the locus of culture. Thus, acting, though still a form of role playing, uses roles intended by modern dramatists, representing the liminoid, developing individual, to undermine the world of respectable, orthodox role playing generated by industrial wealth. In fact, stage roles undermine everyday life roles, declaring the latter "inauthentic." From this viewpoint, it is the mundane world that is false, illusory, the home of the persona, and theater that is real, the world of the individual, and by its very existence a standing critique of the hypocrisy of all social structures that shape human beings, often by psychical and even physical mutilation (foot binding, corsets, indigestible foods), in the image of abstract social status roles. Of course, like all cultural forms, once theater has become a recognized genre of performance, it can be manipulated to support both conformative and subversive social and political positions. I am merely arguing that the rise of modern and postmodern theater contains within it the seeds of a fundamental critique of all social structures hitherto known. The locus of action, such a view would hold, has shifted from "real life" in the "indicative mood" arenas of economics and politics to what has been hitherto held to be the world of play, fantasy, illusion, and entertainment known as theater. This has been especially the case as religious ritual has been stripped of its flexible, lucid components, its sacred clowns, masked tricksters, riddling narratives, to make way for rigorous solemnity, or serious and official discourse about privileged or transcendental "meanings" or "signifiers," to use the terminology of Saussure.

Some modes of experimental theater have recently addressed themselves to the problem of presenting the whole role-playing world of mundane modern society with "acting" as its creative alternative, with the stage as the locus of emergent individuals, alienated from themselves in a world that insists on men and women masking themselves in a flickering series of shadowy personas. These are not the grand personas of tribal or feudal cultures, where the creation of oneself as a "public man" or "public woman" was a work of art, involving high style in dress, manners, and deeds, but the picayune personas of office, factory, or classroom underlings, with only vestiges of familial personas left to manipulate at home for the dregs of a weary day. Here mundane, indicative-mood acting seems to be the domain of the fictive, the false, the rejection of "definite and determinate identity." It is against the "acting" that such masters of experimental theater (who see theater as the counterstroke that annihilates falsehood even when it "puts on plays") as Grotowski, Brook, Schechner, Suzuki, and others, with some ancestry in Stanislavsky, Delsarte, Meyerhold, and even Artaud, have "re-acted" or "counter-acted." Take, for example, some recent notions of Grotowski (Gregory, 1978: 95-7). He is giving an interview to *Trybuna Ludu*:

Action in the sphere of active culture, such as gives one the feeling of fulfilling one's life, widening its scope, happens to be the need of many, but remains the domain of very few. Active culture is cultivated, for instance, by a writer when writing a book. We cultivated it while we were preparing performances. Passive culture – which is important and rich in aspects not easy to talk about right here – is a relationship to what is a product of active culture, that is to say, reading, watching a performance, film, listening to music. In certain, let us say, laboratory dimensions, we are working on means to *extend* the sphere of active culture. What is the privilege of the few, can also become the property of others. I am not talking about a mass production of works of art, but of a kind of personal creative experience, which is not indifferent for the life of an individual person, or his life with others. [Grotowski then states explicitly the view that acting is being, not performance:]

Working in the sphere of theater, preparing productions for many years, step by step we were approaching such a concept of active man/actor, where the point was not to act someone else, but to be oneself, to be with someone, to be in relationship, as Stanislawsky used to call it.

In the past few years Grotowski seems to have abandoned theater altogether to set out on what he calls "culture searches" or "paratheatrical experiments," like the Summer 1977 pilgrimage to Fire Mountain near Wroclaw in Poland, and the Global Village, a "kind of university of research," dispersed among many countries – "creative centers working alongside of various research and cultural centers in those countries" (1978: 103). The distinctive feature of these projects is the disappearance of the audience and the development of ritualized experiences that, to my anthropologist's eye, bear a striking resemblance to the instructions and hazards typical of successive phases of boys' and girls' puberty rites in Central Africa. Here are some of the names of these "experiments" in both small and large groups, which may suggest anthropological comparisons to some of you: "Night Vigil," "The Way," "The Area of Fear," "The Circle of Touch," "The Circle of Play," "The Circle of Rhythm," "The Circle of Darkness and Voice," "The Cutting." (The last is *not*, you will be relieved to hear, an exact parallel to the operation of circumcision, but a "violent though precise" dance. "Cutting" represents a vegetable cutting, "a seed of Meeting," i.e., a direct encounter between persons.)

I use the word *persons* advisedly, for it seems to me that Grotowski, who is very much persona grata with the Polish Communist party, has abandoned the theatrical tradition in order to create new forms of ritual initiation that inscribe desirable personas on human prima materia, that is, form men and women in a humanistic image that is to replace older forms, especially those carried in the great religious traditions. The Western tradition of theater kept the audience well in mind and respected its independent existence as the jury that decided on the rights and wrongs of the case presented by the dramatist, director, and actors.

VICTOR TURNER

Here I would repeat what I wrote in a recent article called "Frame, Flow and Reflection: Ritual and Drama as Public Liminality" (1977: 54):

I relish the separation of an audience from performers and the liberation of scripts from cosmology, ideology, and theology. The concept of individuality has been hard-won, and to surrender it to a new totalizing process of reliminalization is a dejecting thought. [I had distinguished *liminal* from *liminoid*, by associating the first with obligatory, tribal participation in ritual and the second with artistic or religious forms voluntarily produced, usually with recognition of individual authorship, and often subversive in intention toward the prevailing structures.] As a member of an audience I can see the theme and message of a play as one among a number of "subjunctive" possibilities, a variant model for thought or action to be accepted or rejected after careful consideration. [It may be that by paying for a ticket we have "bought" the author's and theater's production as a commodity, but we have not thereby been forced to "buy" his ideas or vision of reality.] Even as audience, people can be "moved" by plays; they need not be "carried away" by them – into another person's utopia or "secular sacrum," to use Grotowski's phrase. Liminoid theater should limit itself to presenting alternatives: it should not be a brainwashing technique.

To complete the sentence of William Blake I half-quoted earlier: "One Law for the Lion and the Ox is Oppression."

It is true that one of the aims of the "Night Vigil" at Grotowski's Laboratory Theater was to enable people to meet "out of their roles." But when one reads accounts of the way the "guides" of the "Night Vigil" "shepherd" persons toward undertaking certain physical acts (dancing, touching) or attaining certain psychological states – in such a way, to cite a psychologist disciple, Janina Dowlasz (1977: 115), "that healthy human emotions could release themselves again" – one is uneasily reminded not only of circumcision rites in Central Africa but also of "triumph of the will." The role-stripped self is to be remolded by what Grotowski calls the "guides" into... what?

I would like to return to Burridge's argument for a moment before returning to postmodern theater. After making the distinction between person and individual, he went on to consider individuality – which is the "apparent oscillation or movement between person and individual (for most people are both), whether in a particular instance the movement is one-way or a return is made. Or individuality may refer to the opportunity and capacity to move from person to individual and/or *vice versa*" (1979: 5–6). I have tended to regard the social dimension of the individual as communitas, essentially a liminoid, voluntaristic mode of relating, a choosing of one another by total, integral human beings, with limpidity of consciousness and feeling resulting. The social dimension of

Acting in everyday life and everyday life in acting

the person or persona is the activated social structure, the public domain of norm- or custom-governed relationships. Of course, nothing is as simple as that. Even Augustine had to admit that in real history the City of God and the Earthly City were hopelessly intermingled and that compromises had to be made continually by the would-be denizens of the Urbs Coelestis if family life and politics were to be at all workable. Individuality seems to be something that has to be won – and one aspect of winning it, Burridge would say, is "an apperception of own being in relation to traditional or alternative categories" (1979: 6). I suppose that this is roughly what I meant to say, when as a kid of twelve or so, I wrote the first line of a poem: "Serenity treads rougher paths than bliss" – a confident announcement, I realize almost half a century later, never followed up (perhaps for a twelve-year-old impossible to follow up). Burridge sees initiation rites as compressed means of posing the person–individual dilemma, especially in their liminal periods.

My own view is that the experimentalism of Richard Schechner is directed toward the realization through theater of individuality – somewhat in Burridge's sense – rather than toward the making of a new classless or "unalienated" man, in the zealot Grotowski manner. Schechner sees himself, in Kierkegaardian language, as a "midwife" rather than a Pygmalion. There was a time, he records, when he did try to mold the actors of his Performance Group in directions he considered "personally liberating." But there grew a rebellion in the ranks, and Schechner came to realize that he had become somewhat of a dictator, or at any rate more than a director. Both Grotowski and Schechner – and indeed all directors in postmodern experimental theater – advocate the supreme importance of "the rehearsal process," which involves very much more than the effectual realization of a playscript and the learning of parts. It involves innumerable workshop sessions, some lasting for hours, others all night, in which breathing exercises, voice workshops, ingenious games, psychodramas, dancing, aspects of yoga, and, in Grotowski's "paratheater" at least, jumping in mudholes in the woods, represent components. All these disciplines and ordeals have the effect of generating communitas in the group. André Gregory, who ran a workshop in Wroclaw, stressed that this process also

means reaching to the inner recesses of the actor and back into his past. An attempt to reach him – as a human being – in his undersoil and roots . . . It is not important whether one creates art, which one gives to people, but it is important that men – beings not indifferent to one another in life and in work – are included in the creative process . . . I needed Grotowski's theater not as someone connected with theater, or even as a spectator – I needed it as a human being. [1978: 42]

Again I would emphasize: The language favored by Grotowski has moved away from that of performing a play to that of self-discovery and unmediated contact with and understanding of others. The rhetoric is religious, even though, for Grotowski's disciples, traditional religion is rejected. One is reminded of Durkheim's search for "secular substitutes" for both religion and ritual, and De Coubertin's conviction that he had found these in international athletics – a conviction leading to his successful establishment of the Olympic Games, a Hellenistic, humanistic, postreligious, international, highly ritualized festival celebrating what all humans have in common: a body capable of being disciplined (a kind of profane ascesis) and an agonistic drive (though this Darwinian competitiveness proved to be mainly a feature of Western culture).

One can see the attraction, the lure, of Grotowski's agenda. Let us create a liminal space-time pod or pilgrimage center, he seems to be saying, where human beings can be disciplined and can discipline themselves to strip off the false personas stifling the individual within. There must clearly be a great sense of relief or release when the man and woman within emerge and are recognized. The idea of a return to nature is clearly connected with this emergence. But it is the experience of anthropologists that there are grave dangers in the initiatory processes. The initiand is usually being initiated *into* something; he or she may be released from one set of status roles only in order to be more firmly imprinted with another. The elders, the gurus, the masters of the circumcision lodge, the "guides," are there to make indelible marks (not merely in the form of bodily mutilation, circumcision, subincision, tooth removal, scarification, etc., but also in the very psyche itself) on the generic human prima materia to which the initiands have been more or less willingly reduced. The subjective dimension of initiation, of all types of passage ritual, indeed, has not been given sufficient attention by anthropological investigators. We can learn a good deal from experimental theater here. But one can see how a totalistic or totalitarian polity or regime might find the sophisticated elaboration of new secularized rites of passage, guided by certificated ideologists who understand the ritual process, very much to its taste.

To his credit, Richard Schechner has never forgotten that theater is theater and that entertainment is a fundamental part of it. Entertainment is liminoid rather than liminal, it is suffused with freedom. It involves profoundly the power of *play*, and play democratizes. Prospero realized this when he threw away his rod at the end of *The Tempest*. Schechner, though he has often been chided for taking liberties with an author's playscript, has never thrown out such a script completely. Rather he regards the script as a vital component in the rehearsal process, though he does not treat it as sacrosanct. It is an essential preliminary frame, to say the least, through which the rehearsal process must flow, though the extent and character of this frame may be modified, sometimes quite drastically, by the inner logic of that process. Other components have almost equal weight: the director, the actors, the environment (that is, the stage setting that is created anew for every production). All these, *and* the playscript, grow together and interact as the rehearsal process matures. Schechner is fond of quoting the child psychologist Winnecott's formulation, "from *me* to *not-me* to *not-not-me*," to express this process of theatrical maturation. The *me*, the biological-historical individual, the actor, encounters the role given in the script, the *not-me*; in the crucible of the rehearsal process a strange fusion or synthesis of *me* and *not-me* occurs. Aspects of the actor's experience surface that tincture the script role he or she has undertaken, while aspects of the dramatist's world view or message embodied in the script and particularly as understood from the perspective of the "character" being played penetrate the essence of the actor as a human being. The director's role is mainly catalytic: assisting at the alchemic or mystical marriage going on as the actor crosses the limen from *not-me* to *not-not-me*. The *me* at this third stage is a richer, if not deeper *me* than the *me* of the beginning. (I am unhappy about metaphors of "depth" here for they often rest on unconscious Western religio-philosophical assumptions.)

But my purpose is not to attempt an exposition of Schechner's rehearsal techniques – he can obviously do this much better than I can. What I am saying is that by keeping in hand the lifeline of the playscript, the saving fiction, as it were, Schechner saves his theater from what Jaques Derrida has called "the monological arrogance of 'official' systems of signification." And by keeping open the possibility of modifying the playscript – which, in a sense, also becomes a *not-me* and a *not-not-me*, like the actors themselves, the script itself may be saved from "the monological arrogance of 'official'" interpretations that have tended to ossify poetic inspiration into "classical modes of presentation." Works of dramatic genius require many ages to be adequately, let alone fully, manifested; it is the task of each theatrical generation to rotate them anew in terms of its own experience. We are back with the loops of the horizontal figure eight again, the relationships of opposition and synthesis between social drama and aesthetic drama.

Entertainment! That's a key word. Literally, it means "to hold between," from the French *entre*, "between," and *tenir*, "to hold." That is, it can be construed as the making of liminality, the betwixt-and-between state. Webster gives it both playful and serious valences, for it can mean (1) "to keep the interest of and give pleasure to; to divert; amuse;" or (2) "to allow oneself to think about; have in mind; consider." Thus, when the penitent confessed to the priest that he had had lustful thoughts, the latter asked him, "But, son, did you entertain them?" His answer, honest enough, came quickly: "No, Father, but they entertained me." This ambiguity is the soul of theater, which is not a mechanism of repression or even of sublimation, but fantasizes reality even while it realizes fantasy. It also allows spectators their human dignity, their right to treat all they see in an as-if, subjunctive way. Schechner has recently tried to move to a general theory of performance as "a binary," one term of which is "efficacy-ritual" (with transformative intention, "changing" the participant), the other being "entertainment-theater." In my nomenclature these would represent a contrast between liminal and liminoid modes of performance. Actually they interpenetrate, though Grotowski would have the former prevail, and much of Broadway the latter. Writes Schechner:

Performance comprehends the impulse to be serious and to entertain; to collect meanings and to pass the time; to display symbolic behavior that actualizes "there and then" and to exist only "here and now"; to be oneself and to play at being others; to be in a trance and to be conscious; to get results and to fool around; to focus the action on and for a select group sharing a hermetic language, and to broadcast to the largest possible audiences of strangers who buy a ticket. [1977: 218]

Let us return to the title of this essay, whose ironies have been by no means dispelled by our peregrinations. When we act in everyday life, we do not merely react to indicative stimuli, we act frames that we have wrested from the genres of cultural performance. And when we act on the stage, whatever our stage may be, we must, in this reflexive age as never before, bring into the symbolic the urgent problems of our reality. We have to go into that subjunctive world of monsters, demons, and clowns, of cruelty and poetry, in order to make sense of our daily lives, earning our daily bread. And when we enter whatever theater our lives allow us, we have already learned how strange and many-layered everyday life is, how extraordinary the ordinary. We no longer need the "endless safety" of ideologies but prize the needless "risk" of acting and interacting.

REFERENCES

Boulton, Marjorie. 1971. *The Anatomy of Drama*. London: Routledge & Kegan Paul.

Burridge, Kenelm. 1979. *Someone, No One: An Essay on Individuality*. Princeton, N.J.: Princeton University Press.

Dowlasz, Janina. 1977. "Psychologist at Grotowski's." *Zicie Literackie*, No. 381538, September 18, pp. 111–15.

Geertz, Clifford. 1980. "Blurred Genres: The Refiguration of Social Thought." *American Scholar*, Spring, pp. 165–79.

Gregory, André. 1978. *On the Road to Active Culture: The Activities of Grotowski's Theater Laboratory Institute in the Years 1970-1977*. Wroclaw: Grotowski Theatre Institute.

Hartnoll, Phyllis. n.d. *The Concise History of Theater*. New York: Abrams.

Schechner, Richard. 1977. *Ritual, Play and Performance*. New York: Seabury Press.

Turner, Victor. 1967. *Forest of Symbols: Aspects of Ndembu Ritual*. Ithaca: Cornell University Press.

Turner, Victor. 1977. "Frame, Flow and Reflection: Ritual and Drama as Public Liminality." In *Performance in Postmodern Culture*, ed. M. Benamou and C. Caramello. Madison, Wisc.: Coda Press.

RICHARD GILMAN

The actor as a celebrity

There is a story about David Garrick told by writer Hannah More that touches closely on one central aspect of what I want to discuss in this essay. When Miss More asked the actor, then at the height of his renown, why Samuel Johnson, his friend, fellow townsman, and, in some sense, mentor, so often spoke disparagingly of him, Garrick, who was not ordinarily known for his humility, said to her: "It is very natural. Is it not to be expected he should be angry, that I, who have so much less merit than he, should have had so much greater success?"

Johnson's rancor was indeed natural, which is to say it was understandable. Many people of intellectual achievement have felt it an injustice that actors should so frequently surpass them in fame, that acting itself – which is not seen by everyone as a real art – should be the source of so much worldly eminence, éclat, and high financial reward. And there's grievance too in the way actors have assumed or have had thrust upon them authority in areas far from their métier. In our own day, when the predominance of films over the stage has made it possible for the actor to succeed and become famous without having to act in any traditional or even recognizable way, the injustice, or at least a crack in the structure of intellectual values, is seen by some more disconsolately than ever.

I might have entitled my talk this afternoon "The Actor as a Famous Person" or as "Hero" or "Demigod." The reason I've chosen the word *celebrity* can be found within the anecdote I just related. The actor may indeed be a famous person, a hero, or a demigod, as Garrick himself was, or as Edmond Kean and Sarah Bernhardt were, or as Laurence Olivier and Marlon Brando are now. But their fame or demigodhood of a peculiar kind. It often seems disproportionate, as Garrick saw, and it's often an embattled sort of fame, subject to numerous vicissitudes, built on nothing solid, created by rumor as it were, transitory, in

The actor as a celebrity

bondage to public caprice, in many cases having to be continually rewon.

It's also a fame shadowed to one degree or another in various eras by its related, we might say inverse, condition of notoriety. Though fame may rest on the traditional basis of achievement of some sort, or on some passive type of position or condition (as in the case of some rulers, political figures, very rich men, or extraordinarily tall or fat ones), it goes past or around such a foundation or origin to something quite mysterious.

This mystery attaches to an actor's person more directly and reverberatingly than it does to other types of famous people who, wrapped in their titles or sets of deeds, are still present, single, unitary, and different from the rest of us primarily through their *size,* whereas the actor seems like an entirely different species, a person in combination with something else. It seems to me that this mystery might best be investigated through the existence of that strange designation "celebrity." I think of celebrity as a category between fame and notoriety. In its use as a personal noun, in the same syntactical realm as *hero* or *outlaw,* the word is of quite recent origin, though the type of being it refers to has probably always existed. *Celebrity* in this sense denotes a person who, in Daniel Boorstin's phrase, is "known for being known." Apart from anything else he may be, what figure does this describe more accurately than the actor, who is known not only by reputation but by his person, by means of his person, and in the era of the movies by his gigantic face?

Celebration and, somewhat less so, *celebrated* are words with depth and resonance, but *celebrity* is thin, brittle, and evanescent. It's a word that carries with it an aura of something more or less unworthy, like a title without a position or a medal without a deed. And the celebrity, the pure celebrity, is nothing other than that: someone lighted by a sun without warmth, a counterfeit of the real one. The celebrity makes himself known, not felt. Elias Canetti writes in "Crowds and Power": "A celebrity collects a chorus of voices. All he wants is to hear them repeat his name. As long as there are enough of them and they are versed in his name it does not matter whether these voices belong to the dead, to the living, or to the as yet unborn."

Hyperbolic as Canetti's formulation may be, this truth touches every actor in his desire and sometimes his fate. However distinguished and accomplished he may be (for the sake of economy I've been using and will mainly continue to use the generic word *actor* for both sexes and the pronoun *he;* such are the biases of language), there is always a dialectic, a tension, between fame in its truest, most deserved sense and celebrity, which might be described as arbitrary fame and which whistles up its appreciation in an abstract realm of nominalism. It's the aspect of fame or renown that need not be earned and that's in excess or defiance of reason (so that the fattest or tallest person in the world is not actually a famous person but a celebrity, of an especially peculiar kind) that Garrick understood, I think, when he made his uncharacteristically modest reply to Hannah More.

With these matters in mind, I'd like at this point to sketch the boundaries of my essay. Except tangentially, I won't be discussing the esthetics or technical aspects of acting. I'll be discussing the stage actor far more than the movie performer or star, because with the latter the elements of myth, public and private appetite, and persona taking the place of creation – all aspects of my subject – have swollen to such an immense size that they constitute a world of inquiry in themselves and have been sifted and explored by many others. At all events, I think that what I have to say about the stage actor – and it's the classic stage actor mostly of the English theater who's my chief subject – can be extended to the movie star, who may not be an actor at all – "I am not an actress, I am a phenomenon," said Brigitte Bardot – but who would not exist had not stage acting, as a human enterprise, existed first.

I'm not going to talk about various other types of performer, the opera singer, for example, or the television personality or rock star. For though they share certain characteristics of the actor as classically understood, especially that of being, as Thomas Heywood wrote in his "Apology for Actors" of 1612, "men who stand in the broad eye of the world," they differ in some fundamental ways. Chief among these is that they are not impersonators, since they appear to us in their own guise and not that of some invented person. Those who don't – opera singers, for instance – present themselves, or rather their chests and voices, under only the thinnest pretense of being someone else. In this regard of course the opera singer and the movie star resemble one another more nearly than either does the traditional actor, who receives recognition precisely through his capacity to appear as someone else, although, as I'll show, he is always being tempted toward a betrayal of what defines him.

We sometimes lose sight of the fact that the actor, so acclaimed and rewarded a figure in our own time, so rich a source of envy and emulation, was for the most part very far from being that until relatively recent times. Garrick himself, only a little more than two hundred years ago, was the first actor in England to break past the narrow boundaries

The actor as a celebrity

of fame described by the stage and its habitual and limited audiences into wider public attention. Burbage and Betterton had been acclaimed for their acting before him, but unlike them Garrick became a personality, a man formidable in the town, a celebrity if you will. He was filled with self-consciousness, he could manipulate his name toward every tongue. Sir Joshua Reynolds, an acquaintance, is reported to have said of him that "great as he was on the stage he was at best equal if not still superior at table, and here he had too much the habit of preparing himself as if he was to act a principal part."

He was indeed acting a part: that of the actor informally acting, behaving as if the stage were everywhere and every man an audience, something almost surely unknown before on the part of a professional performer (men and women do it ineptly in daily life) – unknown before his own flamboyance exhibited itself, in the bursting out of gestures and attitudes previously confined to a formal, circumscribed mode. It was as though it was now possible to act like an actor off the stage, since his own fame had drawn so many more eyes to the activity.

Before I give you the swiftest possible summary of the public and social position of the actor before and after Garrick, I want to pause at his life, since his own career exemplifies so well the shifts and contradictions I'll be recounting. After all, he had his portrait painted by Gainsborough; he was given the freedom of the Borough of Stratford-upon-Avon; and he was responsible during a tour of Ireland for the phrase "Gay as Garrick" in reply to "How d'ye do?" But at the same time he spent a good part of his career just out of reach of the law, and one of his biographers, Carola Oman, tells us that envious rivals "would take a mean revenge when [he] was staying at great houses by having notes sent to await his arrival addressed to Mr. David Garrick, player" – an indication of the anomalous and entirely shaky social position he actually occupied. It was the position occupied by the actor in most periods before Garrick's death in 1777, and for a hundred or more years thereafter.

As far as we know, the Greeks seem to have honored their actors, who in the earliest periods of the theater were often the authors of their own simple presentations for one performer and so perhaps were being honored as much for their writing as for their playing. We know the names of some of the later Greek actors – Thettalus, Athenodorus, Aristodemus – but almost nothing about their lives. We know more about Roman actors, the great majority of whom were slaves. A few of them were able to gain something like prestige and fewer still their freedom, the best known among the latter being the comic actor Quintus Roscius, who died in 62 B.C. and whose name became the generic one for actors, so that two millennia later Garrick would be known as the British Roscius. But there is evidence that for the most part actors in Rome were regarded as queer, if not scurrilous, creatures, without solidity as they were mostly without true status.

The next era in which we know with any certainty about actors is the Middle Ages, when the wandering mime kept up or resumed the tradition of performing as a career. During the Renaissance the true actor emerges again, in Italy with the commedia dell'arte and somewhat later in England. For a long time actors in England had to perform under the protection of noblemen, in whose houses most of their work was done, for they were either outside the law or very close to its margins. Henry VIII once announced his intention, apparently never carried out in the case of actors, of impressing for the navy "ruffians, vagabonds, masterless men and common players." Later various laws against acting – against theater in the widest sense – were indeed passed, culminating in the First Ordinance against Stage Plays and Interludes of 1642, the act that closed the theaters. The same thing seems to have been true of France, where in 1657 the abbé D'Aubignac spoke in his *Pratique du Théâtre* of "the infamy with which the laws have noted those who make an open profession of being players."

For many years plays, and therefore players, were restricted by law to two licensed theaters in London, Drury Lane and Covent Garden, though illegal work was performed elsewhere. But even when the licensing of theaters spread, the actor continued for a very long time in England and in other countries to labor under a stigma, subtle or gross. In France, we know that Molière was refused Christian burial upon his death in 1673 and that as late as 1730 the great actress Adrienne Lecouvreur was buried "at night and without services."

In England, some sophisticated members of the upper class and aristocracy made it a point to cultivate actors, especially after the Restoration; but the great majority had only scorn for the disreputable profession, whose members had no roots, either physical or genealogical, and whose acclaim, which they secretly envied, had no hieratic basis. This was despite the fact that the socially prominent made up a large proportion of theater audiences. Richard Steele commented on the hypocrisy of this, and touched on something crucial to an understanding of one aspect of the actor's ambiguous position, in these lines:

The actor as a celebrity
The player acts the world, the world the player;
Whom still that world unjustly disesteems,
Though he alone professes what he seems.

I want to go back to this poem later, particularly to its last line, but let me first wind up this brief chronicle. Even after society had begun to come round, recognition from the crown as well as from other political and cultural institutions lagged much behind. As late as the middle of the nineteenth century, the great tragedian William Charles Macready could write in his diary that "it is not a pleasing reflection, without caring for the thing itself, that my pariah profession should entitle me to the lavish expression of public praise, and exclude me from distinctions which all my compeers enjoy." It was not until 1895 that Henry Irving became the first British actor to be given a knighthood. As late as 1914, in France, it took great pressure to get the government to finally award the rosette of the Legion of Honor to Sarah Bernhardt, the most famous citizen of the realm.

Sarah Bernhardt is as good a figure as any in whom to contemplate the ambiguities of the actor's position in the world until quite recently. She too of course suffered from snobbery and malicious detraction (Sarah Barnum, an enemy once called her). She was, as I say, only reluctantly acknowledged by her own government, historically so lavish with its decorations, and for most of her career was almost entirely excluded from society, the French upper classes being even more contemptuous of the actor's profession than the English. The latter had surprisingly opened their doors to her during her first appearance in London in 1879, although a letter to a friend by Lady Frederick Cavendish reveals a certain lack of unanimity. "London has gone mad over the principal actress of the Comédie Française," her ladyship wrote, "Sarah Bernhardt, a woman of notorious character. Not content with being run after on the stage, this woman is asked to respectable people's houses to act, and even to luncheon and dinner, and all the world goes. It is an outrageous scandal!"

Yet such was Bernhardt's renown among the general theatergoing public, and with particular fervor among artists, intellectuals, and students, that she could afford to take a derisory stance toward her detractors in society. As early as 1876, when she was 32, Henry James could write that she is "at present, in Paris, one of the great figures of the day." Later a journalist would write that "there are only two celebrities in France today... Gambetta [the controversial political leader] and Sarah Bernhardt." And Edmond de Goncourt would say that "the life of Sarah Bernhardt may prove to be the greatest marvel of the nineteenth century."

On several occasions students unhitched her horses and pulled her carriage through the streets of Paris. Among her friends were Hugo, Zola, Dumas fils, and Oscar Wilde. On one of her American tours she was taken, on a train that bore on its observation platform the words *Madame* and *Bernhardt* circling *New York Central Lines,* to see Thomas A. Edison at Menlo Park, a press agent's notion having been that "the most famous man in America should have the pleasure of meeting the most famous woman in France." Another time an enterprising promoter persuaded her to be photographed with a beached whale in Boston harbor and then advertised the picture as, "the phenomenon of France visits the phenomenon of the sea."

She inspired the most extravagant and most bathetic rhetoric in her admirers. Jules Lemaître wrote that "above any person she will have known glory... concrete, intoxicating, delirious, the glory of conquerors and of Caesars. In all countries of the world she has been given a reception never accorded kings. She has what princes of thought will never have." Pace Samuel Johnson. An unknown admirer wrote this public letter to her:

Among those waiting at the stage door are the rich whose only worth is that they admire you, and there are the wretched who raise themselves up like the great ones of the earth because they will see Sarah pass by, and there is perhaps a criminal, a man abandoned by all, and who will be seized the moment you have passed. But he will say "death does not matter now. I saw Sarah before I died."

This adulation of certain actors in the past is a familiar story, and I beg your indulgence in these tales. My purpose is to make as vivid as I can the extraordinary dimensions and, as I shall soon try to analyze, the strange nature of this worship.

When Eleanora Duse came to St. Petersburg in 1891, the streets leading to the theater were strewn with rose petals. In Vienna, cab-drivers are said to have stopped to applaud her as she drove to a performance. In Lisbon, women spread their lace mantillas for her to walk on from the stage door to her carriage. In Washington, in the early nineties, President Cleveland attended all her performances and is said to have sent her white roses and chrysanthemums each day. At her funeral in 1924, her coffin was taken from a Roman church to a railroad station on a gun carriage.

Garrick's funeral is said to have been the most magnificent London

The actor as a celebrity

had ever seen. When American actress Mary Anderson returned from a tour of England in 1899, a newspaper followed her movements with a series of headlines: "Our Mary is coming." "Our Mary has arrived." "Our Mary is in our midst." "America greets its favorite daughter." Hazlitt said of Sarah Siddons: "The enthusiasm she excited had something idolatrous about it; we can conceive nothing grander... She was not less than a goddess or prophetess inspired by the gods." And the biographer of Macready, Alan Downer, describes his farewell performance in Macbeth, at the Drury Lane on February 26, 1851, in these words: "At first entrance on the blasted heath, the whole house rose to its feet, waving hats and handkerchiefs, stamping, shouting ... in such a crescendo of excitement that George Henry Lewes, from his vantage point in the boxes, wondered whether the actor would be able to go on."

Such stories are regaling and seem to place the actor in the forefront of our species of demigod. But they don't tell us much about the nature of the actor's fame, or rather, in accordance with my own notion, about a fame shadowed and many times contaminated by celebrity. There are many questions that ought to be explored, and the first, I think, is the central one of the coherence, if it exists, between an actor's renown and his merit – a question, it's true, that can be asked about all human activity but is especially pertinent here. In the age of the movie star, fame and merit can be without any coherence whatsoever, but on the stage they ought to bear, and ought to have borne, some relation to each other.

Consuming itself as it unfolds – "an actor's name is writ in water," Garrick said, meaning that he left nothing palpable behind – the art of acting is most difficult to judge; the art of past acting is impossible. What we do know is that every famous actor had vociferous detractors in his own time. Again, this is true of every famous person, but what isn't true of famous generals or painters or athletes, as it is of actors, is that the criticisms made of them by their contemporaries have often been more shrewd, complex, and convincing than the expostulations of categorical praise.

A critic said of Kean, for example, that his much-esteemed "naturalism," something we would most likely scarcely recognize as true to life but the source of his éclat then, went entirely too far: "He is like a poet who disdains metaphor." Leigh Hunt said of the eminent Charles Kemble that his Hamlet "was not the man but his mask; a trophy, a consul's robe; or, if you please, a rhetorician." A critic said of James Quin that he "exhibited the form not the soul of tragedy." Bernard Shaw wrote of Bernhardt that she offered only "her own charm, not that of the character," and of Duse, whom he generally admired, that she was too often perfunctory; on one of her London appearances he wrote that she had given the public not art but her own reputation and he wished her to know that "we do not accept reputations, we give them."

But it is Matthew Arnold's comments on Sarah Bernhardt that go to the heart of what I think the problem must have been with many actors of the most brilliant reputations and that remains the problem now:

> One watches her with pleasure, with admiration – and yet not without a secret disquietude. Something is wanting, or, at least, not present in sufficient force, something which alone can secure and fix her administration of all the charming gifts which she has, can alone keep them fresh, keep them sincere, save them from perils by caprice, perils by mannerism. That something is high intellectual power.

I don't mean to imply that I think greatness in acting depends wholly on "high intellectual power" or that not to have intellectual power is a disqualification from the profession. After all, the actor's motto isn't "I think, therefore I am," but, more truly than for the rest of us, "I pretend, therefore I am." Yet Arnold saw something important. The point is that, historically, so-called great actors, and most others for that matter, have proceeded on the basis of some quality or power or principle that, being irrational, or at least nonrational, is extraordinarily difficult to judge and, more pertinently, is subject to misuses that tend to corrupt the art or skill being practiced. Jean-Paul Sartre once made a remark in this connection that greatly illuminates my subject: "The actor wishes to persuade by contagion."

It is this fever, spread by force of personality – "personness" is a word I wish I could use, to overcome the brittle associations of the other – by the formal display of personality, more magnetic in some cases than in others, more original, richer, or bolder, but a presence of self maintained at an irreducible minimum by every actor, since to display himself formally and so become the object of gazes is the essence of what he does and of his desire; it is this fever that transcends techniques, skills, methods, or rather techniques and skills are employed in the service of personality, in the service of infecting the audience with oneself. Oneself and yet not oneself. For the actor on stage is of course also an invented, imaginary being, and it is this doubleness that is both his glory and his trap. There is still another duality in the theater, the one between the play as artifact to be interpreted and as fiction to be filled with real bodies.

The actor as a celebrity

The word *theater* in its Greek root means "a place for seeing"; what is seen there is first and foremost an exhibition of the self in its sheer, immediate existence, unpredictable, more or less vivid, perhaps strangely violent, and always on the edge of the moment. This exhibition takes place within a network of conventions: the stage, the settings, the rows of seats, the plot to be worked out, the history of all similar occasions, and the acting itself, for that people act on a stage is a convention; and all these conventions are designed to allow the selves on display to pretend to be other. In this behavior – whose strangeness lies in the fact that artificial means are employed to suggest the natural – in these movements, gestures, and speech whose effect, ideally, is in Sartre's phrase to "unrealize" his own being so as to make "real" an unreal being, the actor, poor, glorious double creature, serves as a delegate, a representative for us all. And it is to us, the audience, that I want to turn now in my quest for the nature of the actor's peculiar and haunted fame.

I spoke of the actor as a delegate or representative. Surely the way in which the actor represents us (stands in for us, so to speak, while standing before us) is by presenting us with possible selves, or more accurately with the *idea* of possible selves, more selves than we can in nature have. Of all the discontents of existence, that of being finite has to be, just short of the fact of death, the most melancholy. We are confined in our singleness like an animal in its pelt. "Be yourself," the injunction goes, but we wish desperately to be other, more. The point isn't that we dislike ourselves, though we may – the actor is said to dislike himself more than most, which is instigation to his activity – but that we find it a kind of slavery to be unceasingly this self and not another. And so our common practice is to imagine ourselves as other, to put ourselves through a series of hypothetical transformations in which we become another age, another sex, take on a new vocation, a different set of moral or spiritual attributes, a wholly different face.

In an important book called *Theatricality*, a study in part of the relations between acting on the stage and in everyday life, Elizabeth Burns writes that "the actor... can be regarded as the actual embodiment of these transformations, and beyond these, the living container of the states through which the idea of the self has passed." The actor, she goes on, "is a model of self-images," and a play is "a ritual form of release from the need to act as undivided selves, a reaffirmation of the multiple existential possibilities we incorporate but cannot realize."

Quite obviously, a play is more than that. It's a paradigm of human relationships, a model of emotional or spiritual structures, a delimited world of behavior and thought analogous to – though not necessarily imitative of – the "real" world, an exhibition of fate, a destiny foreshortened and set in motion. But that it's also what Burns says it is, a release from the unitary and ordinarily inescapable self and a reminder of possibilities of transformation, is crucial I think to our understanding of why actors stand in human regard as they do.

On the dark side, these truths about the way actors function for us help explain why they should have worked at various historical times under such contumely. As Burns writes: "The externalization of parts of the self contributed to the suspicion aroused by the pre-professional actor, the mountebank, mummer or fool. As a person who could switch from one role to another by a change of costume or demeanor his integrity was in doubt." In the Middle Ages, "roles" in society were of course far more fixed and inescapable than they later became, and it seems certain that there was far less dreaming of other possibilities for the self than became true when society expanded and grew more various, complicated, and heretical. When the full-fledged professional actor came into being, something of the earlier suspicion remained. The closing of the theaters by the puritans was at least as much due to an awareness, however unstated, of the actor's dubious moral quality as it was to the fear of seditious irreverence that might be spread by plays.

But once the demand for the actor, for theater, becomes unappeasable and breaks down legal restrictions as well as clears spaces in moral realms, a very curious contradiction or tension shows itself with regard to the two orders of reality of a play, which I spoke of a moment ago. It's something we can't fail to notice when we read a favorite play and then see it well acted on the stage. To read a play is to concentrate perforce on the literary, and in a powerful sense abstract, nature of the artifact; to see a play is to be aware of that but to be even more aware of the living presences, the actors in their doubleness, incarnate characters, fusions of fiction and actuality. We may imagine actors while we read a play, or we may perform it ourselves (I sometimes stage, direct, play all the characters in, and produce *Hamlet* or *The Three Sisters* in my head), but this is far different from seeing a play. The bodily presences are decisive; they can't be got round; their opaqueness stands in contrast to the utter transparency, their solidity to the entire indeterminacy of words on a page.

A number of strange things happen when as members of an audience we contemplate and prepare for infection by these actors in front of us,

The actor as a celebrity

especially those who are well known. Through makeup and costumes on occasion but usually by his mere presence on the stage, his having been granted a new name and character by the drama, the actor has become someone else. This we know is the source of his fascination for us, but it's also a source of confusion and paradox, although through another convention we don't consciously dwell on it. But we resolve it throughout the spell of greater or lesser intensity into which the unfolding drama has cast us by holding on, however subliminally, to the actor's *name.* The more famous the actor, the more actively we do this. In the case of an unknown actor, we'll read the biographical notes in the playbill. And when we are told before the curtain goes up that an unkown actor is going on in a star's place, I think we're upset not so much because of our expectation of a lesser performance as because a refulgent name has been subtracted from the proceedings, a name that had previously gathered the almost mystical attributes of acting itself.

It isn't that we're not aware of mastery, not "taken in" by acting in the sense proper to that deception, but that we move between belief and idolatry; we take the interpretation for the thing itself. We are, for example, amazed and convinced by an actor's versatility or force, but these then frequently become detached from their purpose, so that everything else, the play itself, falls back into shadow. The play will often fall into shadow too by the nature of theater as occasion, as a platform for an oratory of the self and a place not for seeing but for staring. "Stop goggling like a bunch of romantics," Brecht's signs said in the theater where he was a young dramaturge.

The things I'm talking about began to show themselves in England almost as soon as the professional, secular theater began. When theatrical activity shifted during the sixteenth century from religious or morality plays to secular dramas in which the actor was an impersonator, not a personification, of various moral and religious truths and values, a professional with a name and not an anonymous member of a religious guild or society, the actor began to dominate the play, to become less its interpreter than its reason for being presented. This trend became ever more pronounced until by the time of Kean in the early nineteenth century, as Joseph Donohue tells us in his book on that theatrical era, the playwright was almost never mentioned in the playbill. What we witness here is an especially sharp phase of the perennial struggle between the self that pretends and the one that uses the pretense as a pretext for its own aggrandizement, the struggle really between the play and the performer. This has often been the fate of classic plays, particularly Shakespeare, during long periods of English-speaking theatrical history. Shakespeare, we know, was bowdlerized, cut into segments, quarried for set pieces. Garrick himself cut the first two acts of *The Winter's Tale* in one production and renamed it *Florizel and Perdita,* and a critic said that he had "minced and fricaseed" *A Midsummer Night's Dream.* In various eras, leading actors tended to exploit their easy successes, to appear in inferior plays that set them off, as did Bernhardt in *The Lady of the Camellias.* Or, like James O'Neill, they would find themselves famous in a particular role and repeat it endlessly, unable or unwilling to break out.

"The force of a unique personality, exhibited within the reassuringly familiar confines of the art," Donohue writes, "is what audiences paid their money to see." The actor had become an attraction, an object in his own right, even a monument. As Sartre says: "The tickets to see Kean as Hamlet sell like hot cakes, just as tourists throng to San Pietro in Vincoli to see a block of Carrera marble as Moses."

The physical conditions of the theaters in London and Paris contributed to the development of what we now call a cult of personality. Most of them were huge, seating as many as three thousand, and this, together with the extremely poor lighting of the age before electricity or even gas, meant that the actor had to overact, to pose, strut, speak boomingly, and so on, even if he were not already disposed to do so. This in turn obviously brought gazes more and more fully upon him, and so encouraged flamboyance and muscular behavior in place of subtlety.

Actors competed with one another on the same stage, an Othello trying to "outpoint" an Iago, a Macbeth his wife. In his book on Shakespearean actors, Bernard Grebanier tells us of a certain Barton Booth, a leading performer of the early eighteenth century, who as Othello was "particularly admired for his stance while listening to other actors during crucial moments." It's difficult to believe that this stance was quiet, dignified, or restrained.

For many years, it was the practice of the more affluent or important members of the audience to be seated on stage during performances. This had some egregious results – gallants grabbing the leading lady for a quick embrace, insults and objects hurled from close range at an actor; more obliquely damaging was that the proximity of so influential a part of the audience encouraged more and more vigorous displays of personality.

What I've been describing is the phenomenon we now call the "star" system, which was to be extended by Hollywood into an attempt to

The actor as a celebrity

displace the very heavens. In the early nineteenth century, when the word *star* gained currency, it had we are told "more the specialized meaning of an actor or actress hired by the theater on the short term as a special attraction," since theaters simply could not be filled without one. But *star* soon came to be applied to any actor whose renown was especially rich. With or without the designation, such a performer grew to dwarf his fellow actors, who, as a nineteenth-century commentator on the American theater describes it, "were reduced to the condition of mere ministers or servants upon some principal performer, whose attractions it was now their sole . . . duty to increase, illustrate or set off."

The star clearly must have begun to amass his fame through some original or especially forceful way of performing. Stardom was certainly not, as it mostly became in the movies, dependent on some type of physical allure; Betterton was described by a contemporary as being "clumsily made, having a great head, a short, thick neck, stooped in the shoulders, and had short fat arms and thick legs with large feet." Sarah Siddons, the most acclaimed actress of her time, had a nose of which Gainsborough, who painted her, said: There "was no end to it." Both Garrick and Kean were well under normal height, and Kean particularly was far from handsome. Nor was the possession of a splendid voice a necessary constituent of stardom; many of the most celebrated actors' voices were said to be inferior, high pitched, or raspy.

No, it was Betterton's passion, Kean's violent naturalness, Macready's dignity and attention to detail, or, in a different era and a different dimension, Sarah Bernhardt's mesmerizing presence (she looked, in Ellen Terry's wonderful phrase, like "smoke from a burning paper") that launched them into public favor. Yet in nearly every case – in every case at one time or another – the ardor of their originality or the beauty of their presence degenerated into mannerisms, poses, or, more fatally for dramatic art, into an unrestraint that saw the personality overwhelm the role. Performances grew into a series of "points" for the famous actor – set pieces, Shakespeare (and to be a serious actor in England was for several hundred years to be a Shakespearean actor), or French classical drama. When Coleridge made his well-known remark about Kean, intended as a compliment – "seeing him act was like reading Shakespeare by flashes of lightning" – he unwittingly informed us of what it must have really been like; the trouble was with all those spaces between the flashes when nothing could be read at all.

From an early time, cliques grew up around leading actors and bitter rivalries set in among them. An audience entirely without inhibitions cheered its favorites and cursed the rivals, sometimes making it impossible for them to go on. Violence swept the pits and galleries, and often the boxes as well, almost always incited by partisanship of this kind. For more than a hundred years, it was the law in London that soldiers had to stand guard at every performance in a theater, but even this didn't prevent frequent riots and the occasional burning down of a theater. The most notorious incident of all, the Astor Place riots of 1848 in New York City, was the outcome of the passionate enmity between Macready and Edwin Forrest, an American star, whose adherents were inflamed by jingoistic newspaper articles.

Something extremely curious can be detected in all of this, something that I think throws much light on the subject of the actor as object of acclaim: It seems to have been impossible, or thought to be so, for any actor to win renown without a corresponding diminution of another actor's reputation. The stars themselves and certain critics contributed to this, in the manner of our own stupid practice of granting the designation "Number One." At the outset of his career, Macready complained that "those already in secure possession of the public favor seemed to leave me little room for success." Kean once wrote to a friend that "The Throne is mine. I will maintain it – even at the expense of expatriation – go where I will I shall always bear it with me." And even as late as this century the critic James Agate included in a list of prerequisites for a "great" actor a "ruthless determination to suppress every promising younger rival." No doubt there were generous souls among the public favorites, but they were surely exceptions.

It was as though there existed an economy of praise and an even more stringent economy of adulation. There is only so much worship to be bestowed before hearts and lungs give out, there is only so much room in the pantheon. Lesser figures will be noted, may even become notable, and every actor, even the inept, will carry a bit of the aura of glamor and enticement of the profession. But a hierarchy has to be maintained, a pyramidal structure of accolade. This is an aspect of the competitive nature of culture that runs through history and that is really quite puzzling, this vertical shape of our appreciations. It is as true today as it ever was, even though stardom and celebrity have spread so widely; precisely because they have spread, a new category comes into use: the "superstar."

Something else follows from this. Once he has been chosen by the public – received its "favor," in older usage – the star actor seems to seal off from at least part of that public the possibility of them appreciating anyone else, or even appreciating him with the same fervor. Choices are made, and it is as though what has been invested has to be guarded. Hazlitt, perhaps the best critic of drama and theater who ever wrote, made an extraordinarily revealing remark about the pain that is felt when someone whom one rationally sees as "better" – at any rate whom one is more taken with – comes along and displaces a previous favorite. "We wish we had never seen Mr. Kean," Hazlitt wrote. "He has destroyed the Kemble religion in which we grew up."

For Hazlitt, the words *religion* as well as *goddess* and *idolatrous* in the remark I quoted earlier about Sarah Siddons are not, I think, intended simply as metaphors. They speak of something irrational, of a preexisting hunger that finds its appeasement in certain figures or, not finding it, creates the beings that will grant it. I don't at all mean, nor have I meant throughout this essay, that there haven't been great actors or that the pleasure taken in them has been spurious, but only that the *idea* of acting and of the actor is oddly more powerful than acting itself, and that for most of the history of the theater the public, not to mention the majority of critics, has had no reliable principle by which to distinguish great acting from good and good from bad, except in the most flagrant instances of the latter. This is especially true of the American public, although it's from England that we take our example and even for most of our early history, our entire theater.

Acting can of course be fine, even sublime, but so taken are we with personality that we are likely as not to miss it. Look at what Henry James says of Coquelin, the splendid French actor he so much admired:

To enjoy the refinement of his acting... the ear must be as open as the eye, must even be beforehand with it; and if... the American spectator in general learns, or even shows an aptitude for learning, the lesson conveyed in his finest creations, the lesson that acting is an art, and that the application of an art is style, and that style is expression, and that expression is the salt of life, the gain will have been something more than the sensation of the moment; it will be a new wisdom.

And look at what Proust says of Bernhardt, whom he seems to have seen at her best and on whom he modeled the figure of Berma in *Remembrance of Things Past:*

... her attitude on the stage, which she had gradually built up, which she was to modify still further, and which was based upon reasonings of a different profundity from those of which traces might be seen in the gestures of her fellow-actors, but of reasonings that had lost their original deliberation, and had melted into a sort of radiance in which they sent throbbing, round the person of the heroine, elements rich and complex, but which the fascinated spectator took not as an artistic triumph but as a natural gift.

The point isn't whether or not Proust was right in his estimation of Bernhardt, but that he saw what most audiences are likely to do: mistake art for nature or, rather, prefer nature to art. This is a subtle matter and I don't mean to ignore the existence of contrary experience, but once again it seems clear that what audiences have mostly wanted and continue to desire, along with the play itself, but often with the play merely as occasion, is that phenomenon I've been talking about so much: the sight, the living presence of someone who is other but whose otherness so often takes a strange kind of subordinate position in order to reveal the power of impersonation itself and the allure of those capable of effecting it.

Caught up, then, in a reputation based to one degree or another on achievement but continually slipping away from that toward his name and aura themselves, the actor, if he can be brought to admit it, is never certain of his true stature, never convinced of his worthiness. This I think helps explain the peculiar terror so many actors feel upon going on for the first time in a new work or each night in a long-running one. It's as though the actor has to create from scratch each time his being, which is based on his nonbeing, his place in the world. The most gifted actor suffers in the same way as the most marginal actor suffers. Sarah Siddons spoke of "the awful consciousness that one is the sole object of attention in that immense space, lined, as it were, with human intellect." Kierkegaard, a marvelously acute observer of theater, wrote that "it lays a prodigious burden on a person to have to support the illusion of the stage and the weight of everyone's eyes." He also set down, in a little-known but revelatory short work, *Crisis in the Life of an Actress,* a description of what it's like to be both talented and fashionably famous in the theater, to be, in other words, half-hero, half-celebrity, which I think you will forgive me for quoting in full:

> Two or three times each week she will be praised and admired, deafened with applause . . . she will . . . have undergone the newspaper critics' total repertoire of platitudes . . . her portrait will have been painted for every art exhibit; she will be lithographed, and if her luck runs very high her portrait will even be painted on handkerchiefs and the crowns of hats . . . she knows that her name is on everyone's lips, even when they wipe their mouths with their handkerchiefs! She knows that she is the subject of everyone's admiring conversations, including those who are in the utmost distress for something to chatter about. She lives on in this way year after year. That seems just splendid; it looks as though that would really be something. But if in a higher sense she had to live on the rich

The actor as a celebrity

nourishment of this admiration, take encouragement from it, receive strength and inspiration for renewed exertions – and since even the mostly highly talented person . . . can become despondent in a weak moment for want of some expression of genuine appreciation – at such a time she will really feel what she had doubtless realized often enough, just how fatuous all this is, and what a mistake it is to envy her this burdensome splendor.

It would be culpably naive of me to imagine that many actors would openly acknowledge the fatuity of their more vulgar kinds of appreciation, the celebrity side of their acclaim, or that more than a handful of renowned performers has ever skipped away from the burdensome splendor. Yet let me, as I come near the end, offer two more quotations, one from a philosopher-playwright, the other from an actress as admired as any has ever been.

In Sartre's play *Kean,* about the actor, the Kean character says at one point: "I was wrong just now to mention Kean. Kean, the actor, died very young. [Laughter] Be quiet, murderers, it was you who killed him."

There are some startling remarks of Eleanora Duse, the source of which I don't know. The theater, she said, "must be destroyed, the actors and actresses must all die of the plague. They poison the air, they make art impossible. It is not drama that they play, but pieces for the theater . . . the drama dies of stalls and boxes and evening dress, and people who come to digest their dinners."

Out of the fictional Kean's type of accusation – "you corrupted me by your mindless praise" – and Duse's kind of disgust and rage (she herself kept going, it has to be said) have come many of the revolutions or revolutionary attempts of the modern theater: the emphasis on ensemble playing, Brecht's and Pirandello's "intellectualization" of the stage, the participatory theater impulses of the 1960s, many "fringe" enterprises designed in one way or another to overthrow the sort of thing Joan Littlewood once inveighed against to me: "all that bloody egotism," she snarled, "all those bloody Sir Laurences and Sir Johns and Sir Ralphs who get up there on the stage and say all the time, whatever else they're saying, look at me, look at me!"

All true. And yet, without intending it, I seem to have placed some of the burden of this talk on the conflict between actors and drama itself, and I won't repudiate any of those ideas. When I watch true actors, even at the expense of a play, I bring to mind, then or later, their chief mystery and boon. They endow us, provisionally, with multiplicity; they elude, for us and for a time, the fixity of nature. We would have to be pure beyond reason, reasonable beyond our capacity, to demand from them, these persons whose task it is to "unmake" themselves in order to make someone else, that they stick always to the whole, larger point, to profess, in Steele's words, "only what they seem" and allow what they "are" to die away each time, that they repudiate their own names and disavow the hectic, so often sterile light that shines on them from the faces before which they exist.

The social impulse to create celebrities clearly springs from an insufficiency of true heroes. But celebrity and heroism are less in opposition than in symbiosis. One is the condition of being only a name, a reputation without a deed; the other is their fusion. Both serve to rescue us from anonymity; if some can have names that are spoken aloud, then mass existence will feel the stings: potshots, or a fusillade, against undifferentiation, against sameness. The fate of the actor, tempted to be a king instead of an emissary, seduced and seducer, himself and not himself, is to move always between the name merely on the tongue and the name, and movement, in the heart.

III

How form in art is related to culture

HAROLD BLOOM

The breaking of form

I

The word *meaning* goes back to a root that signifies "opinion" or "intention," and is closely related to the word *moaning*. A poem's meaning is a poem's complaint, its version of Keats' Belle Dame, who looked *as if* she loved, and made sweet moan. Poems instruct us in how they break form to bring about meaning, so as to utter a complaint, a moaning intended to be all their own. The word *form* goes back to a root meaning "to gleam" or "to sparkle," but in a poem it is not form itself that gleams or sparkles. I will try to show that the lusters of poetic meaning come rather from the breaking apart of form, from the shattering of a visionary gleam.

What is called "form" in poetry is itself a trope, a figurative substitution of the as-it-were "outside" of a poem for what the poem is supposed to represent or be "about." Etymologically, "about" means "to be on the outside of" something anyway, and so "about" in regard to poems is itself only another trope. Is there some way out of this wilderness of tropes, so that we can recover some sense of either a reader's or writer's other-than-verbal needs and desires?

All that a poem can be about, or what in a poem *is* other than trope, is the skill or faculty of invention or discovery, the heuristic gift. Invention is a matter of "places," of themes, topics, subjects, or of what Kenneth Burke rephrased as the implicit presence of forms in subject-matter, and named as "the Individuation of Forms." Burke defined form in literature as "an arousing and fulfillment of desires." The Burkean formula offered in his early *Counter-Statement* is still the best brief description we have:

A work has form in so far as one part of it leads a reader to anticipate another part, to be gratified by the sequence. [p. 124]

HAROLD BLOOM

I will extend Burke, in a Burkean way, by investing our gratification not even in the disruption of sequence, but in our awareness, however precarious, that the sequence of parts is only another trope for form. Form, in poetry, ceases to be trope only when it becomes topos, only when it is revealed as a place of invention. This revelation depends upon a breaking. Its best analogue is when any of us becomes aware of love just as the object of love is irreparably lost. I will come back to the erotic analogue and to the making/breaking of form, but only after I explain my own lack of interest in most aspects of what is called "form in poetry." My aim is not to demystify myself, which would bore others and cause me despair, but to clarify what I have been trying to say about poetry and criticism in a series of books published during the last five years. By "clarify" I partly mean "extend," because I think I have been clear enough for some, and I don't believe that I ever could be clear enough for others, since for them "clarity" is mainly a trope for philosophical reductiveness, or for a dreary literal-mindedness that belies any deep concern for poetry or criticism. But I also seem to have had generous readers who believe in fuller explanations than I have given. A return to origins can benefit any enterprise, and perhaps an enterprise obsessed with origins does need to keep returning to its initial recognitions, to its first troubles, and to its hopes for insight into the theory of poetry.

By "theory of poetry" I mean the concept of the nature and function of the poet and of poetry, in distinction from poetics, which has to do with the technique of poetical composition. This distinction between the concepts "theory of poetry" and "poetics" is a fruitful one for knowledge. That *de facto* the two have contacts and often pass into each other is no objection. The history of the theory of poetry coincides neither with the history of poetics nor with the history of literary criticism. The poet's conception of himself . . . or the tension between poetry and science . . . are major themes of a history of the theory of poetry, not of a history of poetics.

I have quoted this paragraph from Curtius' great book, *European Literature and the Latin Middle Ages* (Excursus VII). My own books from *The Anxiety of Influence* through my work on Wallace Stevens are all attempts to develop a theory of poetry in just this sense. The poet's conception of himself necessarily is his poem's conception of itself, in my reading, and central to this conception is the matter of the sources of the powers of poetry.

The truest sources, again necessarily, are in the powers of poems *already written*, or rather, *already read*. Dryden said of poets that "we have

The breaking of form

our lineal descents and clans as well as other families." Families, at least unhappy ones, are not all alike, except perhaps in Freud's sense of "Family Romances." What dominates Freud's notion is the child's fantasy-making power. What counts in the family romance is not, alas, what the parents actually were or did, but the child's fantastic interpretation of its parents. The child provides a myth, and this myth is close to poets' myths of the origin of their creativity, because it involves the fiction of being a changeling. A changeling-fiction is one of the stances of freedom. The changeling is free because his very existence is a disjunction, and because the mystery of his origins allows for Gnostic reversals of the natural hierarchy between parents and children.

Emerson, in his most idealizing temper, said of the poets that they were liberating gods, that they were free and made others free. I would amend this by saying that poets make themselves free, by their stances toward earlier poets, and make others free only by teaching them those stances or positions of freedom.

Freedom, in a poem, must mean freedom of meaning, the freedom to have a meaning of one's own. Such freedom is wholly illusory unless it is achieved against a prior plenitude of meaning, which is tradition, and so also against language. Language, in relation to poetry, can be conceived in two valid ways, as I have learned, slowly and reluctantly. Either one can believe in a magical theory of all language, as the Kabbalists, many poets, and Walter Benjamin did, or else one must yield to a thoroughgoing linguistic nihilism, which in its most refined form is the mode now called Deconstruction. But these two ways turn into one another at their outward limits. For Deconstruction, irony is not a trope but finally is, as Paul de Man says, "the systematic undoing... of understanding." In this view, language is not "an instrument in the service of a psychic energy." De Man's serene linguistic nihilism welcomes the alternative vision:

The possibility now arises that the entire construction of drives, substitutions, repressions, and representations is the aberrant, metaphorical correlative of the absolute randomness of language, prior to any figuration of meaning.

Can we prevent this distinguished linguistic nihilism, and the linguistic narcissism of poets and occultists, from turning into one another? Is there a difference between an *absolute* randomness of language and the Kabbalistic magical absolute, in which language is totally overdetermined? In Coleridge's version of the magical view, founded on the Johannine Logos, synecdoche or symbol also was no longer a trope, but was the endless restitution of performative rhetoric, or the systematic restoration of spiritual persuasion and understanding. This remains, though with many refinements, the logocentric view of such current theorists as Barfield and Ong.

Whether one accepts a theory of language that teaches the dearth of meaning, as in Derrida and de Man, or that teaches its plenitude, as in Barfield and Ong, does not seem to me to matter. All I ask is that the theory of language be extreme and uncompromising enough. Theory of poetry, as I pursue it, is reconcilable with either extreme view of poetic language, though not with any views in between. The new poet fights to win freedom either from dearth or from plenitude, but if the antagonist be moderate, then the agon will not take place, and no fresh sublimity will be won. Only the agon is of the essence. Why? Is it merely my misprision, to believe that good poems must be combative?

I confess to some surprise that my emphasis upon strong poets and poems should have given so much offense, particularly to British academic journalists, though truly they do live within a steadily weakening tradition, and to their American counterparts, who yet similarly do represent a waning Modernism. The surprise stems from reading historians as inevitable as Burckhardt, philosophers as influential as Schopenhauer, scholars as informative as Curtius, and most of all from reading Freud, who is indescribable as he is now inescapable. These writers, who are to our age what Longinus was to the Hellenistic world, have defined our Sublime for us, and they have located it in the agonistic spirit. Emerson preceded all of them in performing the same definition, the same location for America. These literary prophets teach us that the Greeks and the Renaissance were fiercely competitive in all things intellectual and spiritual, and that if we would emulate them, we hardly can hope to be free of competitive strivings. But I think these sages teach a harsher lesson, which they sometimes tell us they have learned from the poets. What is weak is forgettable and will be forgotten. Only strength is memorable; only the capacity to wound gives a healing capacity the chance to endure, and so to be heard. Freedom of meaning is wrested by combat, of meaning against meaning. But this combat consists in *a reading encounter*, and in an interpretive moment within that encounter. Poetic warfare is conducted by a kind of strong reading that I have called misreading, and here again I enter into an area where I seem to have provoked anxieties.

Perhaps, in common parlance, we need two very different words for what we now call "reading." There is relaxed reading and alert reading,

The breaking of form

and the latter, I will suggest, is always an agon. Reading well is a struggle because fictions and poems can be defined, at their best, as works that are bound to be misread, that is to say, troped by the reader. I am *not* saying that literary works are necessarily good or bad in proportion to their difficulty. Paul Valéry observed that "one only reads well when one reads with some quite personal goal in mind. It may be to acquire some power. It can be out of hatred for the author." Reading well, for Valéry, is to make one's own figuration of power, to clear imaginative space for one's own personal goal. Reading well is therefore not necessarily a polite process, and may not meet the academy's social standards of civility. I have discovered, to my initial surprise, that the reading of poetry has been as much idealized as the writing of it. Any attempt to de-idealize the writing of poetry provokes anger, particularly among weak poets, but this anger is mild compared to the fury of journalists and of many academics when the mystique of a somehow detached yet still generous, somehow disinterested yet still energetic, reading-process is called into question. The innocence of reading is a pretty myth, but our time grows very belated, and such innocence is revealed as only another insipidity.

Doubtless a more adequate social psychology of reading will be developed, but this is not my concern, any more than I am much affected by the ways in which recent critical theories have attempted to adumbrate the reader's share. A theosophy of reading, if one were available, would delight me, but though Barfield has attempted to develop one in the mode of Rudolph Steiner, such an acute version of epistemological idealism seems to me remote from the reality of reading. Gnosis and Kabbalah, though heterodox, are at once traditional and yet also de-idealizing in their accounts of reading and writing, and I continue to go back to them in order to discover properly drastic models for creative reading and critical writing.

Gnostic exegesis of Scripture is always a salutary act of textual violence, transgressive through and through. I do not believe that Gnosticism is only an extreme version of the reading-process, despite its deliberate esotericism and evasiveness. Rather, Gnosticism as a mode of interpretation helps to make clear why all critical reading aspiring toward strength *must* be as transgressive as it is aggressive. It is in Kabbalah, or belated Jewish Gnosis, that this textual transgression is most apparent, thanks to the superb and invaluable labors of Gershom Scholem. Scholem's researches are a demonstration that our idealisms about texts are poor illusions.

HAROLD BLOOM

When I observe that there are *no* texts, but only interpretations, I am not yielding to extreme subjectivism, nor am I necessarily expounding any particular theory of textuality. When I wrote, once, that a strong reading is the only text, the only lie against time that endures, one enraged reviewer called my assertion a critic's sin against the Holy Ghost. The holy ghost, in this case, turned out to be Matthew Arnold, greatest of School Inspectors. But Emerson made my observation long before me, in many contexts, and many others had made it before him. Here is one of them, Rabbi Isaac the Blind, thirteenth-century Provençal Kabbalist, as cited by Scholem:

> The form of the written Torah is that of the colors of white fire, and the form of the oral Torah has colored forms as of black fire. And all these engravings and the not yet unfolded Torah existed potentially, perceptible neither to a spiritual nor to a sensory eye, until the will [of God] inspired the idea of activating them by means of primordial wisdom and hidden knowledge. Thus at the beginning of all acts there was pre-existentially the not yet unfolded Torah.

Rabbi Isaac goes on to insist that "the written Torah can take on corporeal form only through the power of the oral Torah." As Scholem comments, this means, "strictly speaking, there is no written Torah here on earth." Scholem is speaking of Scripture, of what we must call Text Itself, and he goes on to a formulation that I would say is true of all lesser texts, of all poems more belated than the Torah:

> Everything that we perceive in the fixed forms of the Torah, written in ink on parchment, consists, in the last analysis, of interpretations or definitions of what is hidden. *There is only an oral Torah:* that is the esoteric meaning of these words, and the written Torah is a purely mystical concept.... There is no written Torah, free from the oral element, that can be known or conceived of by creatures who are not prophets.

What Scholem wryly asserts does not dismay what I would call *the poet in the reader* (any reader, at least potentially) but it does dismay or provoke many professional readers, particularly in the academies. One of my most instructive memories will be always of a small meeting of distinguished professors, who had gathered to consider the qualifications of an individual whom they might ask to join their enterprise. Before meditating upon this person's merits, they spontaneously performed a little ritual of faith. One by one, in turn, they confessed their belief in the real presence of the literary text. It had an existence independent of their devotion to it. It had priority over them, would be there after they were gone, and above all it had a meaning or meanings quite apart from their interpretive activity. The literary text was *there*.

The breaking of form

Where? Why, in editions, definitive editions, upon which responsible commentaries might be written. Responsible commentaries. For "responsible," substitute what word you will, whatever anxious word might match the social pieties and professional civilities that inform the spirituality of such occasions.

I only *know* a text, any text, because I know a reading of it, someone else's reading, my own reading, a composite reading. I happen to possess a somewhat preternatural verbal memory, particularly for verse. But I do not know *Lycidas* when I recite it to myself, in the sense that I know *the Lycidas* by *the* Milton. *The* Milton, *the* Stevens, *the* Shelley, do not exist. In a recent issue of a scholarly magazine, one exegete of Shelley passionately and accurately declared his faith that Shelley was a far more gifted imagination than he could ever be. His humble but worthy destiny, he declared, was to help all of us arrive at *the* Shelley by a lifetime of patient textual, historical, and interpretive work. His outrage was plain in every sentence, and it moved me deeply, even though evidently I was the unnamed sinner who had compelled him to proclaim his passionate self-effacement.

Alas that words should be only words and not things or feelings, and alas again that it should be, as Stevens said, a world of words to the end of it. Words, even if we take them as magic, refer *only* to other words, to the end of it. Words will not interpret themselves, and common rules for interpreting words will never exist. Many critics flee to philosophy or to linguistics, but the result is that they learn to interpret poems as philosophy or as linguistics. Philosophy may flaunt its rigors but its agon with poetry is an ancient one, and never will end. Linguistic explanations doubtless achieve a happy intensity of technicality, but language is not in itself a privileged mode of explanation. Certainly the critic seeking *the* Shelley should be reminded that Shelley's poems *are* language, but the reminder will not be an indefinite nourishment to any reader. Philosophers of intertextuality and of rhetoricity usefully warn me that the meanings of an intertextual encounter are as undecidable and unreadable as any single text is, but I discover pragmatically that such philosophers at best teach me a kind of double-entry bookkeeping, which as a reader I have to discount. Every poem becomes as unreadable as every other, and every intertextual confrontation seems as much an abyssing as any other. I subtract the rhetoricity from both columns, from rhetoric as system of tropes, and from rhetoric as persuasion, and return to where I started. *Jedes Wort ist ein Vorurteil*, Nietzsche says, which I translate as: "Every word is a *clinamen*." There is always and only bias, inclination, pre-judgment, swerve; only and always the verbal agon for freedom, and the agon is carried on not by truth-telling, but by words lying against time.

Freedom and lying are intimately associated in belated poetry, and the notion that contains them both might best be named "evasion." Evasion is a process of avoiding, a way of escaping, but also it is an excuse. Usage has tinged the word with a certain stigma, but in our poetry what is being evaded ultimately is fate, particularly the necessity of dying. The study of poetry is (or ought to be) the study of what Stevens called "the intricate evasions of as." Linguistically these evasions constitute trope, but I urge a study of poetry that depends upon a larger vision of trope than traditional or modern rhetoric affords us. The positions of freedom and the strategies of lying are more than images, more than figurations, more even than the operations that Freud named "defense." Searching for a term comprehensive enough to help in the reading of poems, I offered the notion of "revisionary ratios," and found myself working with six of these, a number not so arbitrary as it has seemed to some. Rather than enumerate and describe these ratios again, I want to consider something of the limits that traditional rhetoric has set upon our description of poems.

Rhetoric has been always unfitted to the study of poetry, though most critics continue to ignore this incompatibility. Rhetoric rose from the analysis of political and legal orations, which are absurd paradigms for lyrical poems. Helen Vendler pithily sums up the continued inadequacy of traditional rhetoric to the description of lyric:

It remains true that the figures of rhetoric, while they may be thought to appear in a more concentrated form in lyric, seem equally at home in narrative and expository writing. Nothing in the figures of paradox, or irony, or metaphor, or imagery – or in the generic conventions of, say, the elegy – specifies a basis in verse.

John Hollander, who is our leading authority upon lyrical form, illuminates tropes by calling them "turns that occur between the meanings of intention and the significances of linguistic utterances." I want to expand Hollander's description so as to open up a hidden element in all criticism that deals with figuration. Any critic necessarily tropes or turns the concept of trope in giving a reading of a specific poem. Even our most sophisticated and rigorously theoretical critics are at work on a rhetoric of rhetoric when they believe themselves merely to be distinguishing between one trope and another. A trope is troped

The breaking of form

wherever there is a movement from sign to intentionality, whenever the transformation from signification to meaning is made by the test of what aids the continuity of critical discourse. The increasingly scandalous instance is in the supposed critical distinction between metonymy and metaphor, which has become a shibboleth for weak interpreters. Jakobsonian rhetoric is fashionable, but in my judgment is wholly inapplicable to lyric poetry. Against Jakobson, I follow Kenneth Burke in seeing that the fundamental dichotomy in trope is between irony and synecdoche or, as Burke says, between dialectic and representation. There is precious little dichotomy between metonymy and metaphor or, as Burke again says, between reduction and perspective. Metonymy and metaphor alike I would trope as heightened degrees of dialectical irony, with metaphor the more extended. But synecdoche is not a dialectical trope, since as microcosm it represents a macrocosm without necessarily playing against it.

In lyric poetry, there is a crucial gap between reduction or metonymy and the part-for-whole representation of synecdoche. Metonymy is a mode of repetition, working through displacement, but synecdoche is an initial mode of identification, as its close association with the ancient topoi of definition and division would indicate. The topoi associated with metonymy are adjuncts, characteristics, and notation, all of them namings through supposed cause-and-effect. A metonymy *names*, but a synecdoche begins a process that leads to an *un-naming*. While metonymy hints at the psychology of compulsion and obsession, synecdoche hints at the vicissitudes that are disorders of psychic drives. Regressive behavior expresses itself metonymically, but sado-masochism is synecdochic, in a very dark sense. I verge upon saying that naming in poetry is a limitation of meaning, whereas un-naming restitutes meaning, and so adds to representation.

This way of connecting trope and psychic defense, which to me seems an inevitable aid in the reading of poetry, itself has encountered a good deal of psychic defense in my more unamiable critics. What is the justification for linking language and the ego, trope and defense, in relatively fixed patterns? Partly, the rationale would depend upon a diachronic, rather than a synchronic, view of rhetoric, that is, upon an analytic rhetoric that would observe the changing nature of both linguistic trope and psychic defense as literary history moved from the Ancient world to the Enlightenment, and then on to Milton as prophet of Post-Enlightenment poetry. But, in part, the explanation for reading trope as defense and defense as trope goes back to my earlier observations on criticism as the rhetoric *of* rhetoric, and so on each critic's individual troping of the concept of trope. If rhetoric has its diachronic aspect, then so does criticism as the rhetoric of rhetoric. A study of Post-Enlightenment criticism from its prophet, Dr. Johnson, on to our contemporaries would reveal that its rhetoric was reborn out of Associationist psychology, and that the crucial terms of that psychology themselves stemmed from the topoi of a rejected classical rhetoric, ostensibly rejected by the Enlightenment but actually troped rather than rejected.

This complex phenomenon needs to be studied in detail, and I am attempting such a study currently in a book on the Sublime and the concept of topos as image-of-voice in Post-Enlightenment poetry. Here I want only to extract a dilemma of the relation between style and idea in the perpetual, onward Modernizing march of all post-Miltonic poetry. From the poets of Sensibility down to our current post-Stevensian contemporaries, poetry has suffered what I have termed elsewhere an over-determination of language and consequently an under-determination of meaning. As the verbal mechanisms of crisis have come to dominate lyric poetry, in relatively fixed patterns, a striking effect has been that the strongest poets have tended to establish their mastery by the paradox of what I would call *an achieved dearth of meaning*. Responding to this achieved dearth, many of the strongest critics have tended to manifest *their* skill by attributing the dearth to their own synchronic view of language and so to the vicissitudes of *language itself* in producing meaning. A diachronic phenomenon, dependent upon Miltonic and Wordsworthian poetic *praxis*, is thus assigned to a synchronic cause. Deconstructionist criticism refuses to situate itself in its own historical dilemma, and so by a charming paradox it falls victim to a genealogy to which evidently it must remain blind. Partly, this paradox is due to the enormous and significant difference between Anglo-American poetic tradition and the much weaker French and German poetic traditions. French poetry lacks not only early giants of the dimension of Chaucer, Spenser, and Shakespeare, but it also is devoid of any later figures whose strength could approximate Milton and Wordsworth, Whitman and Dickinson. There is also the oddity that the nearest French equivalent, Victor Hugo, remains absurdly unfashionable and neglected by his nation's most advanced critics. Yet the "achieved dearth of meaning" in French poetry is clearly exemplified more even by Hugo than by Mallarmé, just as in English it is accomplished more powerfully by Wordsworth and Whitman than it is by Eliot and Pound.

If this judgement (however unfashionable) is correct, then it would be

The breaking of form

sustained by a demonstration that the revisionary patterns of Modern poetry are set by Wordsworth and Whitman (or by Hugo, or in German by the later Goethe), and by the further demonstration that these fixed or all-but-fixed relations between trope and defense reappear in Baudelaire, Mallarmé, and Valéry, in Hölderlin and Rilke, in Yeats and Stevens and Hart Crane. These patterns, which I have mapped as a sequence of revisionary ratios, are not the invention of belated moderns but of inaugural moderns, the High Romantics, and of Milton, that mortal god, the Founder from whom Wordsworth and Emerson (as Whitman's precursor) derive.

Ratios, as a critical idea, go back to Hellenistic criticism, and to a crucial clash between two schools of interpretation, the Aristotelian-influenced school of Alexandria and the Stoic-influenced school of Pergamon. The school of Alexandria championed the mode of *analogy*, while the rival school of Pergamon espoused the mode of *anomaly*. The Greek *analogy* means "equality of ratios," while *anomaly* means a "disproportion of ratios." Whereas the analogists of Alexandria held that the literary text was a unity and had a fixed meaning, the anomalists of Pergamon in effect asserted that the literary text was an interplay of differences and had meanings that rose out of those differences. Our latest mimic wars of criticism thus repeat battles fought in the second century B.C. between the followers of Crates of Mallos, Librarian of Pergamon, and the disciples of Aristarchus of Samothrace, Librarian of Alexandria. Crates, as an Anomalist, was what nowadays Hillis Miller calls an "uncanny" critic or, as I would say, an "antithetical" critic, a student of the revisionary ratios that take place *between* texts. Richard McKeon notes that the method of Crates led to allegories of reading, rather than to Alexandrian or analogical New Criticism, and I am prepared to call my work an allegory of reading, though very different from the allegories of reading formulated by Derrida and de Man, legitimate rival descendants of Crates.

The breaking of form to produce meaning, as I conceive it, depends upon the operation of certain instances of language, revisionary ratios, and on certain topological displacements in language that intervene between ratios, displacements that I have been calling "crossings."

To account for these ratios, without defending here their name and their number, I have to return to my earlier themes of the aggression of reading and the transgression of writing, and to my choice of a psychic rather than a linguistic model in a quest for tropes that might illuminate acts of reading.

HAROLD BLOOM

Anna Freud, in her classic study *The Ego and the Mechanisms of Defense*, notes that

all the defensive measures of the ego against the id are carried out silently and invisibly. The most that we can ever do is to reconstruct them in retrospect: we can never really witness them in operation. This statement applies, for instance, to successful repression. The ego knows nothing of it; we are aware of it only subsequently, when it becomes apparent that something is missing.

As I apply Anna Freud, in a poem the ego is the poetic self and the id is the precursor, idealized and frequently composite, hence fantasized, but still traceable to a historical author or authors. The defensive measures of the poetic self against the fantasized precursor can be witnessed in operation only by the study of a difference between ratios, but this difference depends upon our awareness not so much of presences as of absences, of *what is missing in the poem because it had to be excluded*. It is in this sense that I would grant a point made by John Bayley, that I am "fascinated by the sort of poetry that is *not really there*, and – even better – the kind that knows it never can be." But Bayley errs in thinking that this is only one tradition of the poetry of the last three centuries, because clearly it is the norm, or the condition of belated strong poetry. The authentic poem now achieves its dearth of meaning by strategies of exclusion, or what can be called litanies of evasion. I will quote a sympathetic British critic, Roger Poole, for a more useful account of this problematic element in our poetry:

If a poem is really 'strong' it represents a menace. It menaces the way the reader thinks, loves, fears and is. Consequently, the reading of strong poetry can only take place under conditions of mutual self-defense. Just as the poet must not know what he knows, and must not state what he states, so the reader must not read what he reads. [The] question is not so much 'What does this poem mean?' as 'What has got left out of this poem to make of it the particularly expensive torso that it is?'

To adumbrate Poole's observations a touch more fully, I would suggest that we all suffer from an impoverished notion of poetic allusion. No strong poem merely alludes to another, and what look like overt allusions and even echoes in strong poems are disguises for darker relationships. A strong authentic allusion to another strong poem can be only by and in what the later poem *does not say*, by what it represses. This is another aspect of a limitation of poetry that defines poetry: A poem can be *about* experience or emotion or whatever only by initially encountering another poem, which is to say a poem must handle experi-

The breaking of form

ence and emotion as if they already were rival poems. Poetic knowledge is necessarily a knowledge by tropes, an experience of emotion as trope, and an expression of knowledge and emotion by a revisionary further troping. Since a poem is necessarily still further troped in any strong reading, there is a bewildering triple intertropicality at work that makes a mockery of most attempts at reading. I do not agree wholly with de Man that reading is impossible, but I acknowledge how very difficult it is to read a poem properly, which is what I have meant by my much-attacked critical trope of "misreading" or "misprision." With three layers of troping perpetually confronting us, the task of restituting meaning or of healing a wounded rhetoric is a daunting one. Yet it can and must be attempted. The only alternative I can see is the triumph of Romantic irony in purified form by way of the allegory of reading formulated by Paul de Man. But this most advanced version of Deconstruction cheerfully accepts the risk warned against by de Man's truest precursor, Friedrich Schlegel: "The irony of irony is the fact that one becomes weary of it if one is offered it everywhere and all the time."

To evade such destructive weariness, I return to the poetic equivalent of Freud's concept of defense. The center of the poetic self, of the speaking subject that Demanian Deconstruction dissolves into irony, is narcissistic self-regard. Such poetic self-esteem is wounded by its realization of belatedness, and the wound or narcissistic scar provokes the poetic self into the aggressivity that Freud amazingly chose to call "defense." Even Freud, like all the rest of us, idealized the arts, it being Nietzsche's distinction that in this too he was the grand exception, though to some extent he shares this particular distinction with Kierkegaard. Because of such prevalent idealization, we all of us still resist the supposed stigma of identifying the strong poet's drive toward immortality with the triadic sequence of narcissism, wounded self-regard, and aggression. But change in poetry and criticism as in any human endeavor comes about only through aggression. Unless a strong poet strongly loves his own poetry, he cannot hope to get it written. When Robinson Jeffers writes that he hates his verses, every line, every word, then my response is divided between a sense that he lies, and a stronger sense that perhaps he tells the truth, and *that* is the trouble. Alas that poetic self-love should not in itself be sufficient for strength, but it is no good lamenting that it should be necessary for poetic strength. Pindar, one of our earliest instances of lyric strength, should have taught all of us that poetic narcissism is at the root of any lyric Sublime. The first

Olympic ode, still the truest paradigm for Western lyric, overtly celebrates Hieron of Syracuse, yet the horse and rider more fully and implicitly celebrated are Pegasus and Pindar. Lyric celebrates the poetic self, despite every denial. Yet we refuse the lesson, even as Freud partly did. A poet, as much as any man or woman among us, scarcely feels complimented when described as narcissistic and aggressive. But what *can* poetry give back, either as successful representation or achieved pathos, and whether to poet or reader, except for a *restitution of narcissism*? And since paranoid thinking can be defined as a complete shield against being influenced, what is it that saves strong poets from paranoid thinking except for their early susceptibility to poetic influence, an openness that *must* in time scar the narcissism of the poet *qua* poet. For those who scoff still at the idea of the anxiety of influence, I shall cite the second and belated Pindar, Hölderlin, in a letter he wrote to his precursor, Schiller:

I have sufficient courage and judgment to free myself from other masters and critics and to pursue my own path with the tranquil spirit necessary for such an endeavor, but in regard to *you*, my dependence is insurmountable; and because I know the profound effect a single word from you can have on me, I sometimes strive to put you out of my mind so as not to be overcome by anxiety at my work. For I am convinced that such anxiety, such worry is the death of art, and I understand perfectly well why it is more difficult to give proper expression to nature when the artist finds himself surrounded by masterpieces than when he is virtually alone amidst the living world. He finds himself too closely involved with nature, too intimately linked with it, to consider the need for rebelling against its authority or for submitting to it. But this terrible alternation is almost inevitable when the young artist is exposed to the mature genius of a master, which is more forceful and comprehensible than nature, and thus more capable of enslaving him. It is not a case of one child playing with another child – the primitive equilibrium attained between the first artist and his world no longer holds. The child is now dealing with men with whom he will never in all probability be familiar enough to forget their superiority. And if he feels this superiority he must become either rebellious or servile. Or must he?

This passage, anguished in its sense of contamination, is cited by René Girard as another instance of the violence of thematicism that he names as a progression "from mimetic desire to the monstrous double." I would prefer to read it as an exercise in self-misprision, because in it a very strong poet evasively relies upon a rhetoric of pathos to portray himself as being weak. The revisionary ratio here employed against Schiller is what I call *kenosis* or repetition and discontinuity. Appearing to empty himself of his poetic godhood, Hölderlin actually undoes and

The breaking of form

isolates Schiller, who is made to ebb more drastically than the ephebe ebbs, and who falls hard where Hölderlin falls soft. This *kenosis* dares the profoundest evasion of naming as the death of art what is the life of Hölderlin's art, the ambivalent and agonistic clearing-away of Schiller's poetry in order to open up a poetic space for Hölderlin's own achievement. Freud, in his final phase, taught us what we may call "the priority of anxiety" – that is, the dominance of the pleasure principle by tendencies more primitive than it, and independent of it. Hölderlin teaches us the same, even as he denies his own teaching. Freud belatedly discovered that certain dreams in traumatic neuroses come out of "a time before the purpose of dreams was the fulfillment of wishes" and so are attempts "to master the stimulus retrospectively by developing the anxiety." Hölderlin, in his greatest odes, earlier discovered that poetic thoughts did not sublimate desires, but were endeavors to master a quasi-divine reality by developing the anxiety that came from the failure to realize poetic godhood. As a poet, Hölderlin knew what as a man he denies in his letter to Schiller, which is that the anxiety of influence is a figuration for Sublime poetry itself.

Defense therefore is the natural language of Hölderlin's poetic imagination and every Post-Enlightenment imagination that can aspire convincingly to something like Hölderlin's Sublime strength. But in language itself defense is compelled to be manifested as trope. I have argued elsewhere for certain paradigmatic links between specific tropes and specific defenses, at least since Milton's day, and I will not repeat such argument here. But I have never elucidated the relation of trope to my revisionary ratios, and that will be my concern in the remainder of the theoretical portion of this essay, after which I will conclude by speculating upon the role of the ratios in the poetic breaking of poetic form. An excursus in practical criticism will follow, so as to apply my sequence of ratios to the interpretation of John Ashbery's recent long poem, *Self-Portrait in a Convex Mirror*.

It is certainly very difficult to chart anomalies, particularly *within* a poem yet in reference *to* the impingement of another poem. Revisionary ratios are thus at once intra-poetic *and* inter-poetic, which is a necessary doubling since the ratios are meant to map an internalizing of tradition. Tradition is internalized only when a total stance toward precursors is taken up by a new strong poet. Such a stance is a mode of deliberateness, but it can operate at many levels of consciousness, and with many shades between negation and avowal. As John Hollander observed, ratios are "at once text, poem, image and model." As text, a ratio names inter-textual differences; as poem it characterizes a total relationship between two poets, earlier and later. As model, a ratio functions the way a paradigm works in the problem-solving of normal science. It is as image that a ratio is most crucial, for the revisionary ratios are, to cite Hollander again, "the varied positions of freedom" or "true position" for a poet.

Freud's patterns of psychic images are the defenses, a tropological system masking itself as a group of operations directed against change, but actually so contaminated by the drives it would deflect as to become a compulsive and unconscious process like the drives. But eventually Freud was to assert that "the theory of the drives is so to say our mythology. Drives are mythical entities, magnificent in their indefiniteness." To this audacity of the Founder I would add that defenses are no less mythological. Like tropes, defenses are turning-operations, and in language tropes and defenses crowd together in the entity rather obscurely called poetic images. Images are ratios between what is uttered and what, somehow, is intended, and as Kenneth Burke remarks, you cannot discuss images for very long without sliding into whole textures of relationships. Cannot *those* relationships be charted? If it is extravagant to create a new rhetoric, this extravagance, as Joseph Riddel says, "simply repeats the wandering or indirect movement of all trope." But trope, or the play of substitution, is purely a temporal process. Ratios of revision between earlier and later poets and poems are as much spatial as temporal, though the space be imaginative or visionary. Rhetorical criticism, even of the advanced Deconstructive kind, treats a poem merely as a formal and linguistic structure. But strong poems manifest the will to utter permanent truths of desire, and to utter these *within* a tradition of utterance. The intention to prophesy is necessarily a dynamic of space as well as time, particularly when the prophecy insists upon finding its authority *within* a tradition of what has been prophesied. As soon as we speak of what is within a previous utterance, our discourse is involved in thematics, in topology or literary place. Themes are things placed into stance, stance is the attitude or position of the poet in the poem, and placing is a dynamic of desire seeking either its apotheosis or its entropic self-destruction.

A power of evasion may be the belated strong poet's most crucial gift, a psychic and linguistic cunning that energizes what most of us have over-idealized as the imagination. Self-preservation is the labor of the poem's litanies of evasion, of its dance-steps beyond the pleasure

The breaking of form

principle. Where a defensive struggle is carried on, there must be some self-crippling, some wounding of energies, even in the strongest poets. But the uncanny or Sublime energies of poetic evasion, operating through the graduated anomalies that are ratios of revision, constitute the value-creating power of the anxiety of influence. Ann Wordsworth summarizes this eloquently, when she speaks of "this ingenious ravelling, a process as determinant perhaps as dream-work" which is "the creative mind's capacity to *know* through the precursor, to *renew* through misprision, and to *expand* into the full range of human experience." Where my formulation and use of revisionary ratios have been most attacked is in their sequence, and in the recurrence of that sequence in so many poems of the last two hundred years. I have meant that we are to read *through* ratios and not *into* them, so that they cannot be regarded as reductive entities, but still their frequency causes disquiet. So it should, but hardly because revisionary ratios are my own paranoid code, as some journalists have suggested. And yet a few closing words on paranoid codes may be in place just here and now in this fictional time of Borges and Pynchon.

Commenting on *The Crying of Lot 49*, the book's best critic, Frank Kermode alas, observes that "a great deviation is called a sect if shared, paranoia if not." Kermode charmingly goes on to recall that "a man once undertook to demonstrate infallibly to me that *Wuthering Heights* was an interlinear gloss on Genesis. How could this be disproved? He had hit on a code, and legitimated all the signs." Kermode's point is that this is the danger that both Pynchon's Oedipa and the novel's reader confront. Warning us, Kermode asks us to remember that "deception is the discovery of the novel, not of its critics." If Kermode is correct in this, then I would call Pynchon, in just that respect, too much of a moralist and too little of a strong poet. If evasion is the discovery of the post-Miltonic poem, it is also the discovery of the poem's critics. Every belated poem that matters ends with either the narrative gesture, postponing the future, *by projecting it*, or else the prophetic gesture, hastening the future, *by introjecting it*. These defensive operations can be regarded as either the work of negation, intellectually freeing us from some of the consequences of repression, or the labor of paranoia, reducing reality to a code. I would hope to have done part of the work of negation for some readers and lovers of poetry besides myself. There is no reading worthy of being communicated to another unless it deviates to break form, twists the lines to form a shelter, and so makes a meaning through that shattering of belated vessels. That shattering is rhetorical, yes, but more than language is thus wounded or blinded. The poet of our moment and of our climate, our Whitman and our Stevens, says it best for me, and so I end with the eloquence of John Ashbery:

> The song makes no mention of directions.
> At most it twists the longitude lines overhead
> Like twigs to form a crude shelter. (The ship
> Hasn't arrived, it was only a dream. It's somewhere near
> Cape Horn, despite all the efforts of Boreas to puff out
> Those drooping sails.) The idea of great distance
> Is permitted, even implicit in the slow dripping
> Of a lute. How to get out?
> This giant will never let us out unless we blind him.

II

I turn to a proof-text, Ashbery's long poem, *Self-Portrait in a Convex Mirror*. It would not have been thought a long poem by Browning, but five hundred and fifty-two lines is a long poem for our damaged attention-spans these days. Ashbery, like Stevens, is a profoundly Whitmanian poet, frequently despite appearances. Throughout Ashbery's career, he has centered upon full-scale poems, the great successes being *Fragment, The Skaters,* the prose *Three Poems, Fantasia on "The Nut-Brown Maid,"* and above all *Self-Portrait*. They are versions or revisions of *Song of Myself,* in some of the same subtle ways that Stevens wrote revisions of Whitman in *The Man with the Blue Guitar* and *Notes toward a Supreme Fiction*. Necessarily, Ashbery also revises Stevens, though more overtly in *Fragment* and *Fantasia* than in the very Whitmanian *Skaters* and *Three Poems*. Both Stevens and Whitman are ancestral presences in *Self-Portrait,* and so is Hart Crane, for the language of the poem engages, however covertly and evasively, the central or Emersonian tradition of our poetry.

Angus Fletcher, in his studies of Spenser, Milton, Coleridge, and Crane, has been developing a liminal poetics or new rhetoric of thresholds, and I follow Fletcher both in my notion of the topoi of "crossings" as images of voice, and in my account of the final revisionary ratio of *apophrades* or reversed belatedness, which is akin to the classical trope of *metalepsis* or transumption and to the Freudian "negation" (*Verneinung*) with its dialectical interplay of the defenses, projection and introjection. I will re-expound and freshly develop these Fletcherian ideas in the reading of Ashbery that follows.

The breaking of form

Ashbery divides *Self-Portrait* into six verse-paragraphs, a happy division which I shall exploit, naming them by my apotropaic litany of evasions or revisionary ratios. Swerving easily away from Whitman and from Stevens, Ashbery begins his *clinamen* from tradition by a brilliant description of the painting that gives him his title:

> As Parmigianino did it, the right hand
> Bigger than the head, thrust at the viewer
> And swerving easily away, as though to protect
> What it advertises. A few leaded panes, old beams,
> Fur, pleated muslin, a coral ring run together
> In a movement supporting the face, which swims
> Toward and away like the hand
> Except that it is in repose. It is what is
> Sequestered.

This abrupt opening is itself evasive, the "As" being one of Stevens' "intricate evasions of as." The hand's defensive gesture is a reaction formation or rhetorical *illusio*, since what is meant is that the hand acts as though to advertise what it protects. Here a swerve is another mode of repose, so that defense does not so much protect as it sequesters, a word whose Late Latin antecedent had the meaning "to give up for safekeeping." Ashbery quotes Vasari's description of the halved wooden ball upon which Parmigianino painted what the poet calls the face's "receiving wave / of arrival." Unspoken is each wave's ebbing, but the absent image of departure informs the poem's countersong, which thus makes its initial entrance:

> The soul establishes itself.
> But how far can it swim out through the eyes
> And still return safely to its nest? The surface
> Of the mirror being convex, the distance increases
> Significantly; that is, enough to make the point
> That the soul is a captive, treated humanely, kept
> In suspension, unable to advance much farther
> Than your look as it intercepts the picture.

The poignance of the extreme dualism here will be almost constant throughout the poem. Such dualism is a surprise in Ashbery, yet the pathos is precisely what we expect from the self-portraitist of *Fragment* and *Three Poems*. Certainly the anguish of *Self-Portrait* has an intensity to it that marks Ashbery, yet generally not to this degree. I will suggest that

Harold Bloom

Self-Portrait, though meditation rather than lyric, is a poem closely related to the *Ode on a Grecian Urn* and to Stevens' version of Keats' *Ode, The Poems of Our Climate*. Three reveries upon aesthetic distance and poetic coldness share a common sorrow, and manifest almost a common glory.

The soul is a captive, but art rather than the body appears to be the captor:

> The soul has to stay where it is,
> Even though restless, hearing raindrops at the pane,
> The sighing of autumn leaves thrashed by the wind,
> Longing to be free, outside, but it must stay
> Posing in this place. It must move
> As little as possible. This is what the portrait says.
> But there is in that gaze a combination
> Of tenderness, amusement and regret, so powerful
> In its restraint that one cannot look for long.
> The secret is too plain. The pity of it smarts,
> Makes hot tears spurt: that the soul is not a soul,
> Has no secret, is small, and it fits
> Its hollow perfectly: its room, our moment of attention.

We can remark that the actual painting looks rather like the actual Ashbery, and that this poet's characteristic expression could not be more accurately described than as "a combination/Of tenderness, amusement, and regret . . . powerful/In its restraint." The secret *is* irony, is the strong presence that is an abyss, the palpable absence that is the poet's soul. Times and places come together in the *attention* that makes the painter's and the poet's room into the one chamber. But this attention is a Paterian music, surpassing both painting and poetry:

> That is the tune but there are no words.
> The words are only speculation
> (From the Latin *speculum*, mirror):
> They seek and cannot find the meaning of the music.

Angus Fletcher, in his seminal study of "Threshold, Sequence and Personification in Coleridge," reminds us that while numerology suggests a timeless ontology, the *poetics* of number accept our time-bound duration. Poetry, as St. Augustine conceived it, is "the mirror or *speculum* of the world," a mirror that "temporalizes and historicizes number." Ashbery, as a rider of poetic motion, labors at the fiction of duration, but his evident ruefulness at becoming what Stevens' *Asides on the Oboe* called "the human globe" or "the man of glass" is strongly emphasized. The *clinamen* is away from Stevens' celebration of Emerso-

The breaking of form

nian centrality, or praise for "the man who has had the time to think enough," and toward a lament for the confinements of art and artist:

> We see only postures of the dream
> Riders of the motion that swings the face
> Into view under evening skies, with no
> False disarray as proof of authenticity.
> But it is life englobed.
> One would like to stick one's hand
> Out of the globe, but its dimension,
> What carries it, will not allow it.
> No doubt it is this, not the reflex
> To hide something, which makes the hand loom large
> As it retreats slightly.

A representation conveyed only as a mode of limitation; this irony is the peculiar mark of the poem's initial movement of *clinamen*, its swerve away from its origins, which truly are not so much in Parmigianino as in Stevens, particularly in the Whitmanian Stevens of *Poem with Rhythms*, written just after *Asides on the Oboe*, a poem where "The hand between the candle and the wall/Grows large on the wall." The painter's hand as seen by Ashbery must stay within aesthetic limitation:

> There is no way
> To build it flat like a section of wall:
> It must join the segment of a circle....

Stevens, like the Whitman of *The Sleepers* whom he echoes earlier in *Poem with Rhythms*, breaks the limitation by an act of will, by the hyperbole of a Sublime power:

> It must be that the hand
> Has a will to grow larger on the wall,
> To grow larger and heavier and stronger than
> The wall; and that the mind
> Turns to its own figurations and declares,
> *"This image, this love, I compose myself*
> *Of these. In these, I come forth outwardly.*
> *In these, I wear a vital cleanliness,*
> *Not as in air, bright-blue-resembling air,*
> *But as in the powerful mirror of my wish and will."*

A mind that can turn to its own figurations and constitute an ego by love of those figurations is a Whitmanian, transcendentalizing mind of summer. Such a mind is also that of Freudian Man, since Freud defines narcissism as being the self's love of the ego, a love that by such cathexis veritably *constitutes* the ego. The *speculum* or convex mirror of Ashbery precisely is not the powerful mirror of his wish and will, and in this inclination away from his fathers, the palpable Stevens and the ghostly Whitman, Ashbery establishes his true *clinamen*. But the cost is severe, and Ashbery accurately observes that his own "pure affirmation," like the painter's, "doesn't affirm anything." Or, to illuminate this properly ironic affirmation by using Fletcher's terms, Ashbery affirms only his own perpetual liminality, the threshold stance that he shares with Hart Crane and with the more delicate, fragile nuances of Whitman's more antithetical moments. Fletcher, writing on Coleridge, seems to be describing the first part of Ashbery's poem:

While epic tradition supplies conventional models of the threshold, these conventions are always subject to deliberate poetic blurring.... poets have wished to subtilize, to dissolve, to fragment, to blur the hard material edge, because poetry hunts down the soul, with its obscure passions, feelings, other-than-cognitive symbolic forms....

Ashbery hunts down the soul, following Parmigianino, and finds only two disparate entities, a hand "big enough/To wreck the sphere" and an ambiguous hollow, a room without recesses, only alcoves, a chamber that defeats change, "stable within/Instability," a globe like our earth, where "there are no words/For the surface, that is,/No words to say what it really is."

A threshold is a crossing, and at the close of this first verse-paragraph Ashbery deliberately fails to negotiate a first crossing, and so fails to get over a threshold of poetic election. The disjunction is from the artist's "pure/Affirmation that doesn't affirm anything" to "The balloon pops, the attention/Turns dully away." Since the attention is the memory that the soul's only room was "our moment of attention," the balloon's pop dislodges the earlier "ping-pong ball" of the painting's stable instability. A failed crossing of election leaves the poet helpless (by choice) as experience threatens to engulf his sense of his own pathos. Ashbery's second verse-paragraph is his poem's *tessera*, its antithetical completion which fails all completion. The poet, necessarily unsure of his poet-hood's survival, is only the synecdoche for voices that overwhelm him:

> I think of the friends
> Who came to see me, of what yesterday

The breaking of form

Was like. A peculiar slant
Of memory that intrudes on the dreaming model
In the silence of the studio as he considers
Lifting the pencil to the self-portrait.
How many people came and stayed a certain time,
Uttered light or dark speech that became part of you
Like light behind windblown fog and sand,
Filtered and influenced by it, until no part
Remains that is surely you.

There is an affinity between this peculiar slant of memory's light and Dickinson's oppressive certain slant of light that imaged death. Both are synecdoches of a kind that belongs to Coleridge's wounding sense of symbol or to Anna Freud's defense mechanism of turning against the self. Anna Freud said of a patient that "by turning her aggressive impulses inwards she inflicted upon herself all the suffering which she had formerly anticipated in the form of punishment by her mother." What I call the revisionary ratio of *tessera* is the poetic transformation of such turning against the self. Ashbery, *as poet,* is compelled to present himself as being only a mutilated part of a whole already mutilated. Why most strong poems in our tradition, from Wordsworth on, manifest this masochistic impulse of representation, *even as they strive to pull away from initial ironies,* is beyond my present capacity to surmise. Yet Ashbery's contribution to this necessity of representation clearly joins the Wordsworthian "enchantment of self with self":

In the circle of your intentions certain spars
Remain that perpetuate the enchantment of self with self:
Eyebeams, muslin, coral. It doesn't matter
Because these are things as they are today
Before one's shadow ever grew
Out of the field into thoughts of tomorrow.

Fletcher remarks that, in the context of poetic thresholds, "'sequence' means the process and the promise that something will follow something else." Such process begins spatially, Fletcher adds, but ends "on a note of temporal description," perhaps because sequence in a poem is a mode of survival, or fiction of duration. I have experienced my own defensive emotions concerning the sequence of revisionary ratios that I find recurrent in so many poems, quite aside from the defensive reactions I have aroused in others. But the sequence is *there* in the sense that image and trope tend to follow over-determined patterns of evasion. Thus, Ashbery's poem moves on to a third verse-paragraph that is a *kenosis*, an isolating defense in which poetic power presents itself as being all but emptied out:

> Tomorrow is easy, but today is uncharted,
> Desolate, reluctant as any landscape
> To yield what are laws of perspective
> After all only to the painter's deep
> Mistrust, a weak instrument though
> Necessary. Of course some things
> Are possible, it knows, but it doesn't know
> Which ones. Some day we will try
> To do as many things as are possible
> And perhaps we shall succeed at a handful
> Of them, but this will not have anything
> To do with what is promised today, our
> Landscape sweeping out from us to disappear
> On the horizon.

This "today" seems not so much uncharted as non-existent. Ashbery displaces "today" by "possible," "promises" or "dream" throughout his third verse-paragraph. A sequence of "possible," "possible," "promised," "promises," and "possibilities" in lines 151–68 is replaced by seven occurrences of "dream" or "dreams" in lines 180–206, where the section ends. All these are metonymies for, reductions of, "today," and perform the self-emptying action of *kenosis*: "out from us." Brooding on aesthetic forms, Ashbery attains to a poignant and characteristic sense of "something like living":

> They seemed strange because we couldn't actually see them.
> And we realize this only at a point where they lapse
> Like a wave breaking on a rock, giving up
> Its shape in a gesture which expresses that shape.

Kenosis is Ashbery's prevalent ratio, and his whole poetics is one of "giving up/Its shape in a gesture which expresses that shape." What but the force of the past, the strength of his own poetic tradition, could drive Ashbery on to his next threshold, the disjunctive gap or crossing of solipsism that he leaps between his poem's third and fourth verse-paragraphs? The transition is from "a movement/Out of the dream into its codification" to the angelic or daemonic surprise of the face of Parmigianino/Ashbery. The Uncanny or Sublime enters both through repression of the memory of the face, and through a return of the repressed by way of what Freud termed Negation:

> As I start to forget it
> It presents its stereotype again

The breaking of form

But it is an unfamiliar stereotype, the face
Riding at anchor, issued from hazards, soon
To accost others, "rather angel than man" (Vasari).
Perhaps an angel looks like everything
We have forgotten, I mean forgotten
Things that don't seem familiar when
We meet them again, lost beyond telling,
Which were ours once.

The great modern critic of Negation, foreshadowing the Deconstruction of Derrida and even more of de Man, is Walter Benjamin. I do not believe that Ashbery cites Benjamin here, but it is inevitable that any fresh Sublime should remind us of Benjamin, who joins Freud as the century's theorist of the Sublime. Ashbery's tentative formula "Perhaps an angel looks like everything/We have forgotten" is very close to Benjamin's meditation upon his angel:

The angel, however, resembles all from which I have had to part: persons and above all things. In the things I no longer have, he resides. He makes them transparent.

This is Benjamin's *aura* or light of the Sublime, truly visible only in the shock of its disappearance, the flight of its repression. Ashbery has lost, he goes on to say, "the whole of me" to the strict otherness of the painter. Yet the loss becomes the Emersonian-Stevensian *surprise*, the advent of power, in a passage that plays against Stevensian images:

We have surprised him
At work, but no, he has surprised us
As he works. The picture is almost finished,
The surprise almost over, as when one looks out,
Startled by a snowfall which even now is
Ending in specks and sparkles of snow.
It happened while you were inside, asleep,
And there is no reason why you should have
Been awake for it, except that the day
Is ending and it will be hard for you
To get to sleep tonight, at least until late.

Even the accent suggests very late Stevens, the perception of "Transparent man in a translated world,/In which he feeds on a new known." But instead of the Stevensian "clearness emerging/From cold," with a power surpassing sleep's power, Ashbery opts for a lesser pathos, for an uneasiness, however Sublime, rather than a transcendence. As always, Ashbery represses his own strength, in his quest to maintain an evenness of tone, to avoid climax-impressions. This results in a spooky

HAROLD BLOOM

Sublime, indeed more canny than uncanny, and the reader of Ashbery more than ever has to cultivate a patience for this limpid style, this mode of waiting without seeming to wait. "The surprise, the tension are in the concept/Rather than its realization." Yet even the concept is hidden, buried deep in the image of depth in this daemonic verse-paragraph: "the face/Riding at anchor, issued from hazards." Throughout the poem, the painting is imaged as a ship, appearing to us "in a recurring wave/Of arrival," but still a "tiny, self-important ship/On the surface." Toward the close of the poem, in lines 478–89, a transumption of these earlier tropes will be accomplished with mysterious urgency, when "A ship/Flying unknown colors has entered the harbor." The portrait as ship suggests the peril of poetic art from Spenser to Stevens, but to Ashbery's reader it seems another version of the oxymorons that concluded his magnificent earlier meditation, *Soonest Mended*, where the poet speaks of

> ...learning to accept
> The charity of the hard moments as they are doled out,
> For this is action, this not being sure, this careless
> Preparing, sowing the seeds crooked in the furrow,
> Making ready to forget, and always coming back
> To the mooring of starting out, that day so long ago.

Parmigianino's self-portrait is another "mooring of starting out," and such an oxymoron (with its quasi-pun on "morning") is for Ashbery a characteristic sublimation of unfulfillable poetic desires. A greater sublimation comes in the poem's *askesis*, its fifth verse-paragraph, where Ashbery "perspectivizes" against both the painter and his own poetic self. The perspectives are bewildering, as the "outside" cities and landscapes are played off against the inner space of painting and of poem:

> Our landscape
> Is alive with filiations, shuttlings;
> Business is carried on by look, gesture,
> Hearsay. It is another life to the city,
> The backing of the looking glass of the
> Unidentified but precisely sketched studio. It wants
> To siphon off the life of the studio, deflate
> Its mapped space to enactments, island it.

If the soul is not a soul, then the inside/outside, mind/nature metaphor is rendered inadequate, aside from its built-in inadequacies of endless perspectivism. Ashbery boldly sets out to rescue the metaphor

The breaking of form

he has helped to bury. A cold wind of aesthetic and vital change rises to destroy Ashbery's kind of urban pastoral, and the painter, as the poet's surrogate, is urged to see and hear again, albeit in a necessarily illusory present:

> Your argument, Francesco,
> Had begun to grow stale as no answer
> Or answers were forthcoming. If it dissolves now
> Into dust, that only means its time had come
> Some time ago, but look now, and listen....

But though Ashbery goes on to urge the normality and correctness of metaphor, such a rescue operation must fail, reminding us perhaps that the prestige of metaphor and of sublimation tends to rise and fall together in cultural history. A third and most crucial threshold-crossing takes place as Ashbery moves reluctantly away from metaphor and into the giant *metalepsis* or ratio of *apophrades* that concludes and is the glory of his poem. The long final sixth verse-paragraph (ll. 311–552) begins with a surprised sense of achieved identification, introjecting both the painting and the poet's death:

> A breeze like the turning of a page
> Brings back your face: the moment
> Takes such a big bite out of the haze
> Of pleasant intuition it comes after.

Before describing this crossing and the superb section it introduces, I digress again into Fletcher's theories of threshold, sequence and personification, as they were my starting-point for thinking about transumption. Coleridge credited Spenser with being the great inventor in English poetry of the "land of Faery, that is, of mental space." Fletcher follows Coleridge in relating such mental space to daemonic agency, personification and topical allusion. What Fletcher's grandest innovation does is to alter our understanding of personification, by compounding it both with transumption and the pun. Complete projection or introjection is paranoia, which means, as Fletcher says, that "madness is complete personification." But most strong poets avoid this generative void, though all pause upon its threshold. John Hollander, following Fletcher, has traced the figurative power of poetic echo and its link to the Post-Romantic transformations of *metalepsis* or transumption, transformations that based themselves upon Milton's transumptive use of similes:

The peculiar quality of Miltonic simile, by which, as Dr. Johnson put it, he "crowds the imagination," is a mode of transumption – the *multitudinousness* of the Satanic legions in Book I is like that of autumn leaves, but unclaimed manifestly for the comparison are the other likenesses (both are fallen, dead) whose presence is shadowed only in the literalizing of the place name of Vallombrosa.

Hollander cites the mythographic commentary by George Sandys on Ovid's story of Echo, where Sandys quotes Ausonius and then adds that "the image of the voice so often rendred, is as that of the face reflected from one glasse to another; melting by degrees, and every reflection more weake and shady than the former." This, Hollander implies, is the predicament that Milton and his heirs escaped by making their images of voice transumptive. And this is precisely the predicament that Ashbery evades in *Self-Portrait*, and particularly in its sixth or transumptive section to which I now return.

The breeze whose simile is a page's turning, and that brings back the self-portrait, returns more than two hundred lines later in the closing passage of the poem:

> ...the ache
> Of this waking dream can never drown out
> The diagram still sketched on the wind,
> Chosen, meant for me and materialized
> In the disguising radiance of my room.
> ....
> The hand holds no chalk
> And each part of the whole falls off
> And cannot know it knew, except
> Here and there, in cold pockets
> Of remembrance, whispers out of time.

The wind transumes the breeze, returning the self-portrait to an introjected earliness, an identification of poet and painter. The pockets of remembrance, though cold as painting and poem are cold, remain the winds whispering *out of* time, in a multiple play upon "out of," which refers us back to Keats' cold pastoral that teased us out of time, as did eternity. The echo of the *Grecian Urn* reinforces the echo of the *Nightingale*'s "waking dream." Death, as in Keats' odes, is what the figurations defend against, quite directly. So, going back to the start of the sixth verse-paragraph, the page-turning similitude is necessarily followed directly by the introjection of death, in a Crossing of Identification that links not only painter and poet, but also the tragic Alban Berg and *Cymbeline*. Reflections upon the common mortality of artists lead to earlier presages of aesthetic whispers out of time:

The breaking of form
> I go on consulting
> This mirror that is no longer mine
> For as much brisk vacancy as is to be
> My portion this time. And the vase is always full
> Because there is only just so much room
> And it accommodates everything. This sample
> One sees is not to be taken as
> Merely that, but as everything as it
> May be imagined outside time –

The vase, emblem both of Keats' *Ode* and Stevens' *The Poems of Our Climate*, is as full as the poet's own time is briskly vacant, the oxymoron strengthening Ashbery's own recovery of strength in the poem. A meditation upon Ashbery's familiar "permanent anomaly," a certain kind of erotic illumination, leads on to a new sense of earliness, a metaleptic reversal of the poem's ironic opening:

> All we know
> Is that we are a little early, that
> Today has that special, lapidary
> Todayness that the sunlight reproduces
> Faithfully in casting twig-shadows on blithe
> Sidewalks. No previous day would have been like this.
> I used to think they were all alike,
> That the present always looked the same to everybody
> But this confusion drains away as one
> Is always cresting into one's present.

What shadows this freshly achieved earliness is the doubt that still more art is needed: "Our time gets to be veiled, compromised/By the portrait's will to endure." Creation being out of our hands, our distance from even our own art seems to become greater. In this intensification of estrangement, Ashbery's meditation gradually rejects the paradise of art, but with enormous nostalgias coloring farewell. A sublime pun, fulfilling Fletcher's vision of threshold rhetoric, is the climax of this poignant dismissal, which reverberates as one of Ashbery's greatest passages, majestic in the aesthetic dignity of its mingled strength and sadness:

> Therefore I beseech you, withdraw that hand,
> Offer it no longer as shield or greeting,
> The shield of a greeting, Francesco:
> There is room for one bullet in the chamber....

The chamber, room of poet's and painter's self-portraits, room as moment of attention for the soul not a soul, fitting perfectly the hollow of its tomb, is also the suicide (or Russian roulette?) of a self-regarding art. Ashbery's poem too is the shield of a greeting, its defensive and communicative functions inextricably mixed. Yet Ashbery's reading of his tradition of utterance, and my reading of Ashbery, are gestures of restitution. Achieved dearth of meaning is exposed as an oxymoron, where the "achieved" outweighs the "dearth." The antithetical critic, following after the poet of his moment and his climate, must oppose to the abysses of Deconstruction's ironies a supermimesis achieved by an art that will not abandon the self to language, the art of Ashbery's earlier *Fragment*:

> The words sung in the next room are unavoidable
> But their passionate intelligence will be studied in you.

NOTE

"The Breaking of Forms" by Harold Bloom. From *Deconstruction and Criticism.* Copyright © 1979 by The Seabury Press, Inc. Used by permission of The Continuum Publishing Company.

STEPHEN SPENDER

The "I" as an other in poetry

When Alexander Pope wrote an epistle to Dr. Arbuthnot, or to some aristocratic patron or friend, he assumed in using the first person pronoun "I" that the recipient was on terms – rather elevated ones – of equality of discourse with him. The poet is, of course, superior as a craftsman, using the tools of his technique and the material of words; but because he is a poet, he does not as a human being belong to a different order of existence from the friend whom he compliments by addressing in his poem. He considers poetry an exalted form of manners rather than an exalted condition of soul. He despises the Grub Street poets not just because they write miserably but because they are *misérables*: members of a kind of social Gehenna, living in conditions of poverty and madness, which is the equivalent of the lack of politeness in their writings. The social equivalent of the polished perfection of Pope's writings is Twickenham and the aristocratic friends, by whom he is received.

The Romantics, and critics who favor Romantic poetry, sometimes criticized the Augustan poets on the grounds that they were writers of verse – prose thoughts skillfully woven into poetic forms – rather than poets. In the present century in his famous lecture *The Name and Nature of Poetry*, A.E. Housman pronounced that Pope was a writer of prose. When I consider the extraordinary fantasy and invention of Pope in *The Rape of the Lock*, and the somber, gloomy power of the ending of *The Dunciad*, I begin to wonder whether the idea that Pope and other Augustan poets were versifiers is not based on the feelings of Wordsworth, Arnold, Housman, and others who have expressed their view about the poets rather than the poetry. Poets who dedicated their poems to aristocrats and who assumed that their polished verses put them on equal terms with the most exalted members of polite society were not, from the standpoint of Romantics, poets. But Byron, who from the Romantic standpoint is very much a poet, thought Pope a better poet than any of his lot – the generation of Romantics. But Byron ostensibly prided himself more on being a lord than on being a scribbler of verses.

Something happened at the end of the eighteenth and the beginning of the nineteenth centuries that (1) made the poet qua poet seem different from previous poets as well as from other people and (2) made the self of the poet appear identical with his poetry.

Wordsworth writes of the poet as a man speaking to men. But the man who is doing the speaking is Wordsworth talking out of what Keats diagnosed as the Wordsworthian "egoistical sublime." And the men to whom Wordsworth as a man speaks in his poetry are again and again invited by the poet to enter into the experience of being Wordsworth as a child who had extraordinary communings with nature. In Shelley's poetry the reader is constantly being invited to enter into the *being* of the poet. In Romantic poetry the reader is promoted by the poet to the position of a Romantic who shares to some extent the nature of the poet's being, but does not write poetry, because his own being has not attained that pitch of intensity that would enable him to do so. The Romantic reader could be called a grade B Romantic poet of existing who does not write poetry.

In Keats's wonderfully apt description, *Wordsworth*, we recognize a whole chain of identifications: the adult Wordsworth ego identifying with Wordsworth's own childhood, the child with the mother, the mother with a mountainous river-run landscape.

When Wordsworth writes in the first person singular, the reader is aware of the pressure of a far greater force of existing than the reader can ever attain. The reader of Wordsworth's poetry feels himself to be a tourist visiting a landscape that is both "nature" and the very presence of the poet. The tourists in charabancs who at this very moment are visiting the English Lake District are acting out a metaphor for the relationship of the reader to Wordsworth's poetry. Perhaps that is why, of all visitors to poets' shrines, they feel in Cumberland closest to the spirit of the poet. It would not be at all the same to go to Pope's Twickenham.

A poem by a Romantic poet is like the bread and wine of the mass – one substance with the flesh and blood of the creator. The "I" of the Augustan poet was that of the gentleman who wrote poetry – or, rather, the poet who wrote poetry for gentlemen. The "I" of the Romantic is that of the poem personified: the poet who in his life as well as in his work is his poetry. The poet is intrinsic with the poem.

The "I" as an other in poetry

One reads:

> My heart aches and a drowsy numbness pains
> My sense, as though of hemlock I had drunk,
> Or emptied some dull opiate to the drains
> One minute past, and Lethe-wards had sunk.

The reader at once identifies with the very existence of the poet, whose existence is also identical with that of the poem.

When I talk here of the "I" of the poet, I do not mean that the poet has to be an egotist. Wordsworth was indeed an egotist – though a sublime one – in his poetry, because his experiences were like funnels of nature, rising like the sides of a pyramid to the apex, which was his separate self. With Keats, on the other hand, the self is the apex of the inverted pyramid, which moves upward and outward into the world and into other poetry outside himself. Nevertheless, every line of Keats is throbbingly Keatsian, colored with his own personality, like the pulse of his wrist: "When this warm scribe my hand is in the/grave." This line, in *The Fall of Hyperion*, has the poignancy of the poet writing his last poem with his dying hand. Yet the "I" of Keats is not an egotistic self into which all his feeling and experience enter: Rather it enters into things outside while endowing them with his subjective life and feeling. Keats distinguishes his poetic aims from the Wordsworthian sublime egotism in his letter of October 27, 1818, to his friend Richard Woodhouse:

As to the poetical Character itself, (I mean that sort of which, if I am any thing, I am a Member; that sort distinguished from the Wordsworthian or egotistical sublime; which is a thing per se and stands alone) it is not itself – it has no self – it is everything and nothing... It has as much delight in conceiving an Iago as an Imogen... A Poet is the most unpoetical of anything in existence; because he has no Identity – he is continually in for and filling some other body. The sun, the Moon, the Sea, and Men and Women, who are creatures of impulse, are poetical, and have about them an unchangeable attribute.

The vanishing of the ego into an everything that is outside Keats is the obverse of everything outside Wordsworth being transformed into the poetic product of his egotism.

When Wordsworth was an adult, he connected his experience of nature with memories of earlier, more intense sensations from childhood, going back to memories of being held in his mother's lap, leading back to still earlier and perhaps prenatal sensations – trailing clouds of glory – and to the idea of a Mind beyond Nature moving through it.

The reader understands all this to the extent that reading Wordsworth stimulates him to remember similar sensations of nature in his own childhood: to become, in short, the infant Wordsworth, a situation in which he may possibly imagine himself when walking through the landscape sanctified by Wordsworth's poetry as being made identical with Wordsworth's sublime self-consciousness.

A difficulty notoriously arises for the reader who tries to objectify the sensations of the Wordsworthian self into a Wordsworthian philosophy, or to follow Wordsworth's argument when the poet attempts to do so. In a famous passage from *The Prelude*, Wordsworth endeavors to draw philosophical conclusions from the sensations provided by his own infancy. At the beginning of the passage, he generalizes from himself and talks about the infant instead of about the particular "I" who is experiencing these things – Wordsworth. He calls himself "he":

> Thus, day by day
> Subjected to the discipline of love,
> His organs and recipient faculties
> Are quickened, are more vigorous, his mind spreads,
> Tenacious of the forms which it receives,
> In one beloved Presence, nay and more,
> In that most apprehensive habitude
> And these sensations which have been derived
> From this beloved Presence, there exists
> A virtue which irradiates and exalts
> All objects through all intercourse of sense
> No outcast he, bewildered and depressed:
> Along his infant veins are interfused
> The gravitations and the filial bond
> Of Nature that connect him with the world.
> Emphatically such a Being lives,
> An inmate of this *active* universe;
> From nature largely he receives; nor so
> Is satisfied, but largely gives again,
> For feeling has to him imparted strength,
>   And powerful in all sentiments of grief,
>   Of exaltation, fear and joy, his mind,
>   Even as an agent of the one great Mind,
> Creates, creator and receiver both,
>   Working but in alliance with the works
> Which it beholds. Such, verily, is the first
> Poetic spirit of our human life,
> By uniform control of after years,
> In most, abated and suppressed; in some,
> Through every change of growth or of decay,
> Pre-eminent till death.

The "I" as an other in poetry

At this point Wordsworth shifts from the generalizing third person to the first person, bringing us back to himself as an infant. He makes it apparent that what he is doing in the previous passage is attempting to deduce thinking processes, true for all mankind, from his subjective sensations remembered, private to him:

> From early days,
> Beginning not long after that first time
> In which, a Babe, by intercourse of touch
> I held mute dialogue with my Mother's heart,
> I have endeavoured to display the means
> Whereby the infant sensibility,
>   Great birthright of our being, was in me
>   Augmented and sustained.

The second passage shows that, in the first quotation, Wordsworth is objectifying from his personal recollections of feelings he had when he was at his mother's breast. The reader can judge the truth of the first passage only according to his capacity to identify his own earliest recollections of infancy with those of Wordsworth in the second passage – by becoming, as it were, the infant Wordsworth. The Romantic poet's writing derives from intensely felt subjective experiences, which are perceived as having an existence in the poetry itself – the subjective poet and the object that is the poetry he makes are one and the same. The reader, through the poetry, enters into the poet's experience of existing. Receiving this experience secondhand, he becomes, while under the blurring of subjective awareness of a very intense kind with thoughts derived from that awareness – thoughts that are conditional on the reader sharing Wordsworth's feelings about his intercourse with nature. This produces the peculiarly hallucinatory effect of Wordsworth's poetry when he is philosophizing, the hallucination being that subjective feeling has at some point passed over into objective thinking, a sensation of thinking into philosophical argument.

William Empson has observed that the Romantics were the first poets to lay down a pipeline connecting them with their childhood experiences. The reason for this surely is that in the newly industrialized modern world, where adults were becoming specialists in whatever activities they pursued, childhood was the only time of life that provided the sense of a world of the imagination and experiences shared with others. Infancy is the stage when distinctions between the infant's world of his own body and that of his mother's body, representing the world outside him, do not exist. Outer and inner worlds are the same. The poet, through awakening in the reader memories of infantile states of being, may make the reader *become* the world of the poet's imagination.

With the beginning of the technological era, poets were forced back on the identification of their own being with their poetry by the collapse of a whole nexus of beliefs and values and the social hierarchy provided by religion, a classical education, the social hierarchy which poets could formally draw on, a language of live objective symbols transferable into the language of poetry, fragmented by the new civilization of cities. Wordsworth chose nature inhabited by men and women who were close to nature as the territory that he would fall back on in a rearguard action, against the de-poeticized city. In the Preface to *Lyrical Ballads* (1800), he states the situation clearly:

A multitude of causes, unknown to former times, are now acting with a combined force to blunt the discriminating powers of the mind, and, unfitting it for all voluntary exertion to reduce it to a state of almost savage torpor. The most effective of these causes are the great national events which are daily taking place, and the increasing accumulation of men in cities, where the uniformity of their occupations provides a craving for extraordinary incident, which the rapid communication of intelligence hourly gratifies.

Wordsworth left the town, rarely visiting London, and went to the English Lake District. But the Lake District, with its mountains, shepherds, and village communities with parson, school marm, old dame, vagrants wandering through, soldiers wounded in the Napoleonic wars, unfortunate women abandoned by their adventurer husbands – though marvelously alive – did not provide an active alternative to the civilization of London and Edinburgh. This vital natural energy was a poignant retreat from the mechanical energy of the cities. For the reader, the interest of the scenery and cast of characters in Wordsworth is the extent to which they become Wordsworth through the force of his transforming imagination.

The Romantic, cut off from the fixed external symbolism institutionalized in the society itself that earlier poets could draw on, tried to make other connections with the surrounding life: with nature, with revolutions arising from Godwinian belief in the perfectibility of man, or in a vision of intense spiritual and sexual connection between individuals, relations so passionate that they would transform humanity through the power of human love. This last we find in Whitman and D.H. Lawrence, just as much as in Shelley, and in Matthew Arnold's *cri du coeur*:

The "I" as an other in poetry

> Ah, love, let us be true
> To one another! For the world which seems
> To lie before us like a land of dreams,
> So various, so beautiful, so new,
> Hath really neither joy, nor love, nor light,
> Nor certitude, nor peace, nor help for pain:
> And we are here as on a darkling plain
> Swept with confused alarms of struggle and flight,
> Where ignorant armies clash by night.

Here the Romantic situation is clearly one into which the poet is driven by external circumstances: driven to find the identification of soul mates with each other as the only surviving value in a world of clashing mechanical forces.

The Romantic is one who finds himself forced by circumstances to regard his own existence as the incarnation of poetry cut off from traditional props. Poetry is isolated and he is isolated; therefore he has to offer himself to the world as an example of the power of the individual to concentrate in his own being values of nature, of living. This is the result of the individual's situation of despair within industrial society. With Whitman we see the obverse, a situation of hope and optimism in an emerging new society, which is still mainly preindustrial – or what he thinks to be so – celebrated in *Song of Myself*:

> I celebrate myself, and sing myself,
> And what I assume you shall assume,
> For every atom belonging to me as good
>   belongs to you.

Whereas the English Romantic poet identifies with one beloved elect person, Whitman identifies with whoever in the crowd of emergent American democracy chooses to respond with all the atoms of his existence to all the atoms of Whitman's.

The phrase *egotistical sublime* applies – though in very different circumstances – really as much to Whitman as to Wordsworth. In directing all his experiences of the geography and nature and life of ordinary people around him into his consciousness of himself as the ego bearing the burden of all this awareness when he pronounces "I," he is the American Wordsworth.

I return now to Keats. At the end of his very short life, when he knew he was dying, and when his powers were clearly failing, Keats made a final attempt to rewrite his projected epic called *Hyperion*, about a mythological struggle between gods. For the new draft he wrote an introductory three hundred or so lines in which he confronts himself with the problem of a poet in modern times – ours as much as his – who sets out to write an epic poem.

It is typical of the Romantic that he asks himself not what the characteristics of the poem should be but what the characteristics of the poet should be. Were Dryden or Pope considering the problem of writing an epic, they would certainly have been concerned with the poem rather than the poet.

Essentially, Keats equates the qualities of the poet with the requirements of the poem. To write a great poem, a poet has to be great. Poets who lack moral stature equal to the greatness of the task they set themselves cannot achieve greatness in their poetry. In the opening of *The Fall of Hyperion*, the poet has to submit to various tests, but they are all tests of his being, not of craftsmanship. And despite his modesty, Keats finds that the only poet qualified to write the epic is Keats: that is to say, a Keats who has submitted his existence to crucial tests in which his contemporaries Shelley and Byron would certainly fail. Keats disqualifies his great contemporaries from attempting such a task on grounds of their moral failure as human beings. He calls upon Apollo in his destructive plague-bearing aspect – with his "misty pestilence":

> to creep
> Into the dwellings, through the door crannies,
> Of all mock lyrists, large self-worshipers,
> And careless hectorers in proud bad verse –

The hectorers are taken to refer to Shelley and Byron.

Keats, like Rimbaud, demands that the poet should be no mere dreamer but a true visionary, staring into the abyss of modern reality. The writer of the modern epic has to be one who in his own being equals the forces of the world that he confronts. Keats depicts himself standing at the bottom of a flight of marble steps, at the top of which stands a prophetess called Moneta (*Moneo*, I warn, and one recalls here that Wilfred Owen, the great English poet of World War I, wrote a Preface to his poems about the experience of the trenches of the Western Front, pronouncing: "All a poet can do today is to warn"). The warning Moneta gives the poet is that in order to attain the spiritual greatness that will enable him to write his epic, he must climb these steps. Doing so is like confronting death with the whole of life concentrated in the poet's being. Moneta sternly warns:

The "I" as an other in poetry

> If thou canst not ascend
> These steps, die on that marble where thou art.
> Thy flesh, near cousin to the common dust,
> Will parch, for lack of nutriment – thy bones
> Will wither in few years, and vanish so
> That not the quickest eye could find a grain
> Of what thou now art on that pavement cold.

The poet makes the prodigious effort required to climb the steps, which almost kills him. Keats here describes symptoms of the consumption from which he knows himself to be dying:

> One minute before death my iced foot touch'd
> The lowest stair; and, as it touch'd, life seemed
> To pour in at the toes; I mounted up.

He then asks Moneta what is required of the poet. She answers:

> None can usurp this height, return'd that shade
> But those to whom the miseries of the world
> Are misery, and will not let them rest.
> All else, who find a haven in the world,
> Where they may thoughtless sleep away their days,
> If by a chance into this fane they come,
> Rot on this pavement...

Keats, who was a medical student working in a London hospital in 1819, and was seeing operations performed without anesthetics, asks:

> Are there not thousands in the world
> Who love their fellows, even to the death,
> Who feel the giant agony of the world,
> And more, like slaves to poor humanity,
> Labour for mortal good?

The Fall of Hyperion, written by a dying man, and mixing negative bitterness, envy, and hatred with the magnificent positiveness of Keats's vision, is a failure, but it is one of the most significant failures in Romantic poetry. For it sets forth the problem of the poet "out of tune with his time," thrust back upon himself, and forced, when he retells what seems to be an old myth, to create the myth completely out of his own qualities as a human being. It was a challenge set down for the nineteenth century and not taken up again until the twentieth, in *The Waste Land* and the *Cantos*.

Stephen Spender

What characterizes the great Romantic poets is this absolute equation of states of being in the poet himself with his poetry. The difference between being a Romantic as noun – in the sense that Wordsworth, Keats, Shelley, and, in spite of himself, though somewhat differently, Byron were Romantics – and being what I call *adjectively* Romantic, in the way that the Victorians were, is this: In the Romantics we feel an intensity of being that makes the poet become poetry, the poetry become poet. Sometimes the Romantic seeks to transfer this identification to another person, not a poet – or, rather, to share it with this person – in whom he reads his own existence identified with poetry. Shelley certainly does this in his love poetry. The object of his passion is invited to become the poetry that is identical with Shelley; invited, in fact, to be Shelley, to be his poetry.

Tennyson and Browning perhaps wrote greater poems than did Keats and Shelley, but they lack the total objectivity and the dedication to the poem as a thing made out of the language of the Augustans, as well as the total identification of subjective passion with poetry considered as expression of the poet's own existing, which we find in the Romantics. That is why, however much we admire them, we feel their world to be tainted with the preoccupations of the society to which they belonged, exemplifying values that are bourgeois. The Victorian poet has a split "I"; with one part he considers himself a representative of the society in which he lives, and with the other part he cultivates the idea of himself as superior to it, qua poet: "Vex not thou the poet's mind/With thy shallow wit." Tennyson runs a line in prophecy, but it is not that of one like Blake; it is essentially that of pre-Wellsian science fiction – of a man who shares many of the values of the scientific industrial bourgeois society even while considering himself as a becloaked poet and prophet to rise above them:

> For I dipt into the future, far as human eye could
>   see,
> Saw the Vision of the world, and all the wonder
>   that would be.
> Saw the heavens filled with commerce, argosies of
>   magic sails,
> Pilots of the purple twilight, dropping down
>   with costly bales.
> Heard the heavens filled with shouting, and there
>   rained a ghastly dew,
> From the nations' airy navies grappling in the
>   central blue.

The "I" as an other in poetry

Reading this, one has the impression of prophecy perhaps but not of vision. One says to oneself: "We are the time he is foreseeing. Some of what he says is wrong, some right." It is materialistic.

Of course, Tennyson had a world of his own individual poetic imagination, a strange and sombre world. One striking thing about his poetry is that in so much of it he seems to regard his world as representing temptation to be avoided at all costs, something a good Victorian should not indulge in. *The Lotos-Eaters* is a vision of *calme luxe et volupté*, which Tennyson regards as time wasted. *Locksley Hall* is Tennyson contemplating the danger of going to some Gauginesque island and there raising a dusky tribe of little Tennysonian half-breeds. *In Memoriam* depicts the love that most people decidedly dare not name. Blake would surely have felt that Tennyson rejected divine satanic energy in his poetry and sided with some Victorian Nobodaddy.

Arnold is probably to us the most deeply interesting – if by no means the best – Victorian poet, because his poetry is so much concerned with the unattainability of the poetic life in the modern conditions. In *The Buried Life*, he contrasts the life we lead in the modern world with the hidden life we instinctively know to be the real truth of our being. He compares these two lives, the one of the surface, the other buried under separate but parallel lines:

> But hardly have we, for one little hour
> Been on our own line, have we been ourselves;
> Hardly had skill to utter one of all
> The nameless feelings that run through our breast,
> But they course on for ever unexpressed.

What splits up in Arnold is two "I's": one the poet, the other the school inspector and responsible liberal-minded nineteenth-century citizen full of progressive ideas. With both Tennyson and Arnold, there is fear of letting the right hand of the responsible citizen know what the left hand of the irresponsible poet is up to. One might think that the result of such fusion would be the explosion of the whole fabric of middle-class Victorian society. And perhaps it would have been. Perhaps we in the twentieth century have seen this happen.

So the "great Victorian" poets in England wrote poetry – reams of it – but lost faith in the idea of the poet in his life, being in his self, his poetry. One reason for this may have been the disastrous effects of Romanticism on Byron, Keats, and Shelley in their lives. Another is that the situation of the Romantic was overtaken by history. Blake,

Wordsworth, Shelley, and Keats could still dramatize a conflict between the poet and the time in which he lived, allying themselves with mystical religion, nature, utopian revolution – forces that they themselves in their poetry incarnated. Tennyson, grappling with scientific learning and ideas of evolution, felt the need to be no mere Bohemian but a respected and honored citizen who could discuss science with scientists. Whitman, in comparatively undiscovered, newly democratic America, could seek alliances for his poetic "myself" in the physical self-awareness of Americans and in the physical continent of the largely unexploited continent. But he lost faith in American democratic institutions, deeming them incapable of producing life corresponding to that of his self in his poetry after the Civil War.

Toward the end of the nineteenth century, the "I" of the poet was felt to be a source of weakness, existential frailty, rather than of strength. The poet must conceal the nakedness of the I, adopt the mask of a deliberately fabricated, artificial persona.

This attitude was partly the result of French influence. Mallarmé wrote, "The pure work implies the disappearance of the poet as speaker, who hands over to the words." And Rimbaud, "*Je est un autre.*" Yet such tactics represent a return to the total commitment to poetry by the poet of the Romantics, rather than an extension of the split ego of the Victorians. Wordsworth through the ego connected his adult self with the self of his infancy, and through that self with the mother, and through the mother with nature – a process that Auden gives a Freudian twist to:

> By landscape reminded of his mother's figure
> The mountain heights he remembers get bigger
> and bigger.

The "I" as the conscious self is felt by Mallarmé and – differently – by Rimbaud to be a point of weakness of the poet. Instead of the subjective poet and the objective poem being equated within the "I" of the poet, the poem, the words, take over and eliminate the "I" in Mallarmé. In Rimbaud, the external sensations – misery, cold, drugs, violence – that press upon the poet communicate below the consciousness, which says "I" to the subconscious. This is the "systematic derangement of the senses."

I suggest that the whole development of poetry since the year 1800

The "I" as an other in poetry

(when Wordsworth wrote his Preface to *Lyrical Ballads*) has been the various attempts of poets who lacked a shared system of public symbolism related to beliefs, values, and the social hierarchy (embodied in Church, State, and education) to compensate for this, first by intense subjectivity and later by attempting to reach beyond individual subjectivity to the forces of the unconscious. What I have said about the Romantics relates, I think, to the present situation of poetry. All the modernist movements are perhaps to be seen as illustrating two tendencies: one to intensify and hot up the subjectivity of the "I" – a tendency that we see in today's "confessional" poets; the other to purge poetry of the subjective solipsist Romantic and post-Romantic characteristics and to present them as impersonal objects, artifacts. This has been the tendency of modernism in Yeats, Eliot, Pound, and Auden.

RESPONSE AND SEMINAR DISCUSSION

Aileen Ward: I am glad to see that the chairs are set around an imaginary round table, meaning that our discussion will be an open one. I would like to start the discussion and then turn it over to Mr. Spender and our panel. I might raise a question from your discussion of last night on Romantic poetry, and that is what I perceive as the profound ambivalence about the self that runs through the career of most, perhaps all, of the major Romantic poets. One thinks of Blake's early exaltation of the self in *The Marriage of Heaven and Hell* and the early "Annotations to Leander," and then the increasing doubt about selfhood that comes out in his later work. I think also at the other end of the development of the Romantic poetry of Keats. What starts as the young man's sense of the lack of selfhood as something to be praised in the poet – as in fact the distinguishing characteristic of the poet – is replaced by an increasing concern with what Keats calls identity. The sense of identity which is perhaps his version of the self is not an assertion of the ego; yet it is not the abandonment of the ego either. We remember what Keats said about Shakespeare, who originally was his idea of the poet with no selfhood. A year after that letter describing him as the chameleon poet par excellence, the poet in contrast to the egotistical sublime, Shakespeare turns into a very different character after Keats's tragic experience. Shakespeare

STEPHEN SPENDER

becomes for Keats "the mighty and miserable poet of the human heart," and this sense of selfhood is something that emerges by contact with the suffering of others.... I think this is the great meaning of selfhood for Keats. But in each case it is a developing thing; it is very hard I think to pin down the sense of the self in Romantic poetry in only one formulation.

Stephen Spender: Yes, when I was giving that paper and using the pronoun "I," I was wondering whether what I was saying could simply be replaced by the word self, but I don't think it could. I would say that, regarding Keats, I was really taking the position of the poet who feels himself cut off from a symbolic medium or various symbolic systems of expression which in the eighteenth century a poet had in common with the reader. I mean Latin and Greek and the Bible, and also the social hierarchy. When a writer like Pope uses the word "I" in a poem, he is addressing himself to a patron, to a friend, or to someone as though they both know what a poem is. It is something quite detached from them, like a craftsman who has made a watch, a beautiful object. The "I" of Pope is one gentleman speaking to another gentleman. It is something quite separate from the artifact that is made which is the poetry. But I think that Wordsworth becomes extremely conscious of this whole system of symbolic communication as having broken down as a result of the growth of the city, the industrial revolution. In fact, he says that very clearly in the Preface to *Lyrical Ballads*. What I meant was that the poet feels cut off; he doesn't want to be completely isolated, so he tries to find an alternative. In Wordsworth's case it was nature. But the alternative doesn't already exist in the mind of the reader. The poet has to prove the alternative to the reader by the reader entering into the actual being of the poet: Wordsworth being in nature. Wordsworth is very persuasive about nature and we go and visit the Lake District as a result. But actually the poet has to invent it through his own imagination. The reader has to identify with Wordsworth, and Wordsworth to some extent identifies with the reader.

Whitman is a very good example of this. In *Song of Myself*, Whitman starts off by saying: Reader, you are the same as I am; you are also made of millions of atoms and so on. But I think that in spite of *Song of Myself* being so called, the poet is not quite conscious of the "I" in the way that he might be conscious of the self. So that

The "I" as an other in poetry

when Keats attacks Wordsworth for the egotistical sublime, he is quite right. Everything in Wordsworth – his experiences in connection with his childhood in nature, his connection through his mother with nature, and beyond nature to the idea of a mind which moves through the universe – always leads back to Wordsworth, doesn't it? The egotistical sublime is a very good phrase, just as Whitman always leads back to Whitman, "I Walt Whitman."

Keats turns the thing on its head by trying to, in a very modern way, like T. S. Eliot, depersonalize and not talk about the "I." He cheats slightly in that famous letter about the poet having no identity, because he is talking about Shakespeare and he is also talking about a playwright. Keats in his letters tends to play roles in Shakespeare; he writes prose in his letters which is like the prose of the speeches of Hamlet.

Richard Sennett: Aileen, what are your criticisms, if you would?

Aileen Ward: Well, I was suggesting first of all that it is difficult in the case of each poet to speak about the single notion of the self or the "I" or whatever we want to name the distinction between those two words. The self is something that develops. In Keats, I think of the development of a selfhood, or what he calls an identity, in that wonderful letter of April 1819. The "veil of soul making" is not something that sets the self off from others, which is what I think he still criticizes in Wordsworth, but is a means of truly entering into the experience of others by having suffered what all men suffer, having suffered in one's self and then becoming able thereby to participate imaginatively in the sufferings of others. I think very much of Wordsworth in *The Ruined Cottage*, the evolution of which is very interesting to watch. It starts out as an absolutely impersonal poem, describing the sufferings and eventually the death of Margaret. Bit by bit as he moves from draft to draft he adds a witness to this suffering – a peddler who eventually comes to occupy the main focus of the poem. I think the idea behind the development is that it is only when a sympathetic and perceptive observer, a self with whom we can identify, mediates the experience that it comes home fully to us. I wonder whether that isn't what Keats was trying to do in *The Fall of Hyperion*, to add that dimension of the poet as witness to the wars of the Titans to bring home fully the nature of that tragic experience. So the self is in some of its dimensions reprehensible as Blake comes to describe it, the aggressive self that centers all of experience in itself and seeks to dominate others. Whereas for Keats, ideally, and I think for Wordsworth, too, it was felt as a bridge to the experience of others.

Joseph Brodsky: If I understand what Stephen was talking about, it is not so much the thematic bridges or the emotional links which the poet tries to establish between the reader and himself; it is a slightly different thing. It is not what the poet tries to establish, but what the reader establishes, what the reader feels toward the poet. Because I think that's what the main subject of Stephen's lecture was: the dwindling of common ground between a poet and his readership. In the nineteenth century, a poet and his audience had quite a lot to share. Whereas . . . in subsequent time it is quite obvious that, for instance today, the charge of being esoteric is leveled against very plain-speaking poets very frequently. It is simply because the common ground rarely exists. If the poet today makes classical references, it immediately opens him to the charge of being obscure. Therefore, this issue of the "I" and the other is basically a question of the common consciousness of the common language. I don't really know where I am taking this, but I was trying to take it away a little bit from stressing this distinction between self and "I." It is what emerges in the reader's mind when he hears the poet saying "I." One question is whether he identifies with that pronoun, or whether he feels estranged and looks at the poem as a kind of purist text or artifact. A more interesting question for me is this: the industrial revolution, the advent of TV and newspapers, creates this disintegration of the previous common verbal ground; but to what extent do you think that the "I" of the poet is influenced by the preceding styles, or by poets working in the same generation? For instance, it is my belief that every poet, apart from genuine reasons, apart from the creative urge of youth, perhaps unknowingly, but I think rather wittingly, reacts against the existing dominant fashion in literature. Would you have anything to say on whether the "I" of the poet is affected or depends on the preceding or current modes of expression in poetry?

Stephen Spender: Yes, I think that the Romantics and the Victorians repudiated the kind of "I" that there was in eighteenth-century poetry. It always seems to me that the reasons that are offered by the Romantics and even right up to the twentieth century with A.E. Housman or Quiller-Couch, the editor of *The Oxford Book of English Poetry;* the real reason they disliked Pope, for instance, and considered him a prose writer was not because they had read *The Rape of the Lock* and thought that compared with *Endymion* it was a much more fantastic feat of imagination. They didn't like the poet in the poem. They had the romantic conception that the poet in the poem had to somehow be completely identical with the poem. The reason why the Romantic poet is so identified with his own poetry is because he feels isolated and shut off; he has to invite or persuade the reader to look at nature. He is always trying to make the reader look at something which is not just him outside himself. But he can only do this by making the reader completely share his experience and, in Wordsworth's case, share the experience of being Wordsworth. With Wordsworth, the reader has to go back to his own childhood, which is really the only common ground Wordsworth has with the reader. In fact, I think he makes this very clear in the passage from *The Prelude* which I read last night, in which he says that when I was on my mother's lap I had this sense of a presence of a life which was hers, and beyond that there was nature, which I was receiving at the same time I the child was giving. He says "he" the child. He turns to "I" at the end of the passage, but he is really saying "I" in order to try to generalize. Then he says that most people are completely cut off when they stop being children and then they are brought back to themselves, while for Wordsworth this sense of presence goes on throughout life. So the poet is forced into this position because he feels so completely isolated; and Whitman does exactly the same thing by saying, Reader, be me, or be yourself. If you are your "I," I am "I" also, and we can not only understand one another, but there is a complete interchange. Whitman would have everyone in America like this, totally sincere and totally existing. I think that this point of view is terribly infectious, and I think we are more romantics really than anything else. Yet the "I" which is a point of identity is also a point of weakness, so that when you have explored all of the possibilities of existence and your sense of your own being, as Wordsworth did, you then relate it to the outer world and you see that, after all, this pure existence is something no one can live up to, including the poet himself. So the Victorians are terribly split; they still have this romantic sense of poetry, they produce these wonderful visions of existing which the reader can share. But at the same time, as Victorians, they don't quite believe in it. Matthew Arnold is a wonderful example of that. He was always writing poetry about how the life of poetry is the real life, but for God's sake don't live it because you have to be a good Victorian. Or just live it when you and I (a lady whose name isn't to be mentioned in the poem) meet together. As the "I" is split, then one tries to eliminate it altogether. I think that the reference to modern poetry is that modern poetry is, as you say, influenced by either accepting or reacting against this situation rather than the concept.

Joseph Brodsky: That is a peculiar thing – every modern poet chooses not to use the first-person pronoun, he tries to be objective.

Mark Strand: That is not entirely true. I think the twentieth-century poet or latter-day romantic is more emotive, more isolated than certainly Wordsworth. One of the differences is, I think, that the certainty about the self in Wordsworth is enormous. There is no twentieth-century poet who writes out of that degree of certainty. When you read *The Prelude*, the presence of the self is so powerful that it acts as an authenticating agent; the experience is there because the self in some way has preceded it. In the twentieth century we have gone so far that when you read Robert Lowell (this is not to say that Lowell is a minor or a weak poet), the self is authenticated by the experience, the self is not emblematic as it is for someone like Wordsworth. There are so many place names in Lowell, so many facts, so many details that it is the kind of journalism that exists in a lot of confessional poetry. No contemporary poet would allow himself the kind of generalities that exist in Wordsworth; there is just not that certitude.

Stephen Spender: Yes, I am very glad you said that. If I were to develop this idea, I thought that I'd find myself defending journalism; and as much as we all despise journalism, journalism is a much stronger element even in Auden and Eliot, for instance. The *Four Quartets* are full of editorializing. What does Eliot mean when he says "I"? It is like "we." "We" arrived and "we" accomplished this. One despises editorializing of the self, but it is not despicable really. It is an element that is being picked up by poets and used for their poetry.

Mark Strand: Well, in poets who write about themselves, the American so-called confessional poets, that element of journalism is absolutely necessary because it is the only thing that allows them to say "I am." I am because I have had such-and-such an experience, I have been here, I have taken these pills, etc., etc.

James Tuttleton: I have to agree with that. What makes Wordsworth a very powerful poet is that sense of self that is projected. What I see

The "I" as an other in poetry

as problematic in much of modern poetry is the very uncertain relation to the identity of the poet that is generated out of this Keatsian idea that the poet doesn't have any identity, that he is a chameleon, everybody and nobody. We are bombarded with this. I am speaking of Goffman's presentational self; in everyday life, we are just a cluster of projections, of various functions or roles. I think the poet suffers that. In much modern verse it seems to me that the only way he can aggregate to himself a sense of identity is through the journalism of names, place, dates, descriptions, and so on.

Mark Strand: It is done in several ways. There are the poets who are representative of something much larger than themselves without subscribing to a religion or a political party but whose desire is to represent the age. A certain amount of detail is necessary for demonstrating that you do belong to the age. That project is a much larger one really than the authentication of the self.

Stephen Spender: But what is the relation of the poet to reader? It seems that one of the signs of the romantic is the romantic is always a hotted up version of the reader. I mean the confessional poet has more to confess than the reader can ever quite believe, and at the end he has to commit suicide.

Mark Strand: I don't think there is that degree of identification because there is not that degree of amplitude. I think that very often the confessional poet becomes an entertainer. I don't think that it is easy to identify with Lowell, in *Life Studies;* I don't think that it is easy to identify with John Berryman in *Dream Songs.* I think that the voice somehow becomes very idiosyncratic and, as a bolster to that, the experiences are very definitely theirs.

Stephen Spender: But how can you communicate unless somehow Wordsworth persuades you? Through Wordsworth entering into Wordsworth's childhood, through your memory of your own childhood, you have the door which enters right into nature. Then, there is a kind of illusion, a hallucination of philosophy which arises from this. You feel you are entering into a state of mind in which you feel philosophy rather than think it. Unless there is some chain of identification, I don't see how one can enter into a confessional. Romantic poetry is really confessional poetry, isn't it?

Participant: It is self-exploration more than confession.

James Tuttleton: That is exactly where the common ground between the poet and the audience is lost. I think we surrender ourselves to a Wordsworth because of that sense of identity. We don't really surrender ourselves, I would submit, to Whitman. He projects a stong sense of self, but he subverts it in claiming that he is simply a composite of all of us; he really is not. I think that to the extent that the modern poet abandons, let's say, the kind of self projected in Pope and engages in this exploration of his chameleon variety, he is likely to focus on eccentricities that estrange him from the reader.

Participant: But when we can read Lowell, we use Lowell as a touchstone for ourselves, as an intensely personal one on one, rather than two in a culture.

Mark Strand: I think it is a little drastic to ask that of the reader in the case of Lowell. Each of us keeps a locked razor, but not all the time. It is much easier to dip into *The Prelude*.

I think that there is a difference between the English and the Americans. To make a distinction between Whitman and Wordsworth, one of the ingratiating things about Wordsworth is that when you read *The Prelude*, it is really the second time around. Part of the authority that he has is because he is going back to something that he has experienced before and reexperiences again in a more powerful way. Whitman, on the other hand, is really creating the world; it is a different kind of attention that you pay and a different kind of experience. It is not one of identification; you are participating in the project. He keeps asking the reader to join him in a belief that somehow exists outside of the poem. It is not part of the texture of the poem. The poem is insistent, it is very often aggravating; the poem can go on too long. It does almost everything to tire the reader.

Joseph Brodsky: You are still talking about the thematic bond between the reader and the poet, whether the reader recognizes himself in this treatment of the subject matter, or even in this detail. In the first place, a poem is the diction, and the subject matter can be as alien as the description of some biological species. The diction would still be recognizable for a reader. It is my understanding of Whitman, for instance, that what makes him so recognizable to an American is not so much what he is saying as the verse itself, which is based on the Protestant Bible. When an American hears an agitated speech, the first thing that comes to his mind is a preacher, and Whitman has that quality. He employs that verse.

Also, Mark spoke of the distinction between the English and the American. I am not in the best position to observe this, but I wonder how much the distinction you make between, say,

The "I" as an other in poetry

Wordsworth and Keats, how much the polarization between Romantics and Victorians, derives from, should I say, the class attitude or the class-oriented conscious. In the eighteenth century we had gentlemen, whereas in the nineteenth century we had, so to speak, rentiers. I think that in what Keats says about Wordsworth there is a great deal of the pose of the rentier talking about the class that he doesn't belong to. Every next class or succeeding class is prone to criticize its predecessors. I just wonder about that.

Richard Sennett: I'd like to go back to the first point, to talk about what seems to me to be very important. There is another way to think about this which is not thematic, but which goes back to the distinction between the "I" and the self. In a psychoanalytic text, the "I" appears as equivalent with what you call verse. I mean the "I" is something that is made through language. The "me" is that thematic content: This is what I am and I make a laundry list.

Joseph Brodsky: To me it is already a lyricism.

Richard Sennett: Yes, but the "I" is something that is much more elusive and strong at the same time, it's emotion: The "I" is an act of speaking. It seems to me that where one would want to add on to what you are doing, or introduce another dimension to how a poem is constructed, is to ask how you construct a discourse or how the action of speech is creative of an "I" as opposed to this thematic content. Whenever you can point to something and say "that's me," the pointer already has a distance from the "that's me." Whenever you can say "This is how it was," there is distance. It is a distance which also creates an activity. Since I can speak about something that is in my past or something I belonged to, since I can make a laundry list, then I exist to the very degree that I can create that distance.

Mark Strand: I think that whether it is you, I, he, she, it, they are equivalent fictions. "I," for the purposes of a poem, might be more powerful, more suggestive, or perhaps better, but I think that when we write a poem we are very far from the raw inchoate self, the real "I," if you will.

Richard Sennett: There is a tremendous trick to that because a really good confessional writer can, in the act of confessing everything, run farther and farther away from the reader. With someone like Nabokov, for instance, the more we know about his various guises, the less Nabokov is an active presence in the prose, the farther away he becomes. It is a tremendous trick. How that "I" exists is something that is made, I should have thought, in the structure of the poem, in its way of speaking, and not in this thematic identification.

Stephen Spender: I think a poet is not really thinking of "I" all the time. When you are writing a poem you are thinking about writing a poem.

Richard Sennett: I think that the problem is the problem about all thinking, all expressive thinking. If one wanted to have that raw Wordsworthian "I" in the sense that Stephen is talking about, the child has to shut up. That is to say, if it is to have that absolute thematical identification between our own childhood and that childhood, that little child can never speak; it exists as a kind of object, as a thing we can identify with. But the moment it begins to talk, a separation occurs, and it is that that seems to me to be a very crucial psychological distinction between the "I" and the "me." The stronger an "I" gets, the more it can push the "me" away from that active voice; that active voice becomes freer – it isn't prisoner, for instance, of a memory, but it can have many memories. That is what I would understand to be an ego. That is, one is capable of producing lots of kinds of "me's" – that's what creativity in ordinary speech consists of. Whenever I talk, I don't have to, as it were, play the same record. That is how speech is enabled to have a free "I" in ordinary speech. It seems to me in poetry the problem in analyzing an "I" has to be how you locate the poet's freedom. To hear different voices in a poem seems to me to indicate the presence of an "I."

Denis Donoghue: Of course, a lot depends on the analogies you are using. I think that a good deal of what you read today about the self is confused, because it is based upon a false analogy. The analogy that most writers seem to have in mind is that the self exists by analogy with the way in which an object exists. Then, of course, it is an appalling experience if you discover there is no such object. But suppose, for example, that we were to shift our analogies: Suppose we were to regard the self not existing on the analogy of an object but existing on the analogy of function, an algebraic function which has no existence except in relation to other functions – then we would talk far more about relations. I notice that Richard Sennett used the word *action*, which seems to me very interesting in this connection as moving one away from the terminology of objects and toward actions and relations. I must say my own feeling increas-

The "I" as an other in poetry

ingly is that it doesn't matter, or it matters only in one connection. If we reify the notion of self in this way, and if then a great deal of evidence is brought to bear which suggests that in fact there is no such thing, then we are defeated into saying that we've been very empty. Now one possibility is to give up the reification altogether, but another way of looking at this is to say that it doesn't matter except in relation to the particular sentiments which the axiom of self provokes in the poet. I'm thinking, for example, of the nineteenth century. To me, the most almost-violent assertion of self, or rather the sentiment of selfhood, is in a note of Hopkins – not in one of his letters, but in one of his more confessional private notes. He says in effect that the only thing he feels absolutely certain about is the self, his own self, and he uses the language very interestingly; he uses the language of taste – that the taste of something, or the smell, is the way in which he has this conviction of his self, and that he has no such conviction of anything else. And, by implication, that includes God, for instance. Now that, of course, to Hopkins was really an appalling predicament, whereas to a more secularly inclined poet it would be wonderful. Yet it seems to me that it makes, literally, all the difference in the world which group of analogies we take. I think in my own case I've often been guilty of appearing to reify the self and then proceed to defend the self as if I were defending a bridge or defending my home. In fact it is, of course, very difficult to think in any other terms. It is very difficult to think in terms which say the visual analogy doesn't apply, and that is why I think it is very difficult when we are being told these days that we are merely to think of these things as relations. It may be that we have to give up our old habits of reification.

Richard Sennett: It is very common in psychology to make a distinction between character and personality. And it is one of those common distinctions that seems very plausible until one begins to think about it. A character exists purely in a world that's moral. It exists in a world of social relations. The poet is a "bad man." We would speak about that as having to do with his or her character. Whereas a personality is something that in a way is the capacity to detach oneself from that world of relations with that attitude about it. The trouble is that this act of detachment is in fact a kind of war on oneself as an object. Then again, it comes down to the question of what you mean by an "I." If you want to stick to the "I" as being a theme, what is it that a poet like Keats is revealing? It seems to me that very little of Keats's personality, as we would now understand that term, is present in his poetry, but a great deal of what we would see as his character is. That is a way of talking about Keats as an object. What I have in mind is the following: If somebody could only tell you one story, confess one story in their poem, this distinction between character and personality wouldn't exist. But if the poet can tell you many stories about his life and if, as the stories change, the feelings that they arouse cohere; then we could say that there is a presence, I would think, of a poetic personality. That means he/she confesses to many different things; she confesses "I did it," "I didn't do it," and so on. The nature of the confession or the nature of the "I" revealed is immaterial. That character is totally plastic, but the qualities of the revelation are, when they cohere, when you hear many different stories being told about one's past but you hear the same speaker telling them, then it seems to me you're in the presence of an "I." And that has to go back to what Joseph was saying, that it has to do with something about the way somebody writes, not what they point to.

Joseph Brodsky: Poetry absorbs all of those things, the "I" means all of those things: It means self, it means persona, it means the character in the poem, and so on. But basically, when a poet sets out to write a poem, the main urge he experiences is not to convey the peculiarities of his psyche, ego, or whatever; the main thing that sends him into motion is a certain noise, a certain sense of harmony to which he subordinates all those notions we mentioned before. This sense of harmony molds this notion into the final product of the poem. It is quite true that every poem, insofar as it is, well, poetry, is an incurably semantic enterprise; and therefore we can discern traces of personality, traces of self, idiosyncracies. But the main thing is that a poem has its own dynamic, and it spins itself off. For instance, you say several things in a poem, and yet you somehow sense it requires two or three or more stanzas to make an audio or phonetic unit. Very frequently you end up by saying things that you had not planned originally to say. The question is, How does the reader take in all those things? What creates a common bond, a common ground? What makes the reader go through that poem? In my view, it is not necessarily the identification or recognition or joy or disgust of recognition of certain statements within the poem; what makes him finish the poem is the more visceral pleasure of seeing those words assembled in this or that fashion. What we are dealing with, really, is the common language, not the common notions, and the common sense of harmony. All those poets differed from one another throughout the history of poetry, because each of them tried to exert a slightly different note of linguistic lyricism – this is what makes a reader hooked or interested in reading that poem. We are all interested in lyrical possibilities, so it is a disagreeable thing in my view to reduce poetry to its paraphrasable content, however intricate the paraphrasing itself may be. And yet we are getting something out of it – lyricism can be rendered as message or as content. The most interesting thing about lyricism is that it bears no relation whatsoever to the reality. What distinguishes a work of art from any artshow experience is that in art, in the material itself, you can achieve that degree, that pitch of lyricism which is absolutely unattainable in any human interplay, for instance. This is what makes poetry different from, say, prose. All those elements, psychological analysis, etc., are just components that are by no means the purpose of the poet's undertaking.

Stephen Spender: I am sure that is correct, but Keats's own question is then a problem of the great poem. *The Fall of Hyperion* is the poem that sets up, establishes a ratio between, a whole world of the imagination created by the poet. In order that the poet can create, this he has to create himself. This is what Keats says, that he has to create himself; that is where we come back to self and being. He divides poets into the poets who write the kind of poetry that they can write, but he says that they are not setting up this ratio. They are just dreamers. The point is what kinds of dreams one has. Are they just the dreams we all have, or does one create oneself in such a way that one creates a dream which is not (I hate the word escape) escaping from the world, but creating a world of the imagination? Yeats was also concerned with creating a world of the imagination, which, to use Arnoldian language, was a criticism of the real world. This is what *The Fall of Hyperion* is about. The poet is one for whom the misery of the world is misery. He must deliberately make that awareness of human misery a part of his consciousness; he must pass these terrible tests of going up the marble steps and, in doing so, nearly destroying himself, nearly dying. It's that sort of distinction.

Joseph Brodsky: Yes, I wouldn't make the distinction so sharply; I would say we certainly have dreams and you are a dreamer. I remember what you said yesterday about the great poems that bear a nearly direct relation to the greatness of the phenomenon they describe. Since the phenomenon is out there regardless of your talents, you are challenged all the time by its scope; and your real task is to produce something on the paper which would bear a certain relation or which would contain such a strength in itself that it would reveal something about the phenomenon.

Let me put it slightly differently. I think a poem or poetic oeuvre should represent to the reader a certain mental or verbal unity, which being by definition far smaller than the world outside would be able to withstand that world's pressure. It should have this kind of spine in itself. It is a dreaming enterprise, and yet poetry is often a cunning enterprise as well. You are making all your choices; you substitute one word for another. It is a very shrewd process; it is a very analytical process. The miseries of the world become your miseries, they are your miseries by definition from the very threshold. There is no point in rationalizing about that because we belong to the same species.

Aileen Ward: I would like to pick up a phrase that Mr. Spender quoted from an earlier letter of Keats. In fact this was not about *The Fall of Hyperion*, but about the writing of *Endymion*: "that which is created must create itself." Keats wrote this long poem in order to prove to himself that he had the capacity for the great poem. It was not a great poem, but he learned from the failure, from the very imperfection that he sensed in himself. This making of the self is central to the Romantics; the world is not given, it is to be discovered in the very writing of poetry.

Stephen Spender: It's very strong in Keats.

Aileen Ward: Yes, I think it is perhaps good to remind ourselves that Keats's condemnation of Wordsworth as representing the egotistical sublime did not apply to *The Prelude*, which was not to be published for another thirty-odd years, but really to *The Excursion*, that editorializing poem that *The Prelude* was the prelude to. When Denis speaks of the self as functional instead of as a thing, I think this is a great formula for *The Prelude* and the way Wordsworth makes himself in it. Each wave of *The Prelude* is going out from the completely self-centered infant, who first of all goes out to his mother who mediates the world around him, which he can then begin to proceed outward to. But the great experiences of *The Prelude* are precisely when each time the self-absorbed little child, or self-absorbed adolescent, or young man comes up against some new dimension of the world outside of himself with great surprise or shock. The shock of encountering the blind beggar, for instance, on the streets of London jars Wordsworth out of self-preoccupation, out of egotisticalness (that is a horrible word to use), and into relatedness. And he becomes bit by bit that man speaking to men. This is my favorite phrase from Wordsworth: "who bears everywhere with him relationship and love." It's the notion that the self has built the relationships that I think is fundamental.

Mark Strand: It doesn't happen often and it doesn't happen in Wordsworth's later poetry. I think he is lamenting the world of men more than relating to it. I think also that those figures that he encounters are projections of his own isolation sometimes. The idea of sympathy can be challenged. For example, in the crowds of London he gives a very unsympathetic view of other people.

Aileen Ward: But that is Wordsworth in what you might call *The Prelude* state, before he has suddenly found a way to relate, and it is these encounters with the beggar and the old soldier on the road that jar him out of that state.

Mark Strand: . . . But he finds a way through nature and in order to be in nature you have to be alone; . . . that old soldier is encountered alone. The mythologizing of these creatures is a way of fortifying his own isolation and his desire for some kind of truth to be found in the unity of his person . . . apart from the world, I mean. *The Prelude* is after all an escape from the city. He leaves London as if it were a jail. That is an interesting departure if we are going to speak of the twentieth century. One of the earmarks of the so-called confessional poets is that they find themselves as city people. There is something determinately urban about Lowell and Berryman – they're always chatting to others. That's one thing the Romantic, or at least Wordsworth, chose not to do.

Aileen Ward: I can't agree with you about this notion of isolation. Wordsworth had an isolated childhood, as a boy growing up in the wilds of Westmoreland, but . . .

Mark Strand: . . . The thing is that you cannot be aware of other peoples' otherness if you are always moralizing about them.

Stephen Spender: I think "Resolution in Independence" is an absolutely wonderful poem, but it doesn't really enter into the nature of the leech gatherer; he is just a moral, a bit of the landscape . . . ; that is what is really wonderful about it, this image of him being like a cloud or a rock. Yet all he really gets from the leech gatherer is a sense of his own inadequacy. He learns something about himself.

Aileen Ward: Yes, but he also ends with a resolution about the future: that he will think back on the leech gatherer on the moor when he feels the need for being fortified in the independence that the leech gatherer is such a splendid example of.

Stephen Spender: Do you think he's entered into a leech gatherer's life? It is not like Tolstoy meeting a leech gatherer.

Aileen Ward: It seems to me a paradigm of that Wordsworthian pattern I was trying to set up of a self-preoccupation broken in on by an encounter with another.

Stephen Spender: I just wonder whether self-absorption shouldn't be qualified by saying that everything outside Wordsworth has to go through the machinery which is Wordsworth and be reinvented, but it all remains Wordsworth. Wordsworth invented the Lake District; people go up and stay at little hotels and look at the Wordsworth country. But it has been created for us by Wordsworth's experiencing of it through his childhood and his maturity. Dr. Johnson would have hated it, wouldn't he?

Aileen Ward: I wonder if this... isn't simply a mark of Wordsworth's power as a poet, a whole area of experience which we can identify in our own minds as Wordsworthian, like an area of experience we call Mozartian, which has been created for us by contact with this great experiencer, this great creator.

Richard Sennett: Stephen, you said you hadn't the time yesterday to talk about modern poets.

Stephen Spender: No, I just felt that now I have to reread Berryman and Lowell. I just think that modern poets still feel the same problems, although they are aware of the limitations of romanticism, and I in my own mind divide modern poets into those who try to write an objective kind of poetry and the confessionals. Eliot believed that poetry is not the expression of self but the gradual destruction of it. In Rimbaud, the self becomes an instrument of sensibility, which is struck by the most terrible experiences external to it, and then produces a cry like a person being tortured who suddenly hears a scream and realizes in a surprised way that it is himself screaming. Then there are the confessional poets. Here we have mentioned Berryman and Lowell. I wonder how far they are really confessional poets...

Mark Strand: Actually, I think it is a misnomer. I don't think they confess

The "I" as an other in poetry

very much. Any man, such as Lowell, who calls one of his books *History* is not confessing. I think of Dylan Thomas or perhaps Sylvia Plath as an example.... The interesting thing about Sylvia Plath is how she doesn't fit in with the others; when you read her, it is not news that you're getting. With Anne Sexton... it is an entirely different experience. Sylvia Plath is almost a Spaniard among these others... It's as though she were hearing those black sounds that Lorca talks about. The matter of her unconscious is very available, and she writes out of an entirely different state. She is not commenting on her existence, the way Anne Sexton is, nor is she dramatizing it the way Anne Sexton is; it's a much more powerful poetry... I think if you examine all of the so-called confessional poets you will find they are all quite different and they don't constitute a viable school. There are those who mythologize the self. Their versions of self are so generalized... that they are almost Wordsworthian. I mean, the self that Wordsworth presents us with is, for example, quite general, which is one of the reasons that we are able to enter in. All of us can identify, all of us can have, Wordsworthian moments.

Aileen Ward: I would like to put one last question to you... Stephen Spender; I think of the poem that begins "I think continually of those who are truly great...," and one thing that strikes me is that you have talked about the sense of self and the "I" in relation to a great many other poets, but not in relation to your own poetry.

Stephen Spender: Well, when I'm writing my own poetry I never think about these things at all. Robert Lowell made a very funny remark about that poem. When he was slightly crazy one of the things Lowell did was to try to rewrite, first of all, all his own poems, and then he started rewriting other peoples' poems. So he rewrote "I think continually of those who are truly great...," and the first line was, "I would think continually of those who are truly great..."

VIRGIL THOMSON

Music does not flow: constant and variable elements in music's patterning

Comparing history to a stream, no doubt a vigorous idea when new, seems nowadays less urgent, especially regarding the arts. So also does belief in their continuing progress, as if any series of related events involved necessarily a destination.

I prefer to think of the arts as a museum or as a wine cellar. These comparisons would leave room for paying honor to great soils, great years, great workmen, and also for preserving ancient methods. Museums and libraries are mainly devoted anyway to conserving works and ways that are no longer fashionable to imitate.

Gertrude Stein used to say that nothing changes from generation to generation except what people are looking at. Actually what people have thought they were looking at, arranged in chronological order, makes up whatever consistent fairy tale that history can be imagined to illustrate. And though repeating patterns do seem to recur in any such narrative, organic developments are notoriously difficult to identify. In the arts, certainly, the creating, elaborating, and transmitting of techniques are basic procedures, but among these there are few long-term growths. They are more like inventions – say the fishnet, the wheelbarrow, or piecrust – which, once they have come miraculously into being, stay on. And as for the game of "influences," which reviewers, and sometimes even historians, like to play, it is in my view about as profitable a study as who caught cold from whom when they were all sitting in the same draft.

Nevertheless, since what people are looking at changes constantly, everything can seem to be changing. Also, the things that don't change, like wheelbarrows and fishnets and piecrust, are always there. Playing games and eating and childbirth and death, for example, change almost not at all; they merely get arranged into stories about people doing

Music does not flow

them, into literature. And in this literature people move around and talk; sometimes they even sing. This makes for plays and films and operas. And in all these kinds of entertainment the element that affects people most intensely, that makes chills run up and down the spine, the digestive apparatus work faster, and the breath hold or catch, is music. This element has no precise meaning and no dictionary. But it does provoke intensities; and it provokes these so rapidly and so powerfully that all the other elements – the verbal ones and the visual ones for sure – more often than not call on music's transports for reinforcing their own cooler communications. Music's lack of specific meaning, moreover, allows it to be attached to other continuities without contradicting them. The way that singing can give acoustical reinforcement to speech – can shape it, help it to run along and to carry – this is music's gift to liturgical observances, to prayers, hymns, and magical incantations, as well as to mating ceremonials like social dancing.

The composition of music not intended for provoking movement or for singing, and involving no spectacle other than that of men at work, is a quite recent invention, dating as a public show from, at the earliest, about 1600. But its elaboration during the last four centuries has made of music in Europe and in the West generally an art independent of liturgical circumstances, of dancing, of poetry, even of the singing voice.

Now how can an activity without clear meaning hold the attention of people who are not doing anything but just sitting there? It would seem that over recent centuries there has developed for instrumental music, if not a vocabulary of meanings, a way of suggesting things that is capable, shall we say, of halfway evoking them and thus of attaching its own intensities to quite a variety of thoughts.

These evocations are of three kinds. There is that of the human voice singing metrical verse or intoning unmetered prose. Everything verbal, from lullabies to oratory to rigmaroles, is receptive to this kind of treatment. Instrumental music of this kind is in Europe called *strophic*.

A second kind, though perhaps it should have come first – it is so ancient and so easy to do – is known as *choric;* and it can remind us, through a one-two one-two beat, of marching, or, through more fanciful countings-out, of dancing, either ritual and religious or social.

There can also be attractions for the mind through the following of some tonal texture, as in Sebastian Bach's fugal patterns. I do not know a Greek origin word for this kind of music; but when it is enlivened by unexpected waits and irregular stresses, this exploiting of the surprise factor, as both Bach and Beethoven practiced it so masterfully or as we encounter it nowadays in a jam session, could be called, I suppose, *spastic*.

In any case, it is one of the things that instrumental music does, music that is made only for being listened to. And the assemblage of all these kinds of musical gesture – the poetico-oratorical, the movement-provoking, the intellectually complex and surprising – into a composition involving many kinds of variety is the very special achievement of our Viennese masters – Mozart, Haydn, Beethoven, and Schubert. And what do all their grand Sonatas and Symphonies communicate? Anxiety-and-relief patterns, I should say, experiences cerebral from their ability to hold attention, but surely emotive and visceral in their immediate effect.

The continuity devices that purely instrumental music has employed toward these ends are the only discoveries I know of in music's history that even remotely resemble new species. And they were certainly not arrived at by organic evolution. Even today they are so far from having a clear morphology that there is no textbook anywhere for teaching them, no *Formenlehre*, old or new.

Now let us look a little into the permanent materials of music: tones, intervals, and their ordering in time.

By time I mean measured time. The recitation of prose and poetry also exists in time, but that time is not a chain of fixed durations. Movies also are a time art; and their small bits joined together into a continuity, though this final cutting can be measured, every second of it, these bits really make up only a psychological pattern not meant to be perceived independently.

Music's time patterns, on the other hand, are there to be noticed. Their rhythmic and metrical structure controls the tonal one so powerfully that it actually gives to music most of whatever clear meaning it may seem to have. Rhythm is therefore both a stable and a stabilizing element and can be viewed as a constant, something of which neither the nature nor the function changes, though its designs may be infinitely various. And these designs, for all their constantly recurring elaborations in different times and places, are limited by the inability of the human mind to perceive as a unit any count larger than two, three, and just possibly a fast five. Rhythm, therefore, is hopelessly tied to footwork and to language, to meaning, to expression. It can copy, but it cannot grow or evolve. Speeds and loudnesses, moreover, being subject to choice by performers, are no firm part of any pattern.

The so-called harmonic series – all the intervals that can be generated

Music does not flow

from one fundamental tone – are another constant in musical organization. The pitch of the fundamental on which a composition is based can vary from piece to piece, or even from one performance to another. But the relation of that fundamental to its overtones remains the same whatever the pitch may be. These intervals are fixed by nature, and our awareness of them is very ancient.

Actually the Greeks knew much of what we know regarding the first dozen or more of these, the Hindus and the ancient Chinese possibly more than the Greeks. Their number, though theoretically infinite, is for practical performance limited to about half a hundred, or fewer. Mixing them gives great variety to sound color. Transposing them into a single octave for use as modes or scales is a convenience that has been available for many millennia. Falsifying them to facilitate pattern-making has long been common practice, the European "tempered scale" of twelve equidistant semitones being already more than two centuries old. A somewhat less acceptable tuning practice is to mix the overtones of slightly different fundamentals. This produces an acoustical interference known as *vibrato*. Mixing those from distant fundamentals is likely to cause more complex interferences and to erase clear pitch. We call these mixtures *noise*.

Arrangements of continuities within any scalar pattern, commonly called "music," have long been thought to be good for the spirits and to give pleasure. Noise has no such reputation; indeed it is known to produce exasperation and bad temper. And though it is easy to compose noises into a pattern, it has been a fancy of only recent times to call such arrangements music. Modern art-workers, I must say, do like joining contradictions into a single concept. Nevertheless, the contradictory terms embodied in the idea of noise-music are not by any means terms of equal semantic weight. In fact the sounds of noise, being governed by no single harmonic series, are only weakly interrelated and thus cannot lend themselves nearly so well to acoustical structuring as the sounds of music do. Entertaining they can be, as we know from percussion orchestras. And in Africa, notably in Nigeria and the Cameroon, persons at some distance are said to communicate words without the help of any pronouncing voice. All this is both lively and useful. Noise-music makes a valued addition, in fact, to our repertory of ear experiences, and it is capable, by isolating the rhythmic element, of encouraging its growth in complexity. There is nothing wrong with it so long as it is not offered as a substitute for music's ancient and visceral tone ecstasies.

Virgil Thomson

Moreover, the harmonic series and its intervals are not only a delight, they are another of music's constant elements. They exist in nature, and though refinements of perception may (just may) show a history of progress, the way these are perceived is built into the human body. I am not a specialist in this matter, but I can tell you a few things I have read. One is about an experiment carried out some years ago in Switzerland that tends to demonstrate that musical intervals are perceived by the brain not as a mixture of tones but as a result of their overlay.

The experiment goes as follows. You channel into one ear an electronically produced pure pitch low enough in volume so that there will be no convection by the skull. Into the other ear you feed a similar sound pitched higher by the interval of a fifth. According to the account published in *Gravezaner Blätter*, July 1955, the brain does not hear these two pitches as any recognizable interval but only as a noise. On the other hand, if you feed both tones into one ear (either ear), the brain will instantly recognize the fifth, a phenomenon preservable in the hearing's memory bank as a perception of external fact. An attempt to reproduce this experiment made several years ago in Princeton, New Jersey, gave indecisive results. The operating engineers from RCA found it successful, but the musicians present all maintained that they could identify as separate tones the pitches produced independently.

More extended speculation about music's relation to acoustical fact is to be found at the beginning of a very long book by a famous Swiss conductor, the late Ernest Ansermet. This is entitled *Les Fondements de la musique dans la conscience humaine* (The Bases of Music in Human Consciousness). Its reasonings are derived from further evidence regarding the human ear's attachment to the harmonic series, even perhaps of its evolution therefrom. This evidence, according to Ansermet, is that the semicircular canals of the middle ear have a shape, definable by natural logorithms, that compels the air within them to vibrate in response to the harmonic series, also governed by natural logorithms.

Our learned conductor argues further that twelve-tone-row music, which uses only twelve intervals, all tempered and all uncorrectable on keyboard instruments, is a road leading to no musically pleasurable destination. Arnold Schönberg, its inventor, has been said to boast that this method of composition would assure for at least two more centuries the predominance of German music. I find in the music of the chief twelve-tone masters – Schönberg, Berg, and Webern – that though it bears many marks of individual genius, the actual sound of its built-in

Music does not flow

off-pitchness tends to be sensuously not very satisfying. Also, I see no reason why music today should seek to perpetuate a German domination. Neither can I do more about the new researches on musical hearing than to hope they are right. And I cherish this hope because I like music to be in tune and to sound well. I also think that the intervals when sounded in tune have a great variety of expressive power, whereas twelve-tone-row music has always tended rather toward monotony of expression.

What I do hope for sincerely is proof that not only do intervals exist as an experience built into the brain but that chords as well may turn out to have a real existence. From my own experience I would willingly award this to six of them, which any musical child can recognize. They include the major and minor triads, the diminished seventh, the dominant seventh, the augmented triad, and any three or four notes out of a whole-tone scale. All mixtures outside of these I tend to identify as either real-chords-with-added-notes, or as tone clusters, or as agglomerates. Real chords sounded simultaneously can, of course, create a polychordal complex, and the acoustical principles that govern the use of these in composition, as well as the psychological ones involved in their perception, merit investigation by composers as well as by psychologists. Polyharmony is, after all, a natural extension of the contrapuntal principle.

In spite of Arnold Schönberg's practice of treating all the intervals as having equal rights, whether they are scored in stack-up to look like chords or laid out in a row like melodies, we all know, I think, that they differ in strength, by which I mean their power to build a loudness. They may well differ in expressive intensity, in their relation to our built-in awareness of them, and thus to some kind of pleasure–pain gamut. In Berlin at the Institute for Comparative Musical Research, there is an instrument that produces electronically (that is to say in a pure state) the first fifty or more of them; and among these there is a major seventh so sharp, as related to our experience of this interval in its more common varieties, that I found hearing it actually painful. The belief of Alain Danièlou, the institute's former director, is that the whole gamut of intervals is allied to our gamut of feelings. And though it is far from certain that any such relation is codifiable semantically, we may well be able to experience fifty shades of emotion.

Certainly we have no such number of names for identifying them. And they unquestionably vary in their *affect* through associations, proximities, colorations, stresses, and durations – their rhetoric, in

VIRGIL THOMSON

short. Actually I see no reason to deny that the constants of music, which begin with rhythm and meter and go on to cover all the possible combinations of tones within any harmonic series, are not only structural elements for aiding memory but expressive vocabularies as well. Not dictionaries of emotion at all, but repertories of device for provoking feelings without defining them.

The defining of our sentiments has long been a preoccupation of religions and of governments. And the most powerful of these tie-ups has always been music's marriage to poetry. Music has no connection at all with touch, taste, or smell; and Musak piped into art galleries has never taken on. Films and dancing do require music, but they don't want it overly complex. Actually Igor Stravinsky's most complex ballet scores – *Petrouchka*, say, and *The Rite of Spring*, even *The Firebird* – have long tended to shed their choreographies and to survive purely as concert pieces.

More durable matings have long taken place between music and words, and the music in any such union is likely to prove stronger than the words. How often has a fine melody worn out its verse and taken on another! Or crossed a frontier and changed its language! Tunes move as easily from the secular to the sacred as from the Ganges to the Mississippi. It is part of the way things people are looking at change.

What does not change, or hardly changes at all, is the way words and music fit when they do fit. That too seems to be a constant. Instrumental styles vary with fashion, but the singing of prose and poetry changes little throughout the life of a language. During the Middle Ages, so long as Latin was for Western Christians the language of worship, the musical settings of liturgical texts, being monolinear, could be melodically quite elaborate. For much of this time, of course, Latin was a dead language, immobilized by its plethora of long vowels and by the progressive erosion of its stresses. Nor was understanding it essential. No wonder church music tended toward the flowery and the complex. With the Protestant Reformation, a German syllabification came into use. With the English Prayer Book of Edward VI (1549), patter was discovered, for that is basically the character of Anglican chant, as it is of spoken English. In Italy and France, where church Latin still survived, the seventeenth-century invention of musical tragedy in the vernacular, or opera, forced each local language to find its own musical characteristics.

My point is that when any language becomes a mature language, with

Music does not flow

a dictionary and a grammar, the musical wing almost immediately establishes a prosodic declamation for singing it. And this prosody remains. Instrumental style in music shifts constantly, vocal style very little. Here is therefore another constant element. Just think of Italian opera from Claudio Monteverdi to Luigi Nono. The handling of words in recitative, aria, and arioso has hardly changed at all, even when the vocal treatment was at its most florid. The stories of Italian opera have changed a little, and the music illustrating them quite a lot. But the words-into-music factor has hardly moved at all. The same is true in French opera from Lully and Rameau to Debussy and Poulenc. And if *Pelléas* contains little in the form of aria or set piece, its vocal line is nonetheless French recitative that Rameau himself might have written.

The German cantatas of Schütz and the oratorios of Sebastian Bach are vocally of the same family. And the songs of Franz Schubert were so clearly the model for all who came after, including Hugo Wolf and Mahler, and even Arnold Schönberg, that Richard Wagner himself, the master of them all for theatrical German, could so nearly copy Schubert's practice while enlarging it for the stage that one might almost call the singing parts of any Wagner opera just louder lieder.

A special treatment of the vocal line needs to be mentioned here, which is that of Arnold Schönberg's *Pierrot Lunaire* and which he called *Sprechstimme*. This is an exaggeration of German speech cadences which, by taking them out of control of the harmonic series, takes them also out of music and into something approaching melodrama, or speech-to-music. They are impressive, convincing, and for the most part easier to perform than would be any on-pitch musical line jumping about like that. Even so, since the German language does jump about and feels right doing so, the voice part of *Pierrot* is not unrelated to the recitatives of Jesus in Bach's *St. Matthew Passion* or to the upward full-octave scoops of Brunhilde's battle cry in Wagner's *Die Walküre*.

As for Igor Stravinsky's cantata in French, *Perséphone*, and his English opera *The Rake's Progress*, though they contain what seem to be faults of prosody, they do come over the footlights quite clearly. And their resemblance to classical French or English declamation is much closer than any parallel that might be drawn between their instrumental textures and those of historic composers, English or French. English musical declamation from Tallis through Purcell, Handel, Sullivan, and Britten is virtually unchanging, especially if you recognize Anglican chant as one of its sources. And the extremely high ranges in certain songs of William Flanagan, or of the Italian Silvano Bussetto, are merely flights of musical fancy. They do not alter very much the vowels or at all the stresses of spoken language.

In enumerating the musical elements that are not subject to change, no matter how much the ways of using them may vary, I must not omit to point out that the invention, elaboration, and eventual abandonment of technical devices do tend to follow a repeating pattern. That pattern is especially clear with regard to the historic periods of music's successive expansions. I speak of the West, of course, of Europe, of the music we know as ours. In Asia, Africa, and Indonesia, music may not behave the same way. From this distance the musics of India and of China-Korea-Japan seem relatively permanent, or at any rate subject to changes in method that come about more slowly than with us.

Our musical energy booms, if I may call them that, have averaged over the last twelve hundred years an active life of about three centuries each. I refer to the monolinear music of early medieval times, which, after its codification in the time of Pope Gregory VII created a large and fully written-down repertory, came to the end of its creative strength in the twelfth century. At that time a contrapuntal music very different in methods and procedures, as well as in expressive content, had been invented. Originally called *organum novum* (the new tool), this music was no longer monolinear but was composed as two and three tunes made for being heard together in pitch relations governed by intervals of the harmonic series. These were primarily fifths, fourths, and octaves, with secondary permissions accorded to major seconds and minor sevenths and, to allow for fluidity of movement, to passing thirds and sixths. (This may sound strange because it is contrary to later practice. It is true nevertheless for the thirteenth and fourteenth centuries.) Superposing metrical observance no less elaborate on all such elaborations came to produce in the fourteenth century liturgical music of a high complexity.

Whether the sound of it was ever as complex to the ear as it appears in score would depend on the technical sophistication of those who heard it. Such sophistication was likely to belong in those days to professionals only. Anyway, toward the beginning of the fifteenth century these particular complexities were quite rapidly abandoned. Their replacement for the Renaissance centuries, roughly the fifteenth and sixteenth, was a polyphony far easier to follow, being dominated by the more sentimentally appealing thirds and sixths and even by common chords and their instrumental doublings. But eventually that music also went

Music does not flow

the way of all repertories. It is rather that these skills, along with the kind of expressivity that they deal in, tend to be abandoned whenever a new kind of expression, embodied in a new technique, comes into favor. And if the high practices are not altogether lost, that is due to their preservation in manuscript and occasionally, in some privileged liturgical corner, preservation of a permitted archaic practice. Such survivals also tend to disappear eventually, so that even the notation of yesteryear's music now needs scholarship for its deciphering.

In cases where older music survives along with the new, the older tends to assume an antiquarian rigidity. Establishments may go on performing earlier music, but nobody writes new music in the old way. These simultaneous existences are visible today in Japan and Korea, where an ancient court music is still preserved and taught, still played as an homage to history, while the new musics – Eastern, Western, and pop – carry on virtually the whole of music's creative life.

It is visible too in Roman Catholic churches, where every modernism, after repeated papal denunciation, finally gets admittd to the service. A researched version of early medieval repertory was decreed in 1906 to be the authorized music for Catholic worship. And twentieth-century styles of composition have still more recently been blest in an encyclical of 1946. But the ancient Gregorian plainchant, however devoutly performed, is not a method by which anybody today is likely to compose. And to make survivals further precarious, the Ecumenical rules, ordering services to be held no longer in Latin but in any convenient vernacular, will inevitably put our still enjoyed modernisms, along with the revived plainchant and restorations of late medieval *organum* and Renaissance polyphony, right back into the library.

Today's music may also be approaching the end of a major expansion. Everything we can still feel as ours dates from, at the earliest, around 1600. From then, or a bit earlier, come the Anglican chant, the Lutheran hymns, the opera, the ballet, the oratorio, and the fully developed keyboard instruments, such as the pipe organ and the harpsichord with their terraced dynamics, all those blessed violins which made possible the orchestra, and the pianoforte with its easy crescendo.

In the late eighteenth century, the stiff continuity textures of canon and fugue came to be somewhat abandoned in favor of the freer, almost organic expansions of symphonic and chamber music. We call the noblest of these layouts – as used by Haydn, Mozart, Beethoven, and Schubert – sonata form, though that term was unknown to any of these masters. Historian Paul Henry Lang once told me that he had found the word only as far back as 1838, when Schubert, the youngest of them all, had been dead for ten years.

It is these masters, rather than Bach and Handel, who occupy the central position in today's repertory. And it is the codification of their practices in harmony, free structure, freely differentiated counterpoint and rhythm, and, eventually, by Berlioz, in orchestral scoring, that define current music. So also, of course, do the operatic procedures of Mozart, the Italian and French theater composers, and Richard Wagner.

With the impoverishment of noble patrons during the French Revolution, and with the building of public halls for the orchestra's growing possibilities of loudness, a paying public had come into existence. Publishers, managers, copyright laws, and a vast reorganization of pedagogy accompanied this. All these still exist. They are today's musical establishment, enlarged of course by the recording industry, which preserves (though for how long we do not yet know) performances of the central repertory and also of music's outlying regions. These last include every kind of music available in every part of the world. And music of all kinds is also distributed by radio and by recordings to every part of the world – indeed, to every hut and palace in it.

All this has created not only a codification of the Baroque and Romantic repertories but also a sales empire so large and so powerful that its eventual collapse, if earlier empires are a model, can be easily envisaged. The date of such a collapse is not available to me, nor do I see it as imminent. Empires take a long time to fall. I must say that many composers in our time have seemed to be working toward a speedup of such destruction. Along with these intellectual efforts there has taken place through radio and the jukebox such a massive distribution of music's mere presence that inattention has long since become quasi-universal. And inattention, we know, can kill anything.

Now the ideas that evolution is a constant and that perpetual enrichment of the musical art is inevitable are ideas I have been endeavoring to disprove here, or at least to discourage. The thought that music, for all the present hypertrophy of its distribution, may be in one of its historic declines regarding creative energy is one that has been pressing itself upon me for some time; and I do not perceive any prospect of a major renewal.

The practical methods of Baroque and Romantic music, their exploitation, expansion, and codification, as well as their embodiment in a repertory of concert and theater pieces that both professionals and

Music does not flow

straight music lovers can accept, seem to have come to term about 1914. The constants of music have not altered, but their utilization within the assumptions of our recent centuries would seem to have reached some kind of a terminus. Their high point of interior organization and of expressive intensity had already come with the work of the Viennese symphonic masters roughly between 1775 and 1825. Some amplification of volume, extension of length, and intensifications of sensuous appeal have taken place since, but these achievements had also been pretty well finished off, I think, by World War I.

One may point out also that the United States came to participate in this European history only about that time, too late to have taken a major part in music's major branchings out or in any decline of its flowering. Our musical needs therefore and our contributions, if any, are likely to lie outside of Europe's narrative. Our folklore and our jazz, now studied in many European academies, are phenomenal creations. Indeed, they may lead us elsewhere than toward joining Europe. If jazz could replace classical counterpoint, it might justify our abandoning the classical line. I find such an eventuality quite improbable. But I have observed that the commercial establishment, by fighting jazz relentlessly, has strengthened it. And in its fight for life, black music, jazz, has developed a remarkable ability to reject impurities. Actually it is a persecuted chamber music with nearly three-fourths of a century's history of survival.

Among our century's incompleted efforts, music for electronic tape has not lived up to what many thought was its early promise. Neither has noise composition. As for the arithmetical overlays that some had put faith in for renewing music, the twelve-tone-row method has now, in spite of a vigorous burst after World War II, virtually faded away. The aleatoric, or accidental, ways of composing have probably, except for John Cage, who is now approaching seventy, lost much of their attraction for the young. Stochastics, or the calculation of probabilities, has one brilliant adherent, Yannis Xenakis. And the electronic big machines, though valuable for calculation, have actually invented nothing. Processed sound effects are what their taped products most strongly resemble.

The philosophers of modernism show, along with some hope for music's renewal, a notable willingness to abandon most of its past except for teaching purposes. But there is also among educated people (today a mass public in itself) a distaste for being manipulated by managers and marketeers. Composer Milton Babbitt has even proposed that musicians go underground – to a laboratory, I presume, in which tape composers would work alone or in small groups.

This idea is a tempting one for circumventing the addicts who make up most of music's public, including the opera fans, the electronic wing, the rock music youth, and the more intellectually oriented but no less maneuverable school and college trade, the complexity lovers. Obviously the only way to escape from them would be to turn toward something fresh. But there is very little available in music today, or in any contradictory nonmusic, nothing existing anywhere to my knowledge that was not in existence thirty years ago.

The question often asked – "Where is music going?" – is to my mind unanswerable because I cannot see it going anywhere at all. Nor is anyone standing on its bank. Music, to my view, is not a stream in which a composer drops his line and with luck pulls up a fine fish. Nor is it a mysterious wave force traveling from past to future that may, also with luck, carry us to higher ground. It is not like that at all. It is rather everything that has been done or ever can be done with music's permanent materials. These are rhythm, pitch, and singing. The first, being mainly imitation, is highly communicative. The second, let us call it harmony, is calculative in the handling, intensely passionate in the result. The third, the words-and-music operation, appeals to everybody and is the avenue, almost the only avenue, to lasting fame. But it is also a discipline, never forget, and a game, like chess or contract bridge, to be played for high stakes against churches, governments, and music's whole secular establishment. That game, which will decide your life or death as an artist, cannot be avoided.

The purpose of this essay is to warn young composers to avoid a relaxed attitude toward their art. Look out, I say, lest its permanent pitfalls trip you. Music itself is not in motion. But you are. So do be watchful. Please. Unless, of course, you are a "natural" and can write music without remembering its past. But that involves the discipline of spontaneity, the toughest of all disciplines. Just try it sometime.

IV

Studies in cultural history

FRANCES YATES

The occult philosophy in the Elizabethan age

What is the occult philosophy? I do not really know because I am not myself an occultist, whatever that may be, and I have no pretensions whatever to having had visionary experiences of any kind. I am purely and simply a historian, and it is solely as a historian that I approach this subject. I feel it necessary to make this clear at the start of this essay because, judging from some of the letters I receive, there may be some misunderstanding about this. It is perhaps disappointing that I am only a historian, and not a magus, but I assure you that this is in fact the case.

As historians, then, we ask ourselves, "What is the occult philosophy?" *De occulta philosophia* is the title of a book by Henry Cornelius Agrippa, published in 1533. It is compounded of Hermeticism and Cabala, the two main strands of the occult philosophy. It expounds the teachings of "Hermes Trismegistus," the supposed Egyptian sage; these include magical practices directed toward religious experiences, toward obtaining the spiritual experience of regeneration by ascent through the spheres of the universe. Similarly, the exposition of Cabala is concerned with meditation on the mysteries of the Hebrew language, on the sacred names of God and the angels, approached through techniques of manipulation of Hebrew letters. This again may be a kind of magic, but directed toward religious experience. If these techniques and this outlook have favored new approaches to scientific investigation of nature, as I have argued elsewhere, this was not the main aim. The main aim was religious, to achieve a deeper insight into the nature of God.

This concentration on Hermeticism and Cabala was the result, or partly the result, of great historical upheavals and movements of peoples. We live in time and in history, and our deepest thoughts are affected by the historical events in our times. We know this very well from our own deep involvement in the history of our own times, affecting not only our lives but our interests and our scholarship. My own work has been largely due to Hitler, who sent the Warburg Institute to London. Similarly, in the Renaissance, emigrations and movement of peoples, their learning, and their books profoundly affected the thought of the times.

The old view of the origin of the so-called Renaissance held that the fall of Constantinople to the Turks in 1453 was a starting point. Recent generations of scholars have weakened this view; yet there is something to be said for it. After all, it was the Greek refugees from Byzantium who spread the knowledge of Greek in Europe, and it was from Byzantium that the works of Plato and the Neoplatonists, and of "Hermes Trismegistus" and other *prisci theologi*, reached Florence to form that rich and confused strain of Renaissance Neoplatonism that we associate with Marsilio Ficino. The Hermetic strain in the occult philosophy was basically connected with Neoplatonism, since the Egyptian Hermes was believed to have been the source of Plato's thought.

Another date that has not been so much stressed but that is equally, perhaps more, important is 1492, the date of the expulsion of the Jews from Spain. Spain had been the great medieval center of Jewish learning and science, and it was in medieval Spain that the Jewish mystical tradition, or Cabala, had developed. After the expulsion, the wealth of Jewish scientific and astrological learning, Jewish philosophy, and Jewish Cabala was spread throughout Europe with the refugees from Spain. It is very strange that although the Greek refugee movement has been so much stressed as an important ingredient of the Renaissance, little has been said about the Jewish refugee movement. The date 1492 does not seem to have made much impact on historians of Renaissance thought. An interesting book by an Italian scholar that I read recently stresses the importance of Leone Ebreo's *Dialoghi d'amore* and compares its mingling of Greek mythology and Jewish Cabalistic thought with the similar blend in Pico della Mirandola's *Heptaplus*. The writer notes that Leone Ebreo (Judah Abravanel) arrived in Naples in 1492 and afterward settled in Venice, but he does not connect the date of Ebreo's arrival with the date of the expulsion, nor his settlement in Venice with the fact that Venice was the great center of postexpulsion Jewish learning in Italy. There is no doubt that the Jewish refugee from Spain spread in Italy a new enthusiasm for the Hebrew language and for the Hebrew mystical tradition.

Thus the Renaissance occult philosophy was in part (not, of course, entirely) the result of the great historical disturbances of the age: the flight of the Greeks from the center of Greek learning in Byzantium and the expulsion of the Jews from Spain and the resultant Jewish diaspora.

In my various books I have stressed the importance of the Hermetic-Cabalist tradition for many aspects of Renaissance culture. I have perhaps laid greater stress on the Hermetic side than on the Cabalist side, though I did devote a chapter of *Giordano Bruno* to Pico and the Cabala and to some analysis of Pico's Cabalist Conclusions and to his remarkable statement that Cabala confirms the truth of Christianity. Pico della Mirandola was in fact the first Christian Cabalist of the Renaissance. He expounds the argument, which was known also to St. Jerome and to Nicholas of Cusa, that through the insertion of an *S* (the Hebrew *Shin*) into the four-letter name of God, Jahweh, the Tetragrammaton, the Cabalist letter manipulations can prove that *Jesus* is the name of the Messiah. This is of course quite contrary to genuine Jewish Cabala, in which the Messiah is still to come and the pious Cabalist is able to hasten his coming through prayers. Thus, though the diffusion of Cabalist texts through the expulsion of the Jews from Spain aroused the intense Renaissance interest in Cabala, this interest usually took the form of Christian Cabala – really a fundamentally different matter from genuine Jewish Cabala.

There was another great difference. Pico yoked together Hermes and Moses, Hermeticism and Cabala, Hermetic magic and Cabalist magic. In fact he actually argues that the Hermetic or Ficinian type of magic, using talismans and incantations to draw down the influences of the stars, should always be combined with Cabalist magic, invocations of angels, and invocations of the sacred names of God. The combination of the two techniques of magical meditation, if one can call it that, strengthens the Hermetic magic and also makes it safe. It ensures angelic and holy protection and averts the danger – always present to the mind of an occult philosopher – that in his efforts to reach the higher powers he may run the risk of encountering bad spiritual forces, demons instead of angels.

Christian Cabala thus combines both Hermetic and Cabalist types of magic, or religious magical meditation, and this combination is foreign to genuine Jewish Cabala. In short, Pico's Christian Cabala encouraged strong magic, with the religious aim of strengthening religion, strengthening a type of religion that still claimed to be Christian through Christian Cabala.

Christian Cabala was in fact a very extraordinary development of the

Judeo-Christian tradition, using Jewish mysticism for the development of a supposedly strong and more magical type of Christianity.

In *The Occult Philosophy in the Elizabethan Age*, I try to fill in the gaps of my previous work through emphasizing the Christian-Cabalist side of the Hermetic-Cabalist movement. I am most imperfectly qualified to attack such a difficult subject because of my ignorance of Hebrew. With my usual effrontery and lack of caution, however, I plunge into the history of Christian Cabala in the Renaissance. For this *was* the occult philosophy that reached the Elizabethan age, largely through John Dee.

In what follows I give an extremely abbreviated and inadequate account of the history of Christian Cabala, and of the reaction from it, as a necessary preliminary to the understanding of John Dee and of the occult philosophy in the Elizabethan age.

The next most important Christian Cabalist after Pico was Johann Reuchlin. In 1494, two years after the expulsion, Reuchlin publishd his extraordinary work *De verbo mirifico* (The Wonder-Working Word). In the third book, he gives the Cabalist proof that *Jesus* is the name of the Messiah. The argument had been given by Pico, but Reuchlin's little book on the wonder-working word was a potent force in the spread of Christian Cabala. Twenty-three years later, Reuchlin published his *De arte cabalistica* (1517), the first treatise on Cabala by a non-Jew. It became the bible of the Christian Cabalists. Reuchlin emphasized the numerological or mathematical side of Cabala. He was called "Pythagoras Reborn" and was intensely interested in the numerical values of Hebrew letters, which he expounds in the *De arte cabalistica*. Cabala could transform into a kind of mystical mathematics. Reuchlin was a Neoplatonist for whom the Hermetic-Cabalist core of Renaissance Neoplatonism was immensely important. He hoped to achieve, through emphasis on this magical core, a strong philosophy and a strong Christianity associated with it. He found this in Neoplatonism, with its core of operative magic. But he knew that many people feared operative magic as possibly diabolical. For him, Cabalist magic did away with this fear, for it was concerned with holy forces, with angels, and with the names of God. The demonic powers of ancient magic were made safe through the angels – hence, suggests Charles Zika, the concentration on angel summoning in Reuchlin's system.

We can already see here the outline of the future John Dee, mathematician and numerologist, conjurer of angels, but fervently asserting that he was a Christian, as indeed he was – a Christian Cabalist.

Another very important Christian Cabalist was Francesco Giorgi,

The occult philosophy in the Elizabethan age

whose *De harmonia mundi* (1525) combines Platonic world harmony with Cabala. That Giorgi was a Christian Cabalist means not merely that he was influenced in a vague way by Cabalist literature, but that he believed that Cabala could prove, or rather had already proved, the truth of Christianity. Giorgi's work was in Dee's library and was an important source for some of Dee's most characteristic ideas. Giorgi's Christian Cabala was fused with his Franciscan mysticism, giving an enthusiastic and lyrical quality to his philosophy of world harmony. He was a favorite Christian Cabalist with poets, including the poets of the French Pléiado, and, in Elizabethan England, Edmund Spenser.

The most controversial of the Christian Cabalists was Cornelius Agrippa. It may surprise you to hear of Agrippa as a Christian, for his general reputation has been that of a black magician and sorcerer. This reputation survived from the age of the witch hunts; recent scholarship has greatly changed our image of Agrippa. His *De occulta philosophia* is now seen as the indispensable handbook on Renaissance "Magia" and "Cabala," combining the Hermetic magic of Ficino with the Cabalist magic of Pico in one convenient compendium and, as such, playing a very important part in the spread of Renaissance Neoplatonism, with its magical core.

Charles Nauert's *Agrippa and the Crisis of Renaissance Thought* (Urbana: University of Illinois Press, 1965) has placed the study of Agrippa's life and work on a scholarly footing. The magician now begins to appear as something of an evangelical, combining pre-Reformation humanism with an attempt to provide a "powerful" philosophy to accompany evangelical reform. In this attempt, Agrippa was undoubtedly inspired by Reuchlin's Christian Cabala. In fact, Agrippa's *De occulta philosophia* can be classed as Christian Cabala, for it leads, in the third book, to the presentation of the name of Jesus as all-powerful, now containing all the power of the Tetragrammaton, "as is confirmed by Hebrews and Cabalists skilled in the Divine Names." Agrippa is quoting from Pico's Cabalist Conclusions. His attempt to combine evangelicalism with a magically powerful philosophy makes Agrippa an interesting reformer.

The picture of Agrippa now emerging is strangely unlike the sorcerer with his black dog hunted in the witch crazes and serving later as the image of the nineteenth-century idea of the necromancer. Agrippa's occult philosophy, based on the amalgamation of Ficino's magic with Pico's Cabalist magic, was in effect the work of a Christian evangelical with reforming tendencies, proclaiming with Reuchlin the more powerful philosophy, the magic of the wonder-working word.

From Pico onward, and throughout the sixteenth century, the occult philosophy was a powerful force nourishing many profound aspects of religious and cultural life; at the same time, however, there was a growing opposition against it. The opposition had always been there: Pico had grave difficulties with the orthodox; Reuchlin was a center of controversy; Giorgi's *De harmonia mundi* was censored; and Agrippa, the most extrememly magical of the Christian Cabalists, became the scapegoat of the whole movement, presented by its enemies as the blackest of black magicians.

The Council of Trent discouraged "Judaizing"; nor was the opposition to Christian Cabala solely Counter Reformation and Catholic. It was also distrusted by many Protestants, particularly Lutherans. The occult philosophy became involved in the growing outcry against magic of the later sixteenth century. In the turmoil of those witch-hunting times, the Renaissance magus turned into Faust, a development related to the growing profound distrust in orthodox circles of Renaissance Neoplatonism, particularly in its association with Cabala. On the title page of a copy of Giorgi's *De harmonia mundi* in the British Library, the censor has written the warning that this book is to be treated with caution because it is full of the errors of Platonists and Cabalists. "Platonism and Cabalism," that profoundly Renaissance combination, added up to magic in the eyes of the censor, and in the case of Agrippa it added up to black magic and necromancy.

The reaction against Agrippa is an extreme form of the reaction against Neoplatonism and its occult associations that developed in the latter part of the sixteenth century, culminating in the burning of that famous occult philosopher, Giordano Bruno, in 1600.

The great crisis of the disappearance of the Renaissance in clouds of witch hunting has not yet been seriously investigated. I believe that the witch crazes of that age were in some way a reaction against the occult philosophy. One of the most influential books in fomenting the witch crazes was the famous *Démonomanie des sorciers,* by Jean Bodin, published in 1580, in which Bodin denounces witches and pleads for their extermination. It is significant that Bodin begins his book with a devastating attack on Pico and Agrippa for their wrong use of Cabala. Bodin thinks that Pico's advice in the Conclusions about strengthening magic with Cabala is a most wicked degradation of the true meaning and use of Cabala. And if Pico is a wicked magician, Agrippa is much worse. Bodin's fulminations against the *De occulta philosophia* are alarming. For him, it is an utterly damnable work. He compares the wrong use of

The occult philosophy in the Elizabethan age

Cabala by such a sorcerer with the true Cabala, which is a spiritual discipline and a method of scriptural exegesis used by good and holy men. It draws out deep meaning through allegorical interpretation and leads the devout into holy mysteries.

Bodin is not against genuine Jewish Cabala, which he reveres as a holy discipline. He is against *Christian* Cabala, against the attempts of Christian Cabalists to use Cabalist techniques to strengthen a magical form of Christianity. He regards such teaching as a degradation of true Cabala, which has let loose bad magic on the world. Though he does not in so many words equate his attack on Pico and Agrippa with his attack on witches, it is clear that there must be a connection in his mind between them.

I come now to the subject of this essay: John Dee – the leading philosopher of the Elizabethan age, and an occult philosopher and a Christian Cabalist.

As is well known, Dee was famous not only as a mathematician but also famous, or infamous, as a conjurer. How did he manage to reconcile his scientific and occult interests with his earnest claim that he was a devout supporter of the Tudor Reformation? The answer to this question lies in realizing that Dee was a Christian Cabalist, supporting the "more powerful" philosophy implicit in Renaissance Neoplatonism as understood by Pico, Reuchlin, Giorgi, and Agrippa, with its access to good angelic powers guaranteed by Christian Cabala.

The manifesto of Dee's movement was his mathematical Preface to the English translation of Euclid, published in 1570, which opens with an invocation to "divine Plato" and quotes Pico and Agrippa. Dee's famous magical sign, the *monas hieroglyphica*, is a compound of planetary magic, alchemy, numerology, and Cabala. It includes the sign of the cross; it is Christian Cabala, and the best approach to its meaning can be found in certain passages in the work of the Christian Cabalist of Venice, Francesco Giorgi.

To view Dee as a Christian Cabalist is to explain his mysterious worldwide religious schemes, including his missionary journey to the Continent. He would see Christian Cabala, the more powerful philosophy, as potentially a worldwide movement of reform that should not be restricted to Elizabethan England.

We can now begin to see Dee in his actual historical context. He appears as truly a man of the late Renaissance, developing occult philosophy in scientific directions, involved in the religious and reforming side of the movement, but overtaken by the reaction of the later sixteenth century. It is important to remember the late date of the Elizabethan Renaissance. It began to flourish when, on the Continent, the reaction against Renaissance Neoplatonism and its associated occultisms was growing in intensity. The building up of Queen Elizabeth I as a Neoplatonic heroine by Spenser was in itself a challenge to the Counter Reformation powers and their attitude toward Renaissance philosophy. In the 1590s, when Spenser published his magical poem about a fairy queen and his Neoplatonic hymns in her honor, the continental reaction was in full swing. Their Neoplatonism stamped the Elizabethan philosopher Dee and the Elizabethan epic poet Spenser as adherents of the occult philosophy.

It is important to distinguish the three periods of Dee's life. In his first period, until 1583, he was the leader of the Elizabethan Renaissance, powerfully patronized by the Earl of Leicester and by the queen herself, his library the center of advanced thought for scientists and poets, frequented by Philip Sidney and his friends. Spenser conceived the idea of *The Faerie Queene* within this hopeful time. In 1583, Dee left England for his continental mission. To this period belong the séances described in Dee's *Spiritual Diary*, with their supposed contacts with angels. Dee was moving on the more powerful levels of occult philosophy, through which he hoped to encourage powerful religious movements. Enthusiastic missionaries of his type were moving all over Europe in these last years of the century. One such was Giordano Bruno, who preached a message of universal reform and relied heavily on magic images, which he copied out of Agrippa's *De occulta philosophia*.

When Dee returned to England in 1589, he entered upon his third period, which lasted from 1589 until his death in 1608. His old position at the center of the Elizabethan world was not restored. Leicester and Sidney were dead. Shunned and isolated, Dee was confronted with a growing witch hunt against him. The cry of conjurer had always been sporadically raised, but in the old days the queen and Leicester had protected his studies. Dee felt obliged to defend himself in a letter to the archbishop of Canterbury, in which he protested that all his studies were holy studies, not diabolical as his enemies falsely asserted. It was the letter of a Christian Cabalist who was encountering the kind of opposition that Pico della Mirandola and Reuchlin had encountered and that had turned Agrippa into a black magician.

Dee was very poor after his return. He appealed to the new king, James I, asking that those who called him conjurer be brought to trial.

James turned a deaf ear. Dee was not cleared, and he died in great poverty.

This last act of Dee's story is impressive. The descendant of British kings, as Dee claimed to be, the creator (or one of the creators) of the British imperial legend, the leader of the Elizabethan Renaissance, the mentor of Philip Sidney, the prophet of some far-reaching religious movement, died an old man, in bitter neglect and poverty.

What happened to Dee's *"Renaissance Neoplatonism"* in his lifetime was happening all over Europe as the Renaissance went down in the darkness of the witch hunts. Giordano Bruno in England in the 1580s had helped to inspire the Sidney circle. Giordano Bruno in 1600 was burned at the stake in Rome. Dee's fate in England in his third period presents a similar extraordinary contrast with his brilliant first period.

The occult philosophy and the vicissitudes through which it passed were, I believe, a major issue with the Elizabethan poets. The poet who most fully identified with the occult philosophy, and with its Elizabethan representative, John Dee, was Spenser. I have published an article on the influence of Francesco Giorgi on Spenser. I cannot reproduce here the detailed arguments on Christian Cabala as the Spenserian religious philosophy, and on the echoes of Dee and his movement in *The Faerie Queene*. Spenser inherited much more than Neoplatonism as formulated by Ficino and Pico. He inherited the movement toward reform in such later Christian Cabalists as Reuchlin, Giorgi, and Agrippa. He inherited the intensified Cabalist Neoplatonism with its emphasis on number, of which John Dee was a leading representative. He inherited the thought of a more powerful philosophy leading to a worldwide reforming movement, with Queen Elizabeth I in the leading role, as Dee saw her. The Cabalist-Neoplatonic influence on Spenser was merged with the Arthurian-British element to form a kind of "British-Israel" mystique. Such a development arose in the highly charged atmosphere of sacred destiny with which Elizabethan Englishmen maintained their morale in their dangerously isolated position. And it seems obvious that the circle from which such ideas could have emanated can only have been the circle of John Dee – Christian Cabalist and builder of the Arthurian mysticism around Queen Elizabeth.

The Faerie Queene is a great, magical Renaissance poem, infused with the whitest of white magic, Christian Cabalist and Neoplatonic, and haunted by a good magician and scientist, Merlin (a name sometimes used for Dee) who is profoundly opposed to bad magicians and necromancers. The Spenserian magic should be read not only as poetic metaphor but also in relation to contemporary states of mind. The white magic of the pure imperial reform, represented by the Virgin Queen who is the heroine of Spenser's poem, is opposed to the bad magic of its enemies. Thus, even for Spenser, the cry of conjurer raised against Dee would not have been without danger. As a magical Renaissance poem, *The Faerie Queene* came rather late in time and ran into the period of the witch crazes.

I cannot support here with detailed argument the picture I am presenting to you of *The Faerie Queene* as an expression of the Dee magical Neoplatonism in its relation to Elizabeth as the Fairy Queen of white magical reform. Nor can I support in detail the next rather revolutionary interpretation of a leading Elizabethan poet that I am going to put forward.

I believe that the misinterpretation of Christopher Marlowe's *Doctor Faustus* is one of the greatest mistakes in literary history. This play should be seen not as the outpouring of a lonely soul deeply concerned with the problem of religion and magic, but as a propaganda play against Dee, newly returned from the Continent. The play was probably written in 1593, the last year of Marlowe's life. The diabolical apparatus used in the productions caused great terror. Shag-haired devils with squibs in their mouths ran roaring over the stage; drummers made thunder in the tiring-house. On the title page of the 1616 edition, Faustus stands within a circle, conjuring up a devil. Surely this play was aimed at Dee, the conjurer. Moreover, Marlowe associates his Faustus with Agrippa, who is mentioned several times. Like Dee, Marlowe's conjurer was a student of Agrippa and was trying to put into operation the magic of the *De occulta philosophia*. This play was not written to be read by literary critics in the quiet of their studies. It was written to be produced in the public theater, with horrific diabolical effects, to audiences working up into hysteria.

The medieval antisorcery formula is applied by Marlowe to a situation that is not medieval. Faustus is not a medieval sorcerer. He is a Renaissance scholar who has taken all knowledge for his province, with a particular bent toward the natural and the occult sciences. In this play we see Marlowe in the very act of turning the Renaissance magus into Faust. Though there are no actual witches in the play, it belongs, with its vivid infernal imaginings, to the atmosphere of the witch craze. Audiences would surely have recognized Faustus as an unfavorable reference to Dee. Had not Dee publicly proclaimed in his Preface that he was a follower of Agrippa? The process of turning Dee of the first period – the leader of the Elizabethan Renaissance – into the Dee of the third period – the banished conjurer whom the queen and the court are afraid to honor – was one in which Marlowe's propaganda in the theater may have played a considerable part. Marlowe's *Faustus*, with its obvious allusion to Dee as conjurer, tended to undermine the Elizabethan Renaissance and could hardly have been welcome to surviving members of the Sidney circle, or indeed to the queen and her government.

The world of John Dee, of the Sidney circle, of Spenser and *The Faerie Queene* is a world diametrically opposed to that of Marlowe's *Faustus*. The purity of the white magical reform, the fairy world in which Spenser places his image of the queen, is infinitely remote in its vaguely Arthurian outlines from the doctrinaire patterns of the European witch craze.

Marlowe's antisemitism would also be connected with his aversion to the occult philosophy and its use of Cabala. The first performance recorded of Marlowe's *The Jew of Malta* was in 1592. It has been conjectured that the play was written in 1589 or 1590, again, at about the time of Dee's return to England. This play is antisemitic propaganda, using all the old legends about poisoning wells, and so on. As with *Faustus,* a quiet literary approach is definitely inadequate for *The Jew of Malta.* We should think of this play being performed in a public theatre and imagine the rising passions as the audience turns into an antisemitic mob.

The most notorious Elizabethan Jew was the Portuguese New Christian Roderigo Lopez, employed as physician by the Earl of Leicester and by the queen herself. Suddenly accused of plotting to poison the queen, Doctor Lopez was hung at Tyburn in 1594, amid the howls of a violently antisemitic mob. Marlowe's play must surely have been somewhat uncomfortable for the queen, who had encouraged Lopez the Jew as she had encouraged Dee the conjurer. Marlowe's plays do not reflect the Elizabethan Renaissance but rather the reaction to it. The occult philosophy is satirized in *Faustus*, Elizabethan imperialism is satirized in *Tamburlaine*; and the Jewish element in Renaissance learning is satirized in *The Jew of Malta.* Marlowe belongs to the anti-Renaissance mood of rigidity and reaction that was sweeping Europe, suppressing Judaizing philosophy and darkening the intellectual scene with witch crazes. The Spenserian world of white magic inspired by the Christian Cabalists is not the world of Marlowe.

What was the attitude of Shakespeare to these issues? This is a vast question on which I can only touch. Let us look first for a moment at *The Merchant of Venice*, which concerns the relations between Jews and Christians in Venice. It was written in the 1590s, and Shakespeare certainly had in mind Marlowe's *Jew of Malta*. It is not, however, an antisemitic play but rather something like a reply to Marlowe, its themes profoundly influenced by the *De harmonia mundi*, the work that also influenced Spenser. The plot of the play is not credible in a realistic sense, though it tells a fascinating fairy tale about the law, the Torah.

The central scene is the trial scene, in which Shylock demands his pound of flesh and is confuted by the beautiful Portia disguised as a lawyer. Portia pleads that justice be tempered with mercy. Her sermon has been interpreted as an allegory of the law, the rigorous Jewish law of the Old Testament superseded by the New Testament law of love. A more convincing interpretation argues that the interaction between the characters in this scene reflects the interaction between the Sephiroth of Cabala, as set out in the Sephirothic Tree, with Portia as Tiphereth, Beauty–Mercy, mediating between Severe Judgement and Loving Kindness, Shylock and Antonio.

The other most significant scene in this play about Jews and Christians in Venice is the scene where Lorenzo sits with Shylock's daughter gazing at the night sky. The Christian lover tells the Jewess about the universal harmony. The immediate inspiration for this was, I believe, the *De harmonia mundi* of Francesco Giorgi. Whether Shakespeare had actually read this book, of which there was a French translation, or whether he absorbed its atmosphere through the permeating influence of Christian Cabala in the Elizabethan age is a minor problem. The general suggestion is that the Judeo-Christian harmony emanating from the Friar of Venice had reached Shakespeare, profoundly influencing his thought and imagery.

The Merchant of Venice is in no sense an antisemitic play in imitation of Marlowe. On the contrary, it is something like a reply to Marlowe. The audiences at *The Jew of Malta* were incited to become antisemitic mobs. The audiences at *The Merchant of Venice* heard the universal harmony pealing forth from the work of the Christian Cabalist Friar of Venice.

It would seem that Shakespeare, like Spenser, found the Christian Cabalist philosophy of the Giorgi congenial.

Shakespeare was writing his plays in, roughly, the last decade of the sixteenth century and the first decade of the seventeenth. These were the years in which, in Europe, Renaissance Neoplatonism with its associated occultisms was being attacked heavily by the forces of reac-

The occult philosophy in the Elizabethan age

tion. In England, these stresses and strains were felt intensely. On the one hand, a late form of the occult philosophy was developed in the Dee movement, was reflected in the magical poem *The Faerie Queene*, and was used in the propaganda for Elizabeth I. On the other hand, the reaction was strongly present. The Jesuit missions had spread Counter Reformation attitudes. The atmosphere of the reaction is felt in Marlowe's *Faustus*, aimed against the whole conception of the Renaissance magus and the allied movement of Christian Cabala.

If it can be accepted, as I believe it can, that the thought of *The Merchant of Venice* is affected by the Christian Cabala of Francesco Giorgi, then it would follow that Shakespeare might be sympathetic to the Spenserian outlook. Can one interpret other Shakespearean themes and images as related to this outlook? Take, for example, the Shakespearean fairies.

Shakespearean fairies are not, I believe, manifestations of folk or popular tradition. Their origins are literary and religious. The use of fairy imagery in the cult of Queen Elizabeth was begun in the Accession Day Tilts. As taken up by Spenser in *The Faerie Queene*, the fairy imagery was Arthurian and chivalric and also the expression of pure white magic, a Christian Cabalist magic. Shakespearean fairies emanate from a similar atmosphere. Shakespearean fairies are an expression of adherence to the Spenserian point of view.

The supreme expression of the Shakespearean fairyland is *A Midsummer Night's Dream*. Into the texture of this magical play is woven a magical picture of the Fairy Queen. Defeating the love shafts of cupid, the fair vestal, throned by the West, the imperial votaress, passes on. A well-known portrait of Queen Elizabeth, the "Sieve" portrait, presents the imagery in visual form.

As I pointed out in *Astraea,* the "Sieve" portrait and Shakespeare's word picture in the *Dream* are triumphs of chastity on the model of Petrarch's *Trionfi*. The triumph is a triumph of purity in both public and private life. It is in exactly such a role that Spenser presents Elizabeth. As Gloriana she is a most royal queen and empress; as Belphoebe she is a most chaste and beautiful lady.

The appearance in the sky of this Spenserian vision in the *Dream* strikes the keynote of the magical–musical moonlight of the play. The vision of the imperial vestal virgin relates the play to the Spenserian fairy world, to the Spenserian magical cult of the imperial virgin, with its undercurrent of Christian Cabala.

I believe that the occult philosophy as interpreted by Dee, and the magical Christian Cabalist movement as interpreted by Spenser, were major influences on Shakespeare's outlook and poetry. The *Dream* expresses the Spenserian mood in hopeful terms. In *King Lear* it is darkened by tragedy and failure.

In terms of the Dee movement and its three phases, *King Lear* belongs to the third period, the period of disgrace and failure when the revered magus of the Elizabethan age has become a hunted figure suspected of unlawful commerce with demons, and much out of favor with Elizabeth's successor. Shakespeare, of course, knew the historical sources of the Lear story, but his main inspiration was the story of Lear and his daughters as recounted in *The Faerie Queene*, where it forms part of the "British Chronicle," which is the preparation in history for the appearance of Gloriana and her Messianic role.

In Shakespeare's telling of the story, it becomes a tragedy. The British monarch has given away his empire to wicked and ungrateful persons. They owe everything to him, yet they turn him out into a frightful storm, utterly destitute and friendless, save for a Fool and a person who seems to be an escaped lunatic, possessed by devils.

The wild figure of Tom o'Bedlam, gesticulating beside Lear on the blasted heath, was an addition by Shakespeare to the story and one that introduced the theme of demonology to the melancholy scene. The extraordinary thing about these demons in the night of *Lear* is that they are faked. Tom o'Bedlam is really Edgar in disguise, and he is deliberately simulating demonic possession.

Why did Shakespeare choose as a companion to Lear in his destitute state a man who was *pretending* to be possessed by devils? In choosing the names of the devils supposed to be in possession of Tom o'Bedlam, Shakespeare used a compilation by Samuel Harsnett, *Declaration of Egregious Popish Impostures*. This is a polemical work in which a Jesuit is accused of having induced a sense of demonic possession in some persons, pretending afterward to exorcise them. The devil names from Harsnett would have been recognized by first audiences of *Lear* as referring to a case of faked demonic possession and faked exorcism. That is to say, Shakespeare, through the device of Edgar's impersonation of Tom o'Bedlam, brought in an allusion to demonology not in order to arouse terror in the audience, after the manner of Marlowe, but to raise the question of whether such scares could be falsely raised, or manipulated against a victim for some ulterior purpose. Or, as Harsnett baldly puts it in his title, as "egregious popish impostures."

The architect of the idea of British Empire had been John Dee in his

The occult philosophy in the Elizabethan age

first period, when he had been at the center of the Elizabethan age and one of the inspirations of Spenser's poem. Dee claimed to be descended from British kings, belonging to the tradition that Spenser had traced, and of which the story of Lear was one of the episodes. Dee in his third period, during which Shakespeare wrote *Lear*, was banished from court and society, and might well have thought himself to be the victim of base ingratitude. He who had given so much received no reward. He was, moreover, pursued by scares against him as a black magician and conjurer of devils, though he never admitted this charge, proclaiming himself to be a Christian, as no doubt he was – a Christian Cabalist.

I believe that the tragedy of Lear is a reflection of the tragedy of Dee, the tragedy of the imperial theme of the Elizabethan age, with its roots in the occult philosophy, sung by Spenser but now broken and dispelled in the reaction.

Finally, what of *The Tempest*, the play about a good conjurer, Prospero, and his enchanted island? What an extraordinary act of daring it was to glorify a good conjurer in that day and age, when the controversy about Dee belonged to the very recent past, when the reaction against Renaissance occult philosophy was raging on the Continent and was present as a vital issue in England.

I argued in *Shakespeare's Last Plays* (1975) that Shakespeare in his last period was influenced by the energetic line of thought and leadership represented by the young Prince Henry, intent on reviving the Elizabethan outlook to which his father was unfavorable. Prince Henry encouraged members of the old Elizabethan school. The fairy imagery revived in his circle. In the masques in honor of Prince Henry written by Ben Jonson and performed at court in 1610 and 1611, the prince appears in an Arthurian setting, as a descendant of ancient British kings and a reviver of chivalry, assisted by the magic of Merlin, who rises from his tomb to aid the prince and his subjects, "the nation of the Fays." The Spenserian fairyland becomes the ideal world of the Fairy Prince, who is continuing the traditions of the Elizabethan Fairy Queen.

The prince died in 1612. His sister, Princess Elizabeth, was associated in the public mind with the late queen of the same name, another pure Protestant heroine. *The Tempest* was produced before Princess Elizabeth as one of the shows celebrating her marriage in 1612 to the Elector Palatine; the Protestant wedding was much disliked by pro-Spanish interests.

That Prospero's magic reflects the influence of Agrippa's *De occulta philosophia* was pointed out by Frank Kermode in 1954 in his Introduction to the Arden edition of *The Tempest*. I have argued that this presentation of a Dee-like magus was part of the Elizabethan revival. That the magic of Prospero is a white magic is underlined by the emphasis on chastity in Prospero's advice to his daughter's lover. The white and pure magic of Prospero is contrasted with the black magic of the evil witch. Prospero is using the occult philosophy to call on good spirits (the name *Ariel* is mentioned in Agrippa's book), and he overcomes and controls the bad magic of the witch.

Contemporary audiences must surely have picked up the trend of this play as a return to the magical world of the late virgin queen, her chastity and pure religion now continuing and reviving in the younger generation. Her philosopher, the white magician Doctor Dee, is defended in Prospero. The beneficent magus uses his good magical science for utopian ends. He is the climax of the long spiritual struggle in which Shakespeare and his contemporaries had been engaged. He vindicates the Dee science and allays the anxieties of the witch craze.

How profound is the change from Lear, the British Spenserian king mocked by faked demons, to Prospero, firmly in control of his magical island!

It is strange that, save for one Italian writer, students of Shakespeare's *Tempest* have failed to draw attention to the fact that another play about the occult sciences appeared at about the same time. This was Ben Jonson's *The Alchemist*, first printed in 1612. As I pointed out in *Shakespeare's Last Plays,* there is an undoubted satirical allusion to Dee's *Monas hieroglyphica* in Jonson's play, and Dee's mathematical Preface to Euclid is parodied throughout. Jonson pokes very clever fun at alchemists, magicians, mathematicians, and Rosicrucians, and in the end Subtle and his gang are cleared out of the house, though not before the clever fun has obviously pointed to the Elizabethan revival within the "Elizabethan age" as the object of the satire.

An influential member of Subtle's gang is a whore. One of his dupes is a weak-minded poet who is fooled by the gang. They fake a vision for him in which Subtle is disguised as a Priest of Fairy and the Fairy Queen is impersonated by the whore. It is an attack on the Spenserian revival. Jonson was writing from the viewpoint of the reaction of the enemies of Elizabethanism, of the Elizabethan occult sciences, and of Spenser and his fairyland.

Yet – and this is a most strange phenomenon – Jonson had himself written the masques in honor of Prince Henry, building up the Elizabethan fairyland around him. As a possible solution to this problem it may

The occult philosophy in the Elizabethan age

be suggested that King James, who greatly feared Spain and the Jesuits and was most nervous of his son's active Protestantism, might have been not displeased by Jonson's indirect way of sabotaging the cause that he had publicly supported in the masques.

There is much detailed investigation of these problems to be done. I am trying to draw only the main outline here. I see a great spiritual struggle going on in the Elizabethan age, an age that inherited the occult philosophy of the Renaissance and adapted it to the Elizabethan situation. Spenser and Shakespeare belong with the occult philosophy, but the reaction was strongly present. I would class Marlowe and Ben Jonson as both belonging to the opposition. Marlowe's *Faustus* and Jonson's *Alchemist* should be compared carefully. Both plays were written from similar attitudes, attitudes of reaction against the occult philosophy and with particular reference to Dee.

I have endeavored in this essay to outline what I believe to be a new historical approach to the Elizabethan age and its literature that may have very fruitful results in the future. Instead of concentrating on personalities, I have concentrated on ideas, trying to trace the idea of the occult philosophy into the age and to trace the reaction to it. This approach suggests new angles from which to view familiar phenomena and links the problems of the Elizabethan age with the wider European scene and with the vast issues raised by the occult philosophy and its antagonists.

NOTE

My book *The Occult Philosophy in the Elizabethan Age*, on which this essay is based, was published in 1979 (London: Routledge & Kegan Paul). Full reference for statements made in the essay are given in the book.

ALAIN TOURAINE

Triumph or downfall of civil society

THE END OF SOCIETY

The age of Enlightenment, the eighteenth century, battled against tradition and fanaticism in the name of modernity; it heralded the triumph of reason over irrationality and arbitrary power; but the cult of reason in France was associated with revolutionary terror, and enlightened despotism enrolled the philosophers in the service of the absolute State. The age of progress, the nineteenth century, heralded the liberation of mankind by science and positivist thinking, but it uprooted and proletarianized millions of men and women, and in the early twentieth century, enforced industrialization was one of the major aspects of Stalinist dictatorship. In the modern period, work was regarded as a means of liberation, but in the mid-twentieth century, both in Nazi Germany and in Stalinist Russia, Europe was covered with labor camps that brought the word *labor* back to its Latin etymology: torture.

But in all these cases, both crisis and progress seemed to be limited by the subordination of the realm of social and political action to transcendent principles, on the one side, and to traditions, on the other. We are entering a postindustrial society, which seems to have an unlimited capacity of acting upon itself.

At the beginning, some people imagined it would be the opposite of industrial society, that after several centuries and especially several recent decades of extensive growth, we were going to recover a sense of balance and – to use Claude Lévi-Strauss's image – were about to come back from over-hot societies to cold societies, or at least cool ones, as the younger generation puts it. This utopian dream of a posthistorical, community-based, convivial society lasted only a few years; it was a belated flower springing from a period of affluence and hegemony. The most highly industrialized countries are now confronted with the consequences of their own economic systems, in particular their uncontrolled consumption and wastage; with the geographical redistribution of the means of production by the multinational corporations; with the sudden rise in the price of certain raw materials, especially oil; and with the arms race; but they are also confronted with the growing pace of technological innovation. And so they are being drawn into a new competitive spiral. For ten or twenty years, people in the West spoke only of culture or consumption; once again they are talking about production, investment, and science. This gives a new force and a new form to the question I have already invoked: Does this move to postindustrial society herald the emergence of a society that will be entirely in control of itself, its choice, and its future, or rather the advent of a society that will be the prisoner of its own technology and power? In fact, we even have to distinguish two pessimistic hypotheses. The first one was originally formulated by Tocqueville in the second part of his *Democracy in America*: The triumph of modernity may mean the decomposition of society and the subordination of its atomized individuals to an all-powerful State. The second has been stated more recently, particularly by the Frankfurt school of philosophers, from Horkheimer and Adorno to Marcuse and Habermas: Science and technology become the only principle giving legitimacy to social activity and political choices. Society is thus in danger of being reduced to its own change and of imposing a new despotism on its citizens – no longer the despotism of the established order but rather the despotism of necessary, unceasing, and enforced change. After the economic proletarianization of the nineteenth century we shall, according to this view, undergo generalized cultural and political proletarianization, strengthening the mechanisms of exclusion and stigmatization that Erving Goffman and Michel Foucault have analyzed so well.

Will this society, which could become a "self-producing society," turn into a "self-destroying society"? After having been animated by social conflicts and political and ideological debates, isn't it now dividing into a technocratic elite and a plebeian mass of merely dependent consumers?

For a sociologist, this question, which concerns us all, must be defined more specifically. For three centuries, our conception of social life has been dominated by the idea of society, that is, by the idea of a social body possessing differentiated functions, called institutions, which contribute to the survival and adaptation of the social body, which is itself endowed with homeostatic mechanisms of social control and is capable of socializing its new members – children and newcomers – into its norms and values. This image is not as static as that of culture; in particular, it has been very closely associated, from Durkheim to Parsons, with nineteenth-century evolutionism. It is still based on the idea of a system that is defined by principles, however, by a "collective consciousness" as Durkheim puts it, or "pattern-variables," as Parsons says, and by boundaries. This image always corresponds to a national society, so much so that the concept of society in classical sociology can be identified with the reality of the nation-state, as constructed by Great Britain and France, strengthened and enlarged by the American and French Revolutions, and extended into Central and Eastern Europe by the national movements that broke up the Hapsburg and Ottoman empires.

That image of social life is now outdated and we must abandon the idea of society. It presupposes a unifying principle that is beyond the will of the actors. This may be the law of God, the principles of Reason, or modernization; more materially, it can even be the complexity and intensity of social exchanges. In every case, however, social and political processes seem to be placed inside society, as elements of specialization and differentiation. In this century of growth and crises, wars, revolutions, and planning, it is impossible to believe that social life is contained within an envelope. It is entirely the result of a political process, which is sometimes rather open but sometimes limited to a despotic will.

A famous biologist wrote that modern biology was born when people stopped asking questions about life and started to study living beings and their functioning. Similarly, we might say that sociology reaches maturity when it ceases to speak of society and starts to study social relations. In this respect, its modernizing and secularizing tendencies are taken to their extreme conclusions.

Society no longer has a nature, it is no longer based on any value or invariant; it is only what it makes itself, for better or for worse. It is irrelevant or superficial to appeal to moral principles, natural law, human rights, or religious values in order to organize social life. Society is nothing but the changing, unstable, loosely coherent product of social relations, cultural innovations, and political processes. Social behavior can no longer be explained in terms of the society in which it takes place; society itself is the product of social actions and interactions.

These expressions are not abstract. They concern not only sociologists but each one of us. That is why we are now living through a period that

Triumph or downfall of civil society

is marked both by very great confidence in the future and a very great fear of catastrophes. Confidence was more visible ten or fifteen years ago than it is now, but what confidence remains is based on a great expansion in the fields of cultural innovations and expressions, and especially of higher education. To speak of mass society is also a way of pointing to the enlargement of all kinds of audiences. The political field, which for a long time was limited to legal problems and, above all, the taxation issue and which was then extended to the world of work, with the unions, labor legislation, and collective bargaining processes, is now being expanded to include the whole of social life, from medical care to energy policy. The women's movement is an immense force for change. But at the same time, there is *fear:* fear of nuclear catastrophe, fear of the planet's self-destruction predicted by the Club of Rome, and more recently fear of a new and terrifying world war. Are we entering a society that will be much more open than the commercial and industrial society of recent centuries, just as the latter was more open than the rural societies of the Middle Ages? Or are we witnessing the disappearance of civil society, to give it the name invented by Hegel? Long dominated by empires, the world saw the opening of small spaces – civil societies – first in Western Europe and then in various parts of the world. Are these spaces now closing up again, and are we now entering a new age of empires? Has our modern civilization been merely an interval of a few hours between two long nights, like a winter day in Alaska? Such questions have no simple answer, but in order to examine them and discover how to avoid the worst solutions, we must first of all carefully define the possible choices, the various types of social life that may take the place of the classic civil societies now decomposing as a result of their own success. So we must examine one by one the three hypotheses I have formulated – first, permanent change; second, statism; third, expanded democratic society – before looking at the factors that are pushing us one way or another.

PERMANENT CHANGE

Modern societies have been analyzed from two different standpoints. One is from the viewpoint of their internal functioning, their structure, which is essentially a form of domination exerted over the whole population by those who control investment and knowledge: merchants and lawyers dominating craftsmen and the urban *popolo minuto*, industrialists dominating the workers. The other is from the viewpoint that may be called their mode of development: in other words, the nature of the principal agent of their historical change, in particular, of their industrialization. In the West, this agent was essentially the national bourgeoisie. Some thinkers have dreamed of a society that would become purely industrial, thereby ceasing to be bourgeois. Saint-Simon and Auguste Comte were already thinking along these lines in the early nineteenth century; so too were Thorstein Veblen and Howard Scott in the United States in the 1920s and 1930s, and all those thinkers who, from Burnham to Djilas, have spoken of a managerial revolution and of a new class. The hypothesis I am considering is the opposite one. It starts with the idea of progressive dissolution of the social structure and the relations of production, resulting in the process of social change. It foreshadows a society that will be purely entrepreneurial, purely capitalist, while ceasing to be industrial. This image corresponds to the ideology of the new entrepreneurs. Let us recall how this ideology developed, often hidden behind the theory of organizations. It is part of the Taylorian idea that there is "one best way," scientifically definable and measurable. Between the two world wars, a certain number of "business consultants" sold this pseudoscience, while keeping secret the principles by which they calculated the speed of production lines or the optimal methods of work. After World War II, these methods of work organization were replaced by "management studies," which were more or less directly inspired by classical sociology. And so in the business schools, generations of students were trained to consider the problems raised by combining two organizational principles: "staff and line." But at the same time the psychologists were developing the theme of "human relations," which gradually led to a firm – or any other type of organization – being seen as a site of social and political relationships, mainly managing its relations with its environment, that is to say with its competitors, with technology, and with the personalities and life histories of its workers. The greater the convergence between organizational studies and psychological studies, the weaker the idea of a social structure of organizations. The idea of a rational type of social organization gives way to the search for what Herbert Simon calls a limited rationality. In a more general way, attention shifts from functioning to strategy. Nowadays companies, especially the great multinational corporations are more and more consciously defined in terms of the management of change. The chairman of a major multinational firm said recently: "For several years we thought we had to manage a crisis and find a new equilibrium; we now know that this idea is incorrect, and

Triumph or downfall of civil society

that change has to be permanent." He went on to say that the main social problem now is to reconcile this need for permanent change with the demand for identity, stability, and continuity expressed by individuals and groups.

I have referred to large corporations because this image of social life as permanent change is specific to elite groups. In fact, if society is identified with its change (I am here using the word *society*, as in ordinary speech, to denote a nation-state, a country, or a political and economic grouping, such as the United States or the Common Market countries), the importance of the social actors varies with their capacity to develop a complex strategy. Now to be able to avoid putting all your eggs in one basket, you have plenty of eggs, like an investor who can have an effective savings and investment strategy only if he has substantial funds; if he has small savings, he puts them in a savings bank and generally loses through inflation. The upper stratum of our societies consists of the *players*, those who can develop a strategy; they are few in number. Below them is an ever-growing stratum, which forms the majority in Western countries: the *operatives*, in other words, the blue-collar and white-collar workers, and the technicians directed and protected by the players and represented by their unions, whose defense of their rights and privileges often amounts to a new corporatism. Finally, at the bottom, is the increasingly large mass of marginals: the unemployed, the inhabitants of underdeveloped regions, members of dominated ethnic groups, temporary workers, and workers in subcontracting firms who suffer the stresses of the economic situation – categories whose size has been amply demonstrated by American radical economists. These categories are not classes, since classes are defined by relations of production, like master and slave, craftsman and merchant, or worker and industrialist. They are not defined in relation to a social structure, but in relation to change: the first leads it, the second is protected from it, and the third suffers it. Of course if, instead of considering a country or a group of Western countries, we followed the thinking of Immanuel Wallerstein and considered the whole world economic system to which they belong, we would see that this category of marginals constitutes the majority of the inhabitants of the planet. These marginals are not outcasts, they are not subjected to the power of a totalitarian State, they are not slaves, but nor are they defined as workers; they are deprived of any recognized status. A certain number come from the operatives category, others are dragged down by the crisis, then locked up in institutions where they are labelled sick or deviant. Most remain in a marginal situation while still having a much higher standard of living than that of the population of the Third World.

This destruction of any permanent social structure for the sake of permanent change provokes behavior aimed at defending identity, or personal identity – the search for self in a fragmented experience that depends not only on the intermittent initiatives of the players but on community identity. Voluntary associations, which sometimes even work to establish "alternative life-styles," are created on the edges of the major official organizations. Sometimes they are counterculture utopias; more often, at present, they are purely defensive groupings, sects recruited mainly from the intermediate categories rather than from the marginals, who put an element of "social protest" into their countercultural experiments. In fact, this quest for identity is not intrinsically an expression of protest. Sometimes it organizes marginal groups; sometimes it opposes the nonsocial to the social; sometimes, as Richard Sennett has suggested, it even adapts perfectly to social domination, by retreating entirely into private life and leaving the players the monopoly of public life.

What makes these attitudes of refusal, withdrawal, or counterculture so attractive nowadays is that they manifest both an opposition to the existing power structure and a rejection of the old ideological and political forms of social struggle. The permanent-change society is the more readily accepted since the projects or hopes embodied in the labor movement are exhausted. When a working-class movement leads to a totalitarian regime and ideological arbitrariness, or, at best, to a prudent management of the capitalist economy, it is not surprising that the desire for opposition takes the form of a refusal of the social order rather than opposition to a specific adversary. The permanent-change society causes an appeal to identity that is as void of content as the change, which becomes an end in itself. A film by René Clair shows a funeral procession that starts moving faster and faster. Soon the relatives and friends following the hearse have to run to keep up with it; a magician waves his wand to make them disappear one by one, and finally he makes himself disappear. That is the permanent-change society.

STATISM

This wild race is disorderly; that is its main advantage, but disorder is acceptable only for rich countries. In the poor, dominated countries, a society that identifies with its own change, with a development that encounters immense internal and external obstacles, disappears behind its State. There the State is the agent of change. Only in the hegemonic societies does it merge with the ruling class; elsewhere it takes the place of the ruling class. Those societies that have most strongly identified with an evolutionist vision of history, communist societies, are the ones that have become most completely subjected to a despotic, modernizing State. To free the forces of production from social relations of production that obstruct their development, they have destroyed social organization and left only the party-state, midwife of the future and sole interpreter of the laws of history. The State reigns as absolute master, awaiting the birth of the New Man. Many analysts, especially those trained as Marxists, have tried to analyze communist power in terms of social classes; they have always failed. Not that social classes do not exist in these countries: There too, the workers are subject to the managers of industry and, in the absence of independent unions and the right to strike, they manifest their opposition through slowdowns, absenteeism, and theft. But the ruling class is subject to the party-state. Sometimes it tries to achieve a degree of autonomy; that is surely the chief significance of what is known as economic reform in communist countries. But it remains subordinate to the State. The theoretical analyses of the praxis group in Yugoslavia or of the young philosopher in Hungary who writes under the name of Mark Rakovsky are parallel to the action of the dissidents. The latter, even when they are liberals or Marxists, like Sakharov or Plioutch, attack first and foremost the total State. The State is even more directly opposed by that defender of the Russian land and people, Solzhenitsyn, by the man of total refusal, Bukovsky, and by the analyst of the bad faith and double dealing in intellectual and administrative circles, Zinoviev. But statism is not unique to communist societies. It also governs a large number of former colonies and has gained ground in countries where an active participation in the international capitalist system has meant the elimination of populist or left-wing movements, particularly in Latin America. In every case, society has disappeared behind the State. Instead of taking a modern, democratic form, the representation of local interests works only in an indirect and distorted way, through rivalry between different sectors of the State apparatus. Intellectuals cease to be critical and independent observers and instead become the ideologists of the regime. Trade unions become nothing more than a means of exercising social and political control over the workers.

In countries where the national bourgeoisie carried through the process of industrialization and in which civil society, since the seventeenth century, has achieved its fullest form, it is also possible to perceive a similar trend toward social integration and the subordination of society to the State. Because of the strongly felt need for a fully worked out economic policy, big business and the State are more closely linked today than in the past. Indeed, the present function of social democracy might be described as that of encouraging the integration of business, trade unions, and the State. If outside pressures increase and feelings of insecurity grow stronger, then calls for unity become louder, intellectuals are requested to confine themselves to scientific or utilitarian questions, and protest is considered a form of deviance. Western Europe, the mother of civil society, is no longer hegemonic. Its period of dominance was linked first with the importance of the Mediterranean, and subsequently with that of the Atlantic, the British sea, but it has now been reduced, as the most advanced forms of production have moved toward the Pacific, to the coasts of Japan and California. The question must be asked: Will Europe's relative decline bring with it a decline in civil society and an increase in the strength of integrative States? Fortunately, there have been only limited indications in recent years of such development. But the danger could rapidly increase.

For a long time, the image we had of our own society was dominated by class power and class struggles. Now, surely, it is dominated by the almighty State. In Europe, the century of proletarian poverty has been followed by the century of concentration camps. That is why ideas of domination, imprisonment, and exclusion are more frequent than ideas of conflict in statist or near-statist societies. The strongest protest is expressed by groups who do not have opposing interests but have a different identity, above all a different national and cultural identity. For two centuries, the most important image in our history was that of the Revolution, of a popular uprising that destroyed the ancien régime and opened the way to progress. The future and the interests of the people seemed to be one and the same. Hence the optimism of the American, French, and Soviet revolutionaries. But this period has come to an end. Today, we see more and more national or religious movements opposing the modernization that authoritarian State power, linked to foreign interests, attempts to impose from above. The most recent revolutions have quickly run out of steam, and they have almost immediately been transformed into a State power that destroys society – as has been demonstrated in Ethiopia and, even more dramatically, in Cambodia. But there has appeared simultaneously the first major instance of an

Triumph or downfall of civil society

antirevolution in Shiite Iran, which fought the White Revolution by appealing to fundamentalist religious populism. These new antirevolutionary movements were prefigured in the Irish Revolution as long ago as 1916; and Gandhism, in India, shared many of the same characteristics. But it has gathered most force in the Muslim world and has extended beyond Iran to Syria, Egypt, Tunisia, Saudi Arabia, and even the Palestinian camps. In Afghanistan it has been reinforced by the Soviet invasion. According to many observers, the strongest threat to the present rulers inside the Soviet Union comes from the resistance of the different nationalities, whereas the liberal opposition is weak, and tends to be confined to higher social strata within the population. All these things seem to suggest that the last part of this century will be marked by the recognition of the importance of nationalism, following a short period when internationalism seemed more significant, when the problems of society seemed to prevail over the problems of the State.

A MORE "CIVIL" SOCIETY

Is there still room between the model of permanent change that is being forced on the most advanced industrial societies and the model of an authoritarian, modernizing State that dominates the communist world and the greater part of the Third World for a civil society that is not just the wild dream of the dissidents who are excluded by totalitarian states or of the marginal groups who are left behind in the race for change? It is not an easy question to answer. There is no point in clinging to the ideology that underpinned old social and political struggles. But though we must leave behind outdated issues, we should not be overeager to speak of new hopes and new conflicts in too voluntarist a fashion. We are living through the end of a historical period, especially in Europe. And just as, in the last century, there came a moment when the ideals of the French Revolution were nothing more than the ideology of the victorious bourgeoisie and workers were shot in the name of the Republic, so, today, the socialist ideal that has upheld so many popular movements is little more than a form of statist power, which is particularly dangerous and especially powerful because it concentrates economic, political, and cultural power in the same hands. Our descendants will find a certain continuity between new forms of social protest and socialist protest of the nineteenth century. But at present, it is important to emphasize that an age has come to an end and that certain words now mean the opposite of what they used to mean. That is why I gave the title of *Post-Socialism* (L'Après-socialisme) to the essay I published on French (and European) society and politics. My view is that whereas some political experts still talk of the transition to socialism and of the ways to achieve a kind of regime that they do not describe in any detail, our urgent need is to find a way of emerging materially and intellectually from socialism. I hope I shall not be misunderstood in saying this. I opposed all the colonial wars, I remained in opposition throughout the Gaullist regime, I was physically present on the barricades in Paris in 1968, I supported the Allende government in Chile and fought against the Pinochet dictatorship, I have been involved in the antinuclear campaign. So what I am saying now can hardly be understood as the profession of faith of a conservative. I want to make it clear that in moving away from socialism today I am only following the labor movement when *it* moved away from the parliamentary republic and toward socialism. But where am I going when I leave socialism? All that I have said so far seems to show that there is no longer any room for basic lasting structural social conflicts.

It is not so. My conclusions have not been quite as negative as that. I have described the increasing power of the State and the ideology of the managers of large organizations, but now let's look at the bottom of society. When industrialization first took place, capitalist ideology talked only of progress and change, while there stirred in the shadows at its feet those whom Victor Hugo called *les misérables*, the poor, the people who, through uprising and repression, illegal trade unions and opposition parties, gradually turned into the working class. Let us search at the feet of today's technocrats; we might find vague movements in the shadows, which, through demands and revolts, utopian ideals and protest campaigns, could be in their turn transformed into a new social movement of the future, a social movement that could play the same role that the labor movement and, before that, the defense of the rights of man played in the past. But before looking at what is hidden in the shadows, we ought to discover what causes the shadow. The new ruling class, like all ruling classes, is concerned with both modernizing and establishing, maintaining and transmitting its power and its privileges. It changes the world and sets up an order. What is peculiar to a technocracy is that it is extremely concerned with modernizing and at the same time able to impose not only a legal, political, and economic order but a cultural order as well; that is to say, it is able to produce needs, ways of living, and forms of economic development. Its power does not consist in controlling technical systems, as was the case with the

Triumph or downfall of civil society

directors of the industrial society. Its power consists in inventing products and patterns whereby individual and collective experience can be shaped. Thus the way hospitals are organized forms our image of the body and of illness; the way we see the world is formed by television; data banks will increasingly determine the shape of our collective memory; the choice of nuclear energy will determine the kind of economic development and organization we achieve in the very long term. It is true that these are not total or authoritarian determinations and that they still leave open a way for refusals or counterinitiatives. The same was true in the age of industrialization, when the way work was organized did not prevent the labor movement from coming into existence. But it did hinder it – to such an extent that semiskilled factory workers almost never became active trade unionists. More or less the same thing is happening today. The way supply determines demand does not make social and cultural opposition movements completely impossible, but it has to be acknowledged that it makes their existence more difficult because it reduces social actors to a mass of consumers.

The action of a ruling technocracy or of an authoritarian, modernizing State is to create and attempt to impose upon citizens a certain type of social life. A more civil society, on the other hand, a society that is an extension of democracy, is inevitably the product of social struggles and political processes. What we must discover, therefore, is how, in our kinds of countries, defensive reactions against permanent change can be transformed into social conflicts and antitechnocratic action, and how such struggles may extend the area of political activity or create what one might call a new *Öffentlichkeit*. The study of such social movements and of the institutional treatment of the new conflicts is extremely complex, and I shall merely outline four major aspects of it here.

The major problem is to move from the defensive to the counteroffensive, from the quest for identity to collective action, to control the process of change. It is nowadays impossible to conceive of a significant collective action attempting to liberate a group defined by its ascription, by its roots, since what now defines the masses are only the changes they undergo, the new behaviors they learn to prefer. A social movement can no longer make a positive appeal to needs, principles, or history; it can only have a political aim – that of claiming responsibility and influence in the political control of change. That is why the word *self-management* (*autogestion*) is a good definition of the aims of the new social movements. Then they become directly democratic – what they have not generally been in the past. Take the example of the antinuclear movement. It began with a defensive reaction, the fear of nuclear accidents, made stronger by the memory of Hiroshima; it has been supported by local authorities who are worried by the upheavals that a huge construction site will cause to the life of the community. But as I showed in the *Anti-Nuclear Prophecy* (written with Zsuzsa Hegedus, François Dubet, and Michel Wieviorka), no lasting antinuclear movement can be formed unless campaigners move beyond these initial reactions to a point where a large section of the population demands a say in the choice of energy policy and therefore in the choice of economic policy. Similarly, in the nineteenth century, the fear of machines, bad working conditions, and unemployment only gave rise to sporadic outbreaks of unrest among workers, while the labor movement only took shape when workers' organizations, political parties, and intellectuals attempted to alter the way decisions were taken and economic policy shaped. In Austria, Switzerland, Sweden, and Denmark we have seen the formation of political processes for the discussion of energy policy. In France, immediately after the accident at Three Mile Island, the idea of an antinuclear petition was launched, not making an appeal to people's fear of accidents but demanding, instead, that a referendum should be held and that regional energy development plans should be drawn up in a democratic way. This is how a social movement has acquired a directly political aim, which is the control of change. But the most interesting case is the women's movement. I am not referring here to the movement of a classic, liberal type, what one might call the emancipation movement, which demands liberty and equality for women, very much in the spirit of the nineteenth-century liberalism, in order to abolish the traditional domination of woman by man. I am referring to women's liberation movements, which, I believe, are different from such emancipation movements and even opposed to them. Women's lib does not fight the vestiges of patriarchy but rather fights against a society in which commercial goods and administrative interventions have invaded private life, in which women were hitherto both confined and protected, and have therefore strengthened the domination of the technocracy, which is exclusively male, over consumers' behavior and personal services with which women are strongly identified. Their first reaction is a defensive one: Women shut themselves off in forms of refusal and affirm both their collective identity and their difference from men. But the women's movement is only created when women move to counterattack and speak on behalf of all those who are dominated, against technocratic domination. In this way women create an autonomous

Triumph or downfall of civil society

capacity for action, by refusing to accept the hypothesis of an exclusively male libido, or the idea that women should be subjected to the desire of men, that they should be transformed into consumer objects and status symbols. In a similar way, regional or local movements are also attempts to control changes that affect citizens by demanding the right to discuss town planning or regional development.

Here we come across the second major problem. Social movements today are very well aware that their struggles are about the political control of change. They usually know whom they are fighting against. But what they find extremely difficult is defining their constituency. A trade union knows that it defends the workers in a specific factory, a specific trade, or a specific region. The new social movements, on the other hand, speak for a population that has been reduced to nothing more than an unorganized mass. There is therefore a very great risk that movements of this kind, which speak for huge sections of the population, will become nothing more than extremely militant counterelites, that have only very tenuous links with those women and men they wish to represent and to mobilize.

This leads me to the third problem: the great importance of intermediate agents in the shaping of collective action. Their role is not a new one. In the industrial age, political parties served as intermediary agents for the trade union movement. Today it is possible that political parties, or even trade unions, will once again become political agents for the new movements. This is what has happened in France, where one of the two great trade union organizations, the CFDT, is clearly fulfilling such a role. But wherever the political parties remain highly preoccupied by the problems of industrial society and strongly imbued with its ideologies, and wherever the parties of the left identify themselves most clearly as socialist, it is likely that the new social movements will try to find some form of autonomous public expression, as indeed they are attempting to do in both Germany and France.

The final major problem is that the formation of these movements depends very much on outside political and economic conditions. When outside pressures are strong and when a country feels threatened, it is difficult for new social and cultural movements to be formed. One cannot forget that the student movement and all that came with it, in the United States, in Germany, or in France, was linked to a period of rapid expansion and absence of external threats, particularly as it became associated with the struggle against the imperialist wars, which these same Western countries were waging. And it is when external constraints are weak that social protest can most easily be met by institutional means and can cause social, administrative, and political reforms. But what is striking today, when constraints are much stronger than they were ten years ago, is that the new social movements are still very distant from the revolutionary model and still much closer to a libertarian model. This is what separates them from the mainstream of the labor movement in Europe, which has long associated social protest with the desire to take control of the State. Today's movements are wary of the State and this, more than anything else, indicates their break with the socialist model. They are outright "civil" and attempt to extend, diversify, and even break up the field of politics. They make no appeal to a central institution, such as Parliament, or even to highly institutionalized political mechanisms, such as collective bargaining. They make use of a multiplicity of very informal mechanisms, such as debates, local initiatives, and experiments. In this respect, they have remained faithful to the great American tradition of grassroots democracy.

CONCLUSION

The history of our societies may already be described as that of the tensions between three opposing forces. These are the *domination* of large organizations, which impose permanent change and thus reinforce their own power and atomize the rest of society; the *strengthening* of the State, which substitutes its will for a huge variety of social relations; and the growth of new *social movements* and schools of thought, which attempt to open out and extend the area of politics. The future of democracy does not depend simply on the representative institutions' capacity for resistance or on the influence of the trade unions. It is above all linked to the vigor and independence of these new social movements.

The optimism that has given rise to a rediscovery of opposition forces and to the extension of democratic processes must not be limited to Western societies. Even if the power of statism is overwhelming in the major part of the world, we should not lose hope for democracy in the Second World – the communist world – or in the Third World. We feel acute emotion when we hear, once again, after so many years, the voices of the living or of the dead from civil societies that some State has tried to subdue completely. In the voices of the humblest "zeks," as in those of Mandelstam or Anna Akhmatova, we can today hear the lives, the sufferings, the hopes, and the struggles of all those who continued to form a society when the State attempted to reduce them to subjects. And

Triumph or downfall of civil society

we cannot avoid being sympathetic to the united struggles of intellectuals and workers in Eastern Europe against the State apparatus, from the Budapest and Warsaw uprisings in 1956 to the recent riots in Gdansk, Ursus, and Radom, or the creation of the KOR in Poland.

In quite a different part of the world, my very old links with Latin America make me particularly sensitive to the rebirth of Brazilian political society: The *distensão* has replaced the repressive authoritarianism symbolized by the Institutional Act No. 5, relatively free elections have taken place, the press is no longer censored, and unions that are independent of the government are beginning to be organized, especially in the industrial suburbs of São Paulo.

Social life cannot be reduced to change. Only the dominant ideologies – the ideology of the ruling class and the ideology of the State – assert that there are no longer any structural social relations, that the opposition between the classes has finally given way to international competition and the resistance of the past to the future. That is indeed the choice before us: Either we define our societies solely in terms of their interrelations, so that the only fundamental conflicts are those between States, or we recognize the existence of internal social problems. We then acknowledge that our social life is based on the domination exerted by those who produce and manage economic, social, and cultural change over those who undergo that change, and we consequently maintain, in new forms, the idea that society is the product of conflicting social movements, their conflicts, and their bargaining. It is not true to say that we have to choose between two opposing views of social life, one based on consensus and the other on conflict; there are indeed two opposing visions, but one is based on conflict and the other on violence. The sociologist knows that violence cannot be avoided, that it appears whenever social problems are dominated by the problems of the State, whether it be conservative or autocratic, dominated by foreign imperialism or engaged in authoritarian modernization. He even knows that, in many cases, if he identifies himself with democracy, he is liable to be the accomplice or the agent of an imperialist domination that brutally imposes its power on foreign countries while seeking to legitimate it in the name of the freedom, which actually prevails in the empire. But he certainly cannot accept the language of the State and make himself a direct tool of the destruction of civil society, starting with the destruction of popular protest movements. Nor can he be neutral. He has to search for the conditions of the existence, the autonomy, and the development of civil society – in other words, of the social relations, conflicts, and political processes that weave the texture of social life – and he has to be able to recognize their hidden, degraded, and repressed forms wherever domination, whether of the total State or a ruling class, exerts its pressure. This search cannot be conducted coldly, as if the sociologist himself were not concerned by the problems he studies. For sociological analysis exists only where civil society has a certain autonomy. The authoritarian regimes of the last century often banned the teaching of history and philosophy; in our own times, they start by banning sociology. From the destruction of the great tradition of German sociology by the Nazis and the banning of the social sciences by the Stalinist dictatorship to the repression social scientists are suffering even today in Uruguay, Chile, and Argentina, there is a long list of efforts to destroy the critical conscience of society.

If we intellectuals reflect now on the chances of the downfall or triumph of civil society with so much anguish, it is because what is at stake is our own survival.